Finding My Niche

Finding My Niche

An Autobiography

Virginia Atkinson

Copyright 2012
by Virginia Atkinson

All rights reserved. No part of this book may be reproduced in any form, except for brief passages quoted within reviews, without the express written consent of the author.

Virginia Atkinson
721 West Second Street
Little Rock, Arkansas 72201

ISBN: 978-0-9838992-1-1

Front cover: Ginger Atkinson. attorney at law

Cover and book design: H. K. Stewart

Printed in the United States of America

This book is printed on archival-quality paper that meets requirements of the American National Standard for Information Sciences, Permanence of Paper, Printed Library Materials, ANSI Z39.48-1984.

Preface

This book is dedicated to my parents, John and Amanda Harkey, my big brother John, my daughter Gretel and her husband, Allen, my son Everett, my grandson, Matthew, my granddaughter Liberty and her husband, Tim, and my great grandchildren, Spencer and Rian, and to my granddaughter Chandler who left all of us way too early.

Also to "Miss Ruby," AKA Ruby Davenport, without whom I never would have finally made good on my threat to write the damn thing in the first place.

Ginger Atkinson

1.

I am Virginia Estella Harkey Keeney Ham Atkinson. Three husbands? How could that happen to a hardshell Baptist woman who, growing up, was not allowed to date?

One of my earliest recollections is an incredibly embarrassing time when my father ordered a group of my schoolmates, largely male, off his property when all they had done was ride their bikes, along with me on mine, home from a pep rally. "I'm not going to have a bunch of young boar shoats hanging around here," he shouted, as they quickly dispatched. I had no idea what a "boar shoat" was, but somehow I knew the connotation was something dirty.

I certainly did not set out to be a pioneer, and did not really know I was being one. But for a woman to become an attorney in 1955, as I did, is enough to qualify her as a pioneer. Law degrees were conferred upon only 288 females in the entire United States that year. I was one of them: the only woman in my class at the University of Arkansas School of Law, in Fayetteville, Arkansas—and the top honor graduate to boot! That accomplishment, while taking care of a three-year-old daughter, working, and financing the operation. Not only a pioneer; a miracle worker.

* * *

One thing for sure: I come from pioneer stock. I was born in Booneville, Arkansas, on August 13, 1921, to John Henry and Amanda Parks Harkey. My mother's family came from Kentucky and Tennessee after the Civil War in wagon trains, with all their possessions aboard, their livestock tethered at the rear. Her great grandfather dedicated 40 acres of land for a graveyard near the foot of the Blue Mountain Dam, necessitated I think by the deaths of so many family members, largely children, from various epidemics. It was named the Scott Family Graveyard and it is still there. It is a beautiful graveyard with tall old tombstones and many small graves, enclosed by a rose-covered fence. My parents, when they were well into their eighties, built an open pavilion near the gate of the graveyard, the roof supported by poles set in concrete, with numerous bench-type seats, the backs of which could be turned to form a flat space to accommodate the picnic lunch parishioners brought on Decoration Day. Both Mother and Daddy are buried.

There's also room for me and my family, a necessity that had never occurred to me until I stood, locked in grief, as my daughter called a neighbor in Jackson Hole, Wyoming, from Children's Hospital in Salt Lake City, Utah, instructing her to purchase a grave site for my beautiful infant granddaughter. Chandler Elizabeth Hannibal Adams Branton had just lost her battle with leukemia. Her name? My daughter maintains that all princesses have multiple names.

* * *

My father was from Harkey's Valley, an area settled by the Harkey family during the Civil War. It is now under water: Lake Dardanelle, which spreads westward, behind Dardanelle Dam into Pope, Yell, Logan, Johnson, and Franklin Counties. I remember visiting my paternal grandparents and—after my grandfather, Isaac Wilson Harkey, divorced her—my grandmother in her "dog-trot" house, the living area and kitchen separated from the bedrooms by a long open hallway down the middle of the house.

My grandparents had a large number of children, some of whom died at birth. Eight of them lived. There were two boys: my father and my Uncle "Virge" (Virgil), who served in World War I and had a severe lung problem from exposure to mustard gas. The six girls were Aunt Maudie, Aunt Lorena (Renie), Aunt Ola (Aunt O), Aunt Lillie, Aunt Icie, and Aunt Mable.

Aunt Mable had spinal meningitis when she was very young, resulting in her being totally deaf and unable to talk. My grandfather enrolled her in the School for the Deaf in Little Rock, but Grandma ("Aunt Jenny") missed her so much that she brought her home before she completed her training. She did learn sign language, however, and could say a few words. She was a gifted artist and eventually married one of the hired hands who turned out to be very prosperous from money he made in the timber business. Since Aunt Mabel's deafness was not genetic, none of the children were affected. One daughter is now working as an interpreter for the deaf in the California court system.

Aunt "O" was my favorite aunt. I loved visiting her when she lived in Harkey's Valley, several miles from her parents' home. She was a powerful swimmer and would swim for hours with me on her back. Aunt Maudie was a very devout woman, speaking in tongues and rolling around on the floor in bursts of religious ecstasy. Aunt Lillie wasn't "quite right," as they phrased it. Rumor had it that she had borne a child out of wedlock and given it away, and that she had repented and spent the rest of her life trying to find the child, to no avail. She married the father, my Uncle Lee, and there was never a finer, gentler person. He took great care of Aunt Lillie and assisted her in the search for their child, but they were unable to find it. After they married they had a daughter, whom they named Lilac.

As for Aunt "Rennie" (Lorena), she, recognizing that there were very few eligible suitors in Harkey's Valley, answered an ad published by a man seeking a wife. I don't think she was quite prepared for the dark-skinned man who appeared in person at the Harkey residence in Harkey's Valley. His name was Frank Trow and he said he was Spanish. He well may have been—who knows? After they married, he established a plumbing business in Russellville, Arkansas, where my father later worked. Their two children, Helen and Thurman, were my favorite cousins.

The only villain in the group was Aunt Icie. She married a man who had been in prison, although we never knew for what. Aunt Icie kept strictly to herself, had no children, and caused a great deal of trouble when my grandfather died, fussing over a virtually non-existent estate.

* * *

I never knew either of my Mother's parents, both having died long before I was born. Her mother died when Mother was only five, and repeatedly Mother told the story of how distraught she had been at the funeral. Over and over she had screamed: "Don't put my mama in that hole! Please don't put my mama in that hole!" And to make matters worse, her father remarried five times. None of the women he married were particularly happy with having to care for his numerous children, one of whom was my mother, and she, for the most part had to do a great deal of the housework and care for the younger children. One stepmother was particularly abusive, and my mother, who was almost grown by that time, retaliated by grabbing her stepmother's long hair and dragging her through the mud of the pigpen.

All of this was reported to my mother's father upon his return home that evening, who, after severely whipping her, told her that she could no longer live there. A friend of her mother's, Bob McMullin and his family, took her in, but he was not able or willing to support her. He found her a job in a Booneville hotel, cleaning and washing dishes. Her education ended at that time.

It was there that my father first saw her, and he delighted in repeating the story about how he told everyone he was going to marry that "little black-headed, black-eyed Parks girl." And he did, on Sunday, September 16, 1906, the ceremony being conducted by the Circuit Judge of the District because all the preachers were conducting Sunday services. The following morning, Mother packed a few of her belongings, and they set out for Harkey's Valley. There was an abandoned, run-down house on the "back forty" of my grandparent's farm that housed flocks of geese, and before he proposed to my mother, he repaired the chimney, put in a new floor, dug a well, and patched the roof. The "goose house" was my parents' first home. My father worked with his father as a sharecropper that year. I am sure they had very little money, but they had pigs to butcher and Mother always had a vegetable garden, so they had plenty to eat that summer, and she canned enough to carry them through the winter.

* * *

My father's mother, Aunt Jenny—the woman for whom I was named—was a very unhappy woman. My earliest recollections from visiting her were that she hid the bananas, if she had any, rather than allow the grandchildren to eat them. They were far too precious and difficult to obtain from the distant grocery store to share them with anybody. And when her crop of peanuts had been harvested and stored in the barn loft to dry, she would not allow the grandchildren to eat them. They were to be sold, not wasted on grandchildren.

In spite of my grandmother's disposition, I loved riding in my father's model T automobile over the dusty roads from Russellville to visit with her and all the cousins in Harkey's Valley. There was always an argument between my parents as to whether we would go to Harkey's Valley to visit my father's kinfolks or drive to Belleville, Arkansas, where my mother's sister, Aunt Vera, lived. "The only sister I have in the State!" my mother would sob, and that was certainly true. Most of mama's family lived quite far away, her oldest sister in Idaho, and a brother in Colorado.

Aunt Vera was married to a blacksmith, whose services were still needed because almost everybody had horses to shoe, and they had numerous children. On one of our Sunday visits, we arrived at Aunt Vera's house just as all the children were being allowed to return home, having been placed with neighbors while Aunt Vera, assisted by a mid-wife, gave birth to their only brother, Noble.

Aunt Vera and her husband were indulgent parents, allowing the children to eat whatever and whenever they wanted to—a routine that drove my father crazy. In our house there were three meals a day: breakfast, dinner, and supper. That's when we ate—not all day long or just whenever it occurred to us. And you were not allowed to waste food. You "cleaned" your plate, and if you failed to do so, the residue was put back for you to finish at the next meal. My parents were not stingy—just parsimonious, which they had to be to survive. Many times I saw my father slice the lean part of his helping of meat and place it on his children's plates, keeping the less tender or fat portions for himself.

Needless to say, Mother did not like her mother-in-law, and the feeling was entirely mutual. I think Aunt Jenny was jealous of my mother. One day, Mama was out in the yard of the Goose House, washing clothes. She had a fire going under a huge black wash pot and was punching heavy work clothes and patched bedding into the boiling water, a weekly task. She was expecting no one until her husband returned from work, but suddenly her father-in-law, "I.W" who was working in a nearby field, crossed over to get a drink of water, which my mother pumped for him, welcoming a chance to break from her wash-day chores. Suddenly who should appear but Aunt Jenny, who immediately assumed that her husband was paying too much attention to his young daughter-in-law, and that his intentions were far from honorable.

"So!," she screamed. "You think you're slick, but you can't slide on barbed wire!" And without waiting for an explanation, she turned and went back where she had come from.

Of course, her father-in-law apologized to Mama, and she did not blame him, but she was furious. When Daddy came home, he found "Mandy" packing.

"John Henry," she began, and she had his immediate attention. She always addressed him in that manner when she was angry or when she had made an unchangeable decision. "You can stay here if you want to, but I am leaving."

He decided to look for a different occupation. With the help of his father, he purchased a horse-powered well-drilling rig and a team of mules, and began to drill wells for the public. Mother worked along with him, keeping the team moving around to provide power. She also did some of the "witching" to locate the water.

In the meantime, Mother's father had died, and she inherited an undivided one-eighth interest in a very fertile 160-acre farm in Petit Jean bottom. Daddy managed to borrow enough money to obtain 80 acres of that property, once the land was divided. Before long, combining farming with well digging, Mother and Dad were out of debt. They had acquired a six-room house, livestock, farm tools, and a new gasoline well-digging rig.

2

My parents' first child, my brother John Henry Harkey, Jr., was born August 20, 1917. The First World War, which had begun in 1914, was waxing stronger, and young married men were being called into service. My parents traded their farm for a five-room house with a grocery store in Waveland, Arkansas, thinking that my mother could sell the business or operate it in the event she elected not to go to Idaho to live with her sister should my father be sent into service. The Armistice was signed on November 11, 1918.

Shortly after that, my father made two very bad deals and ended up changing careers again. This time he became a book salesman, selling an encyclopedia known as the *Book of Knowledge* to rural schools and making enough money to purchase a small house in Booneville, Arkansas, where their second child, me, was born on August 13, 1921.

* * *

My father was not your stereotype traveling salesman who enjoyed being away from home, courting the farmer's daughter. In fact, he wanted his family with him so much that he had built in the shops in Peoria, Illinois, a "house car," as we called it, in which we lived and traveled. Mounted on a Reo Speed Wagon body, it was very much like today's Winnebagoes that are everywhere. It was beautifully paneled in wood and had two leather-covered seats that extended into beds at night, the steering wheel being detachable. Since I was the shortest member of the family, that's where I slept. The table on which we ate all our meals came down and across the interior of the car, supported by a folding leg. We children sat on the car seats to eat and my parents had folding chairs, one on each side. When the meal was finished, the table folded back against the wall. The kitchen extended across the back, and though it was small, it was complete, with an oven where Mama baked cornbread while Daddy was driving down the highway toward the next rural school, pulling a Model T Ford behind. There was even a shower and a toilet, and underneath the seats were large storage bins where Mother kept bedding, quilts, and clothing. After work, Daddy parked in a shady park, and John and I played until bedtime. An evening never went by that people did not request permission to go through the vehicle, for this was long before the highways were dotted with this type of mobile home. How I wish he had patented his idea! As for people who went through the vehicle, I well remember a horde of hooded men in white sheets who solemnly dismounted and walked through one door and out the other. It was a group of Klansmen—Ku Klux Klansmen, admiring it through the slits in their sheets.

* * *

Daddy was very successful in selling the *Book of Knowledge*. Always aware that he had been unable to obtain an education, my father believed very strongly that an education was necessary for success and had no trouble convincing the rural school board members that his books were necessary for their students. We traveled all over the greater parts of the Southwest United States, and in one year my brother, who was of school age, attended 11 different schools, in almost as many states. Although he passed and was promoted to the next grade, my parents realized that it was not a good situation, and I was nearing school age. Daddy knew his time as a traveling book salesman was drawing to an end.

My sixth birthday found us living in Shawnee, Oklahoma, the house car parked on the back lot belonging to a woman named "Ma" Baxter. I really don't know how we came to know her, but I suspect it was through a Baptist Church because no matter where the house car was parked, my mother located a nearby Baptist Church and took both John and me to every service they had, including prayer meeting on Wednesday nights. Ma Baxter's son was one of Shawnee's leading physicians, and what a blessing that turned out to be, for there was a crisis about the time the school term began that year, and I had been the unknowing cause of it. Daddy put me in the front seat of the Model T that he was going to crank up, telling me to pull a certain lever. I pulled the wrong one; the Ford reacted, breaking my father's right arm. A working man without a right arm has a problem, even though Ma Baxter's son set it, all without charge. There was no money. Mother was working wherever she could find "honest" work—in a candy factory, ironing shirts in a laundry, cleaning houses. Daddy's broken arm became a problem; he was unable to work and contribute to the household expenses.

Mother took me to enroll in school and learned that first-grade children attended school only half a day. What to do with me the rest of the day? "She's smart enough to go into the second grade" Mama said, having watched the tutoring her son had done on his little sister, and set about to accomplish it.

It happened. "She knows her alphabet; she can read and write, and I don't have anyone to take care of her," Mother explained to the school authorities, and they capitulated, I graduated as Valedictorian from high school in Russellville, Arkansas, when I was 16 years old.

During Daddy's recovery, the family had some very lean times. One day a grocery truck drove into the yard with a big box of groceries. Well we certainly had never had groceries delivered. Mother informed the deliveryman that he had the wrong address, but he was insistent, rechecking his order. He was in the right place. Suddenly "Ma" Baxter, our landlady, emerged from her house and assured him he was right; he was, indeed, at the correct address. The church that "Ma" Baxter had taken us to had learned of the plight that the Harkey family was encountering and had sent the groceries.

My mother was distraught. "We don't want charity!" she declared, proudly. "We can't accept the groceries."

At that time "Ma" Baxter took over. "You certainly can!" she declared, waiving the delivery boy off after he had dropped the groceries at the steps of the "house car." As for John and me, we had spotted bacon, milk, and apples, and had no difficulty at all accepting this bounty!

It was in Shawnee, Oklahoma, that I experienced the only natural disaster that I had ever experienced, although every time a heavy rain and windstorm raged, Mama found the nearest storm cellar and herded the family into it—underground, dark, cold, and spider infested. I really couldn't tell which scared me the most—the storm cellar or the driving rain and roaring wind. But there was no escaping it until the twister had passed over us, uprooting trees and destroying buildings in its wake.

It was 1927, and a devastating flood hit Shawnee. There was water, water everywhere; the house car was submerged. I remember Daddy with me on his back swimming to safety in "Ma" Baxter's storm cellar.

* * *

Once the waters subsided and the house car was renovated, Daddy began to make plans to stop traveling. Both children were now of school age and taking them from pillar to post during the school term was unacceptable. He advertised the house car for sale, asking $2,000 for it, and a prospective buyer, the owner of a small traveling circus, answered the ad and came from Tulsa, Oklahoma, to see it. It was obvious that he was impressed by the unusual vehicle, but he offered only $1,500 for it, and Daddy stood his ground. Loading up the family and bidding our faithful friend "Ma" Baxter goodbye, we set out for Russellville, Arkansas, the home of Daddy's sister, Lorena. Her plumber husband was in need of an assistant, and since Daddy was a Jack-of-all trades, Uncle Frank hired him. Once he became a plumber's assistant, he no longer needed the house car and he did need money. He contacted the circus owner and told him that he would accept $1,500; the man jumped at the deal. It seems that he had decided to pay Daddy his asking price, but we were en route to Russellville and couldn't be contacted. The deal was made, and it included the delivery of the vehicle to Tulsa, Oklahoma.

Daddy made his last trip in the house car, delivering it into the hands of the circus owner. He accepted the $1,500, which was paid in cash, put it in his shoes for safety, and hitch hiked back to Russellville. I shall never forget his return. He arrived after dark, waking us up to tell us he was home. Stretching out both feet he said: "Boy, am I tired. And my feet really hurt. Take my shoes off." John took one shoe, and I took the other. Imagine our surprise when hundred dollar bills began to flutter out. We had never seen that much money in our entire lives. I doubt if our parents had either. We accompanied Daddy to the bank the following morning, where he opened a checking account. We later learned that the spacious storage bin under the seat where Mother kept her quilts had been transformed into a cage for the new owner's pet python!

3

September, and the beginning of a new term of school for my brother and me, was growing near, and my mother was anxious to be settled in order that we could be enrolled in school. Education was, to Mother, the panacea for all social and economic ills; only in ailments of the spirit were its remedial powers ineffective. Each day, she set out from my aunt's house, where our family was billeted—as my aunt hoped, I'm sure—temporarily, and walked from place to place, searching for a house that was large enough for a family of four, yet unpretentious.

Mother was never one to bother with false pride. She knew in what part of town she would be most likely to find such a house: the North Side. To anyone who lived in our particular town, or one like it, the North Side needs no description. The railroad tracks cut the town in half, the populace as well as the terrain, and crossing those long rows of shining steel, blisteringly hot in summer to bare feet, meant entering another world—a world of narrow, muddy streets lined with rickety buildings housing general mercantile stores that sold feed, flour, and stick candy to the farmers every Saturday. Seedy shops run by "Syrians" displayed tapestries brought from the "Old Country" depicting various scenes in monotonous tones, but bursting into flaming shades of red, green, and gold in the silk fringe around their edges. A few second-hand furniture marts offered scarred baby beds and dressers with wonderfully untrue mirrors, and one dingy motion picture house with a sloping concrete entrance and garish posters advertised one week a cowboy picture and the next, one for adults only. The world of the South Side, with its tree-lined pavements, orderly lawns, and cool, gracious homes, was as remote as the millennium.

The house Mother finally selected was a small, once-white bungalow with an unimaginative cone-like roof sitting squarely and defiantly on its eaves, for all the world like my aunt wore her Sunday sailor disapprovingly above her heavy brows. Weeds had sprung up around the house and small outbuildings to such unlikely heights as almost to obscure the buildings from the view of a casual passer-by, and the incorrigible children of an earlier tenant had, with oily, colored crayons, practiced their penmanship and art on the clapboards, woodwork, and wallpaper. However, the advantages of the house were as marked as were its drawbacks. First of all, it was adjacent to the business district and provided a profitable site for my industrious brother, John, who had purchased and was operating a popcorn machine, but who, being only eleven, was in need of his mother's supervision. The bullies of the North Side had been known to knock down such young entrepreneurs and make off with the stock. It was within easy walking distance of the school that both my brother and I would attend, and it could be rented, or so we had heard, for the sum of $15 a month, which was a third of our monthly income and therefore the amount allotted by economists as that which could be safely expended for rent. (More often than not, I was nearer two-thirds.)

A brief conference with the owner, a shrewd old fellow who operated, among other things, a large wholesale store near the tracks, and we were all set to move in, with the understanding that we were to have the premises for an uninterrupted period of at least nine months—the school term—for $15 payable each month in advance. To my father, whose word was his bond, an understanding was all that was necessary. There was nothing in writing.

In we went—fruit jars, feather beds, oak furniture, and all—but not until the whole family had spent four back-breaking days cutting weeds, washing windows, scouring floors and woodwork, and white-washing everything in sight. The acrid odor of disinfectants permeated the place and bit into our nostrils before Mother declared the house fit to live in.

* * *

As it developed, we were to live there only a short time, but to my unsophisticated eyes it was a delightful neighborhood, inhabited by all sorts of interesting people. There was a large house next door that seemed to be a boarding house. The lady who owned it was a friendly, bosomy person with long, heavy red hair, coiled like a shining copperhead in a figure eight, pinned on top of her head with great tortoise-shell hairpins, and held off her neck by combs made of the same material. She smoked innumerable cigarettes and appeared always to be in the process of dressing or undressing, for she was rarely ever clad in anything but a trailing kimono and loose, flopping house shoes (the kind called "mules" in those days), and she was constantly replacing one of the yellow combs, catching between its teeth a wispy bit of the bright hair and raking it carefully back into place. Mother did not encourage the familiarity of the boarding house lady, but then that lady needed no encouragement. Almost every day, she dispatched me to the nearby grocer's for a loaf of bread or a package of cigarettes, offering as inducement a new penny, or sometimes even a nickel, and it was she who brought over a vaporizer when I developed what everyone thought was a heavy cold, but was later prove to be diphtheria.

Directly across the street was a mattress factory, or that was what the proprietor liked to call the one large room in which he, his blubbery wife, and numerous children tore up old mattresses, re-fluffed the stuffing, rewired the springs, and then put the whole business back together again in satiny new coverings, tufted here and there with little tabs of cotton. It was great fun to dart into the lint-filled structure and stay, watching the renovation process, until the dust and fuzz from the disemboweled mattresses choked me and made the tears start.

I remember once they made for my doll a diminutive mattress, bright blue with white flowers on it, a cunning replica of the regular sized ones. It fitted exactly into the homemade cradle my father had put together from scrap lumber for my bisque-faced child with the sawdust body.

And of course the swarthy, smiling foreign shopkeepers, with their quite impossible mixture of English and native tongue, provided a constant source of delight.

* * *

Our stay in that rented house was interrupted abruptly one morning when my father returned from town with his jaw clamped tight, the way he did when a principle had been violated. The landlord had refused Father's proffered $15 and had informed him that the new rental would be $25 a month, else he would like us to vacate his house. Remonstrations about their verbal agreement and the fact that the school term was only a little more than half-finished had produced no results. Rudely, the landlord had walked away, leaving my Father standing with the money—a $10 bill and a wrinkled five—in his hand, still protesting.

The next afternoon—shortly before suppertime—the arrest was made; Father and Mother were "wrongfully upon another's land"—or so the charge read.

Mother was, by turns, frightened and indignant. Father was never anything but outraged. My brother and I were excited; we were going to court! What's more, we were not mere spectators: we were participants, protagonists, defendants. It was a topic for boasting at school—a thing of such proportion as to make us the envy of all our classmates. To be ashamed never occurred to me. My father was a hero; the landlord a villain. My father was St. George; the landlord a dragon. My father was Daniel; the landlord a whole den of hungry lions—for, there being no money to hire a lawyer, *Father was going to defend himself!*

It was like waiting for Christmas. The delay common in legal circles arose, and there developed among my playmates certain skeptics who didn't believe that the sheriff had come to my house at all or that there was ever going to be a trial. My disciples rigidly defended me, and their faith was rewarded. One day I was absent from school; it was the day of the trial.

I do not now remember the day of the week, or even the month. I am not sure of the name of the lawyer who represented the landlord, or that of the presiding judge. But the courtroom, with its lofty, ornate ceilings, its darkly polished rails and benches, its round brass spittoons, and its awesome atmosphere of dignity and solemnity, engraved itself on my seven-year-old consciousness with an indelible clearness.

There was a large crowd of spectators, not present specifically, as I thought at first, to see my father's performance, but because there was a number of other cases to be tried. Many of the people were to be witnesses, but also in attendance, of course, were the curious, the morbid, the town loafers who needed new subjects for argument.

Mother, Father, John, and I filed in and found seats on a hard wooden pew down front, next to the balustrade that separated the stage, as it were, from the audience. We were taking no chances that latecomers might interfere with our vision or interrupt our attention. A rotund and unintelligible bailiff marched portentously and chanted that the court was now in session, *Oh Yes!*, and a respectful company rose to its feet as the black-robed justice entered the room, climbed to his high perch, and settled himself deliberately, pulling at his bat-like sleeves. Then, clearing his throat with a magnificent rumble, he picked up his gavel and seated the assemblage with a resounding rap.

The case was called, and my father stood, waiting uncertainly by his seat.

"Have you counsel?" asked the judge, and my father replied, "No, sir. I will plead my own case."

And then I was frightened. Was it possible that the dragon might turn on St. George after all and rip him into bits or melt him with one consuming belch of flame? What were they going to do to my father? A whimper almost escaped me, but I choked it back and watched in awful fascination as the jury was selected and took their seats. One, two, three, and now there were 12—all men, all dignified, all deadly serious.

The procedure of that trial I can no longer remember—that is, who appeared as witnesses or what evidence was offered—but my father's speech to the jury I can never forget. With a straightforwardness and a simplicity that an experienced attorney might envy, Father outlined, in homespun language, the situation to his listening peers. He touched lightly, but did not dwell upon his circumstances: his was no tear-jerking appeal. He did tell of our labor, of the improvements made to the property, and explained that it was his personal opinion that someone had passed, observed the now neat and orderly property, and had offered the landlord more money—a proposal which that greedy individual could not reject. My father was not vituperative; there was no bitterness in his tone. It was understandable, he said, that the man wanted to get the most he could from his investment, but here, gentlemen of the jury, principle was involved. A contract, verbal or otherwise, was simply a contract. It was unfortunate that the landlord's foresight had not been as good as his hindsight. Then, abruptly my Father sat down. Mother drew a quivering breath.

The jury went out slowly. A babble of voices rose in the courtroom; it was recess. John and I raced downstairs, beating the crowd to the soft drink stand in the basement, where we drank tall bottles of cold, syrupy, strawberry-flavored concoction and licked our ice cream cones, proudly mimicking Father's address to the jury. We never once doubted the outcome of the trial.

Nor should we have. The jury deliberated less than 30 minutes.

"Gentlemen of the jury, have you been able to reach a decision?"

"We have, Your honor," this from the foreman, a tall, sparse man with a balding head.

Then, "We, the jury, find for the defendants," and it was over. We had won!

Father was jubilant. Mother was in tears. Suddenly, in the conclusion which follows one trial before another begins, the judge leaned forward and called my father's name. Diffidently, with fast-beating heart, Father approached the bench, his hat in nervous hands. "Bring the others," the judge's gestures indicated, so Father held back the swinging gate, and we found ourselves standing directly in front of His Honor, looking up into eyes that were incongruous twinkles in a grave face.

"This your family?" He surveyed us approvingly and turned toward Father. "Fine youngsters, fine! By the way, you missed your calling. You should have been a lawyer!"

That night, after the trial had been re-enacted at least twice by everyone, I was carrying the last of the supper dishes to the sink when Father dropped his bombshell.

"How soon do you think we could be ready to move Mother?"

"Move!" It was both an exclamation and an interrogative. "But I thought the jury said," Mother replied impatiently. "I just wanted to show him I could do it! I wouldn't live in his house if he gave it to me!"

A principle had been defended and reasserted. We moved the following week—to, as it happened, the South Side.

Father never forgot the judge's words and remained convinced that he did indeed miss his calling. He should have been a lawyer!

And of course, Mother complied. Women of that era thought they had to, I suppose, because it was a rare occasion when Mama defied Daddy about anything.

4

Mother had a cousin who was a prominent attorney in Russellville, Arthur Priddy; he even had run for Governor at one time. He liked Mama, and she had no problem getting in to see him. I went with her to talk to him about a place for us to live, and I saw my first law office. It was impressive, with enormous desks, walls covered with bookshelves full of beautiful leather-bound books, oriental rugs, and the ever present leather couch—a fixture in all law offices at that time.

Arthur Priddy had practiced law a long time, and I suspect that some of his real estate had been acquired for services rendered, or from foreclosures, because he had numerous properties. I also suspect that many of them were liabilities, for he seemed eager to show them to us. But then a wonderful, unexpected thing happened. My grandfather, I. W. Harkey, really left "Aunt Jenny," my disagreeable grandmother.

This had happened before. I remember Daddy saying that his earliest recollections were of hearing arguments between his father and mother, arguments that sometimes were interrupted with loud thumping noises when his father lost his temper. Of course, divorce was unheard of in those days, especially with church-goers, as everyone involved claimed to be, but my father was completely fed up.

"Why don't you just get out of it?" he asked my grandfather.

And that's what happened. Arthur Priddy had shown us a magnificent two-story, antebellum home on South Commerce Avenue in a beautiful up-scale community in Russellville that was made up of big dwellings occupied by very successful and influential people. Directly across the street lived a doctor, Dr. Emerson, and next door to him Judge Ward, a chancellor; on the other side were the Roys and the Cardens, wealthy landowners and farmers, and next door to them the Leonards, who owned the biggest hardware store in the county.

* * *

I remember the day we went to look at the house, opening the great front door with its oval, floor-length, cut-glass center, to enter the spacious high-ceilinged rooms with shining hardwood floors, something I had never seen before. There was a butler's pantry, another unknown, and an enormous kitchen. We were speechless.

And "cousin" Arthur Priddy was going to sell it to us! Fifteen hundred dollars, but it might as well have been a million, except that I. W. had made up his mind to leave his wife for good—divorce her. And when that happened, he would need a place to live. Again the Aladdin lamp was lit, with the grown-ups talking together long after I had been put to bed.

Here's what they worked out: Grandpa would lend Daddy the $1,500, and once the divorce was final, Grandpa would move in with us in the beautiful house on Commerce Avenue. In lieu of interest on the loan, Mama would "take care of him," which meant cooking his meals, cleaning his room, washing his clothes, and doing whatever else he decided that he needed her to do. Never was there a more usurious debt incurred! Grandpa had "stomach trouble"—real or imagined. His diet was complicated, making the preparation of meals time consuming. And he had a habit of filling his bed with small Irish potatoes at night, having heard from someone somewhere that potatoes were beneficial in the treatment of rheumatism, an ailment from which he had suffered for years.

But the Harkeys would no longer pay rent.

We had furniture enough for only three rooms, and that's the number of rooms which our family utilized when we moved into the house, plus a hallway which housed Grandpa's bed; the other rooms were turned into apartments, unfurnished at first, but rentable, insuring a much needed cash flow. The third room, a large front room, was converted to a bedroom. There were two beds, one for my father and brother; the other for my mother and me. If my parents had any sex life during that period of time, it was not evident to John or me. The middle room was the "stove room," containing a large black pot-bellied stove, its smokestack piercing the ceiling. Of course, there was no central heating system, and as powerful as the coal-burning stove was, it heated only part of the huge room. I remember my father rising before anyone else was awake to build a roaring fire for John and me to dress by, and of course, for Mama to get ready to prepare breakfast, which was one of the most important meals for our family. I remember shivering as I pulled on the "long-handled" underwear, sometimes getting too close to the red-hot stove and being burned. Mother had to blow on it and rub it with butter.

It was also in that room that my father's proudest possession, a roll top desk, sat, and a library table, which had nothing on it except a King James Bible, and our school books that we studied. There was no money for newspapers or magazines, and I saw my first "movie star" magazine when I visited the tenants who rented the rooms on the other side of our living quarters. Later on, my father raised the roof of the house several feet, turning the attic space into additional apartments, thereby increasing the family income.

The kitchen was very large, the butler's pantry having been made a part of it, and all our meals were eaten on a big table covered with a white tablecloth and with the condiments bunched together in the center. Mother's great wood-burning range had a hot-water bin attached to the side, from which we dipped water on Saturday nights for our weekly baths. A long back porch, with a well in the middle, led to the storage room which housed an ice box, with great blocks of ice in it, where Mother kept the milk she coaxed from our jersey cow and the wonderful fresh butter she churned with a manual churn, until Daddy rigged it up to an electrical attachment. The ice man came every day during the hot summer months, driving a heavily loaded wagon pulled by a white horse who knew exactly where to stop while his master, wielding a heavy pick, delivered the chunks of ice to his customers, filling the boxes where the food was preserved. All the children, including John and I, hitched onto the back of the wagon, nibbling the delicious slivers that fell, or melted, off the great blocks. It was during the darkest days of the Depression, but there were endless hours of sunshine. We played Run, Sheep, Run under the streetlights every night until bedtime.

* * *

I can only imagine how the affluent and genteel residents on either side of our house on Commerce Avenue must have felt when the Harkeys and their tenants arrived. Needless to say, the apartments which Mama put together, with linoleum-covered floors and second-hand furnishings, were certainly not luxurious, and the tenants they attracted, were for the most part hard-working people—bus drivers, waitresses, and the like. The police even raided the place one night! Two young women who shared one of the apartments were engaged in the world's oldest profession. Of course, my mother had not an inkling of her tenants' criminal behavior. I remember her in her nightgown, accompanying the police and severely lecturing the culprits as they were being taken away, even advising that they should pray and ask God's forgiveness for their wicked behavior.

Both my parents solicited jobs in the neighborhood. I remember that Daddy built a beautiful outdoor bridal altar for our neighbor, Judge Ward's wife, when their daughter married, and Mother cleaned their lovely home twice a week. I always accompanied her, helping to dust the beautiful furniture and pushing the amazing vacuum sweeper. It was in Mrs. Ward's living room that I saw my first living room suite with a matching rug. The Wards' grown-up daughter was away at college, and I discovered her room as a child, with an unbelievable collection of children's books.

Once I slipped away from Mama and had very carefully taken down a book, sitting on the floor absorbing it, when I looked up to see Mrs. Ward standing at the door observing my every move. I jumped up, unsure as to whether I should replace the book or just what to do, when Mrs. Ward very gently said, "Do you like the book?"

To which I nodded and replied, "Oh, yes, ma'am."

And then she said, "Would you like to take it home and read it?"

I was speechless; I could only nod.

"Well, you certainly may," she continued. "You may take as many of them as you like." I did remember to thank her. School started that year much too soon, for I was reading every spare minute. As it happened, Mrs. Ward was on the board of the Russellville library, which required a fee for membership, and although it was not a very large fee, it was out of reach for us. In her capacity as a board member, Mrs. Ward requested that the Harkey children be allowed to become members and use the library without having to pay anything, a very generous gesture which John and I took full advantage of. I have no doubt that our use of that library through the years contributed to our scholastic achievements.

5

Although our parents did not complain, both John and I were acutely aware of their struggle simply to feed and clothe us. Daddy even tried to go back to selling his encyclopedias, with disastrous results, having to pay back money that had been advanced by the company. The Depression had deepened, and to make matters worse, there was a draught in Pope County that year.

Mother had, on her own, decided to sell flavoring, and she was good at it, displaying colorful lemon, chocolate, and other flavors, but always returning to, and touting, vanilla. She knocked on doors or rang doorbells and displayed her collection, telling the potential customers that she used them herself and knew that all flavors were wonderful. When Daddy came back from his failed effort to sell books again, he joined her, and they expanded their territory to the neighboring towns of Clarksville and Pottsville.

John was 11 when Daddy fell on the idea of turning him into a popcorn salesman. There were many occasions where people got together for various events, like Memorial Day or Veterans' meetings, and Daddy thought popcorn would sell. He was right. John not only took his portable popcorn popper to those events, but set up a daily operation on the streets of Russellville. The brand of popcorn he sold was Jolly Time, and at that time my brother was roly-poly, so everybody called him Jolly, and the nickname stuck.

The freshly popped corn was sifted in a wire basket to separate the "hard grains" from the fully popped kernels, and the "hard grains" were the ones that my family and I ate, saving the other popped kernels to be sold. Hard grains became my favorite, and remain so today. When I popped popcorn for my children, I always sorted out the partially popped kernels, leaving the choice grains for them. One of my most treasured gifts was given to me by my son, Everett, when he was 10 years old. I had married "Duke" Atkinson (the third mistake!), and Everett was enrolled in Columbia Military School, Columbia, Tennessee, Duke having convinced me that putting him in military school was a very beneficial thing to do for my son. My 20/20 hindsight now tells me my law-enforcement husband did not really want either of my children around. Fortunately, Everett loved military school, although he went only one year, after which I brought him home. I missed him too much to send him back, and so did his sister.

Parents were not allowed to visit the first two weeks of the military student's enrollment, and that was the longest two weeks of my life. I remember that I had just bought a new car, and the first place I drove was to Tennessee to visit Everett. I went alone, as Gretel was spending the weekend with friends and my husband was on duty. I was surprised that Everett loved military school. Proudly he took me through his quarters, pointing out how he had learned to make his bed, the sheets so tight he could bounce a coin off them, and hang up his uniforms, all arranged in the same direction; tasks which had been unknown to him when he lived at home and attended regular school. I praised him profusely, and we were just about to leave for lunch in the mess hall when he reached into a drawer and pulled out a small sack. "I have a present for you, Mom," he said and added, "they were going to throw them away." I gingerly opened the sack to discover a cache of partially popped popcorn—"hard grains." He had attended a ball game, bought popcorn, and noted that the "hard grains" had been separated and were destined to be destroyed. Knowing that I loved them and always ate them when we popped corn, he had salvaged them to give to me. Everett may someday give me precious stones, a trip abroad, or even a convertible, but he can never give me a gift that will surpass that small batch of "hard grains" saved for me!

My brother John was receiving only a nickel for two sacks of popcorn, but he did a thriving business and earned enough to buy all his school supplies and clothes, as well as mine, which was a great help to my low-income parents. John adored his sister, me, and realizing that I had no source of income, elected to give me all the pennies he received. I soon had enough pennies that Daddy helped me roll them up and take them to the bank. I suppose it's safe now to reveal that when I knew my friends were contemplating buying popcorn, I always urged them to use pennies, and even told them to exchange their nickels for pennies. I guess there are people who might say I was destined to become a lawyer!

* * *

I shall never forget one disastrous day when Mother and I watched a sobbing John as he returned one afternoon, pushing his popcorn popper slowly back from town, his basket still full, no sales having been made. "What's happened?" Mother asked, rushing toward him, and he told an almost unbelievable story. A constable had apologetically ordered John off the Street.

It seems that there had been an ordinance passed prohibiting salesmen on the city streets, an event which had gone unnoticed by my politically naive parents. But why? John was extremely popular and caused no trouble.

It was my father who figured it out when he observed popcorn still being sold in the lobby of the motion picture theatre, two blocks from John's usual location. Mr. Butler, the owner of the theatre, was obviously tired of sweeping Jolly Time popcorn sacks out of his establishment and losing sales to "Jolly."

He simply pulled his popcorn machine inside the lobby, and it was no longer on the street.

"That ain't right!" my indignant mother allowed. Well, of course, it wasn't, but what could she do about it? She had heard of "petitions"—had even signed them to keep lotteries and other sinful pursuits from occurring, but how to go about it? Another visit to Cousin Arthur's law office was in order, and he complied. A petition was drafted, copies printed, and our whole family set out to obtain signatures.

It was a cinch. Mama declared that some of the people whom she contacted were so eager to sign that they even asked if they could do so more than once! John went back on the street. I never cease to be amazed at the accomplishments brought about by sheer determination on the part of my relatively uneducated parents.

* * *

In that connection, nobody ever regarded education and the necessity of obtaining it to be as important as did my father. He even exerted a Herculean effort to attend school himself after he attained majority. His schooling in the one-room schoolhouse, conducted only three months during the year, had been constantly interrupted by his necessary work on the family farm. He enrolled in the Keys Institute of Training in Little Rock, only to find out that he lacked the foundation to be successful. His instructor suggested that he switch to telegraphy, which he did, but that, too, failed.

Largely as a result of that experience he was determined that his children would obtain educations, and he made no distinction between his son and his daughter, an attitude that was not universally held at that time.

Although we had very little reading material, we always received a copy of the Sears & Roebuck catalog, the document we utilized when it became absolutely necessary that we obtain work clothes or underwear. I never remember my mother shopping anywhere else, although lack of money made all shopping a very limited operation. One day, however, my father noted an extraordinary offer in the latest catalog. It was the height of the Depression, and Sears was seeking new customers. The company came up with an unusual scheme. An individual could sign up to promote customers for the company, receiving for his or her efforts money to finance a college education. The company's order blanks were printed with the participant's name and address attached, and if an order was made on that order blank, the participant would receive a percentage of the total purchase price. The money went directly into a trust account allocated solely to finance a college education, with the money being paid directly to the college. My father immediately contacted Sears to see if the plan was transferable, as John, being older, would need it before I did. The answer was no, and as a result, it was I who was enrolled into the program. It truly was an unusual proposition, with no limitations or restrictions. It could be a junior college or Harvard, and the participant need not purchase a wardrobe from Sears & Roebuck. His or her clothes could be purchased from Neiman-Marcus!

Once the order blanks with my name on them were received, my parents systematically mapped out Pope County where we lived, and later on all the surrounding counties, reaching every rural address and either mailing or hand delivering the order blanks, with typed requests that they be used when ordering merchandise from Sears & Roebuck, explaining that it was at no extra cost, the merchandise was of high quality, and a percentage of their payment would help a very deserving young person obtain a college education.

It worked. After I was graduated from Russellville High School (at age 16 as Valedictorian), I enrolled in Arkansas Tech in Russellville, which was only a two-year school at that time, but I could remain at home. My parents charged me room and board, which Sears & Roebuck paid on a monthly basis, and every dime of it was put in an interest-bearing account to subsidize my subsequent enrollment at the University of Arkansas at Fayetteville.

Every month after my enrollment at the University, I visited the registrar's office to pick up my check from Sears & Roebuck, which, with the money I earned grading papers for one of my instructors and the money my parents contributed as they could, covered my tuition and made my college attendance possible. I remember being ribbed by the registrar and his employees—"Here comes our project mail order girl!"—which bothered me not one whit. I though it was a very clever move on my parents' part, and so successful was our family in obtaining orders, Sears actually contacted my father and tried to pay a lump sum of money to end the process, a proposal which my father promptly vetoed. I don't remember how long I collected the monthly checks, but it lasted the greater part of my term at the University of Arkansas.

* * *

John was successfully selling popcorn again; Mother was renting apartments, cleaning houses, and selling flavoring; my father was helping both, in addition to doing the milking and the gardening, but he felt that he needed to be earning money. There were taxes to pay, and he still owed his father for the purchase of the Commerce Avenue home. Of course, he did all of the repairs, kept it painted, and even cut down two gigantic trees in the front yard which had sapped the soil and kept the lawn bare of grass, filling and sodding the yard until it was beautiful. So anxious was he to locate a paying position that he would sift through the abandoned mail at the post office and answer all ads that might lead to an opportunity for lucrative employment.

Believe it or not, one of the discarded letters was promoting a real estate company, the United Farm Agency of Kansas City, Missouri. The company was searching for agents to sell farms on a commission basis, all advertising to be provided by United

Farm Agency, and my father's letter seeking information about the operation was answered by none other than one of the company's top executives, Mr. Roscoe Chamberlain, who made an appointment to come to Arkansas to interview Daddy.

Such excitement, expectation, and hope: Daddy picked him up at the airport, and Mama readied a bed in an empty apartment, inviting Mr. Chamberlain to save the expense and trouble of procuring a hotel room.

Daddy and Mr. Chamberlain talked at great length before retiring, and it was evident to Mr. Chamberlain that Daddy had sales experience and certainly was well acquainted with farms and farming. The required three letters of recommendation posed no problems, but the posting of a $1,000 bond would take a little time.

The next morning, Mama set up an elaborate breakfast with not only a batch of her incomparable buttermilk biscuits, but fluffy pancakes as well. Mr. Chamberlain's girth gave an indication of his appetite, and he took ample helpings of everything, to Mama's delight. However, when our guest raised the bottle of maple syrup to pour it over his pancakes, he saw a colony of dead ants floating in the sticky liquid. Mama almost had a stroke. She was chagrined, but more importantly she was afraid Mr. Chamberlain had ingested some of the mess. "I'm so sorry!" she kept saying as she seized his plate, dumped it in the garbage pail, and provided a clean one, almost simultaneously.

Mr. Chamberlain's reaction made him her friend for life. He immediately filled his clean plate with scrambled eggs, and assured her that that sort of thing just happens, particularly in such hot weather. It was evident to Mr. Chamberlain that the incident was an anomaly in the Harkey household.

Daddy became a United Farm agent and enjoyed a very close relationship with Roscoe Chamberlain for many years before establishing his own real estate business, J. H. Harkey's Farm Sales, with Daddy as the broker and Mama as his licensed salesman.

6

Our Commerce Avenue address was on the dividing line that required me to attend West Side Elementary School, which was located quite a distance away, rather than a much closer school. John was in high school, which also was much closer to our home. The only transportation we had was John's bicycle, and he pedaled it with me sitting on the handle bars from our house to West Side School every morning before he went to school. I remember some bitter cold days when it was difficult for John to pump against the whistling wind, but he never failed to deliver me on time.

I returned the favor the summer I was 12 years old. John was taking a course in bookkeeping at the Weedin Business College, and I would pedal from our house on Commerce to the high school where the college had its classes and pick John up when it was time to go home.

The Weedins, a man and his wife and their two sons, taught typing, shorthand, and bookkeeping to students who could afford the training, for it was not part of the school system. I never knew if John worked out the idea of trading mounds of roasting ears, okra, green beans, and other vegetables for his course, or if Mama arranged it, but that's how he was able to attend business college.

Sometimes when I arrived at the business, John would have a few things to do before he could leave, and I would walk around, looking at the typewriters whose keys had been covered up and the notebooks that were full of mysterious symbols the shorthand students had written. Mr. Weedin must have been a grandfather, or wanted to be one, for he always talked to me. Once, he typed out "The skunk sat on the stump; the skunk thought the stump stunk, and the stump thought the skunk stunk."

"I want to learn how to type—and write that stuff," I remember saying, "Could you all use some more vegetables?"

Mrs. Weedin was in earshot, and I remember her saying, "I wish you were older. I need somebody to clean my house."

"I can clean houses," I declared, and I could. Mama had taught both John and me to help with the chores and take care of ourselves when she was working outside the home. I must have sounded convincing, because I became a student in the Weedin Business College, riding my brother's bicycle to the Weedins' apartment located quite far from our house, near St. Mary's Hospital, cooking breakfast for their two grown sons, then the older one would ride the bike, with me as a passenger, to the school.

I became a very competent typist, reaching a hundred words a minute on a manual typewriter and winning an area contest. It was Greg Shorthand that the Weedins taught, and I was drawing the symbols and trying to memorize each one. I don't remember whether it was her son or Mrs. Weedin who explained to me that the symbols were phonetic—that you could write anything if you could sound it out. I felt like Helen Keller when her teacher poured water over her hand, writing the word "water" on her hand at the same time. From then on, I could write anything and went on to become a bona fide court reporter without any additional training.

Down the street from us, but still in the neighborhood, lived Boyd Keathley, who was the official court reporter for our district. I used to go to the courthouse and watch him write the swirling symbols as the witnesses were talking. I had my shorthand tablet and tried to keep up with Boyd, an exercise that I did for several years at various times. Boyd got quite a kick out of my learning shorthand at such a young age and was instrumental in my becoming a court reporter after I was married the first time.

* * *

Grandpa Harkey died, from pneumonia, when he was 77 years old. I remember my father propping him up in his bed and shaving him, honoring his last wish that he not be embalmed.

I don't know if it was just my grandparents, or if people of their era regarded death as part of life, but I remember my grandmother showing me a very special dress that she had never worn, but had carefully put away "to be buried in." Grandpa had designed and had his son-in-law, my Uncle Lee, build his casket in the family graveyard. I remember accompanying Grandpa and Uncle Lee to the site during its construction, and watching Grandpa lie down and stretch out, patting his head to be sure the tomb was long enough and that it would be high enough for people to sit on comfortably when they were attending Decoration Day.

Decoration Day occurred in the early spring, not long after Easter, and was quite an event. Great crowds of people—relatives, parishioners, and probably many people simply looking for entertainment and a hearty meal—attended. Housewives brought their finest dishes—baked hams, potato salad, coleslaw, sweet potato pies—and there was great a cappella singing by people from hymnals with shaped notes.

My father's father was certainly one of a kind: Mama told me the story of how once he and some other whittlers were congregated outside the general store swapping yarns. "I. W." had become angry about something and stabbed the offender. Fortunately, the wound was not fatal, but it was serious enough that Grandpa was charged with assault and tried by Brooks Hays when he was prosecuting attorney.

I remember that the Hays family lived in Russellville in the most elegant house I had ever seen, with marble pillars. Brooks' father and mother were members of the Baptist church where we were members—at least Mama, John, and I were members. My father never darkened the door and really didn't like our going, but there was no other Baptist church available, so he grudgingly allowed us to attend. We could not, however, contribute any money to an organization attended by anyone who had attempted to put Daddy's father in the penitentiary. Apparently, Daddy thought the injured man deserved to be stabbed, for he never forgave Brooks Hays and/or any member of his family. Mother always waited until we reached the church before she tied up in a handkerchief the pennies we were giving and gave them to us to put in the collection plate.

Once, my grandfather and my mother were cutting wood when his knife slipped and severed his left thumb. Mother recalls his recovering it from the block of wood in which it had lodged before he was taken, by horseback, to the doctor, who was unable to reattach it, but did manage to stop the bleeding. Grandpa preserved the finger, and it was placed in one of the drawers of my father's rolltop desk. I remember how my friends and I giggled when I surreptitiously displayed it to them when no one was around. When Grandpa died, Daddy placed it in the casket with the body, just before it was lowered into the ground, making sure all body parts were together.

* * *

Grandpa died before Daddy had been able to repay the $1,500 that had made it possible for us to buy the house on Commerce Avenue. During his last illness, he and my father discussed the manner in which the debt could be settled. Of course, Daddy had put far more than that back into the upkeep and improvement of the home, but Grandpa was concerned that his other children would receive nothing, that debt being the bulk of his estate, if not all of it. After a great deal of puzzling over the matter, Daddy thought he had a solution. Not counting himself, there were seven heirs. "How about this," he asked his father, "I will give each of the children $200 as I earn it from my farm sales, paying the ones who need it the worst first. Would that be all right?" And Grandpa nodded agreement.

Daddy had obtained many listings, and was steadily showing farms to the many prospective purchasers that United Farms Agency's extensive advertising had produced, but he had not made a lot of sales, and one half of the commission went to United Farm Agency. Also, Daddy incurred a great deal of expense when he drove the farm seekers all over the county, relying, for the most part, on Mama's earnings from the sale of her flavorings or rent money paid by the tenants to buy the gasoline. Nevertheless, the first $200 he earned, and could do without, went to Aunt Mabel, whose husband had not yet made sufficient money from his timber business to care for his handicapped wife and numerous children.

All of Daddy's siblings went along with the plan, knowing that their father had approved it, except Aunt Icie. She hired an attorney, put the whole thing into probate court, challenging everything, even demanding that she receive Grandpa's anvil, which had been at our house since Grandpa brought it there. As for the house, Daddy could not pay the entire balance, and the Court ordered it sold at the Courthouse steps. On the day of the trial there was one bid made: my father's, for $1,500. Daddy honored the death-bed agreement made with his father. Excluding Daddy, there were seven heirs, and each received $200 from my father as rapidly as he could pay—$1,400 in all. I guess you could say Daddy realized a hundred dollars from his father's estate.

* * *

The year following Grandpa's death, Daddy's farm sales increased, and each succeeding year thereafter he did a little better.

When the prospective farm purchasers, who came to Russellville from all over the United States in response to United

Farm Agency's extensive advertising, arrived in town, Mother and Daddy directed them straight to our house, where Mother always had a spare bedroom and could whip up breakfast the next morning, then Daddy took them to see his many listings. In that way, Daddy could show them the farms he had listed before the other dealers could spot their out-of-state license plates and try to interest them in the farms they had for sale.

One day, the Johansens entered our lives, and no one knew what drastic changes were in store. It seems that Mrs. Johansen had been widowed, and she answered Mr. Johansen's advertisement for a wife. Mr. Johansen was a dirt farmer from Kansas who had struck oil, and he had come to Arkansas to look at farms, with the idea of purchasing farms for each of his children. Daddy spent many hours showing Mr. Johansen his finest properties.

When he had seen a sufficient number, Mr. Johansen said to my father: "I think I'll take that one located off highway so-and-so, the one next to that cemetery, and the one that has the big lake on it."

My father thought he was joking. "Yeah," Daddy said, "That would certainly be great."

"You can sell them to me, can't you? I really think my boys could make a good living, if they had those farms paid for. Figure it up, and I'll write you a check."

Daddy was overwhelmed. The man was serious! Daddy had never sold multiple farms at the same time, and certainly not for cash money! Even though one half of Daddy's commission went to United Farm Agency, he still would get what was to him a fortune!

Mr. Johansen, my folks, and I met Mr. Johansen's step-son, "Pete" Keeney, at the same time he met him, in the front yard of our Commerce Avenue home in Russellville. He flew in to be with his mother and meet his new step-father. He was my age, 17, and a very good looking boy.

The Johansens bought still another piece of property, a lovely home just a few miles west of the elementary school I had attended, in a newly developed, beautiful subdivision. As a result, his family and ours saw a great deal of each other.

* * *

Pete, the new boy in town, became very popular. From the very first, he liked only me, and since he was the first and only boy I had ever been allowed to see, the love stories that I had secretly read when the apartment dwellers threw away their movie magazines became realistic.

Mr. Johansen had a daughter about my age, and she and I became good friends, so I spent more and more time with the Johansens and, of course, Pete. His real name was Marble Woodruff Keeney, but he had an older brother who was his idol, and his nickname was "Pete," so he decided that he, too, would be "Pete."

One Sunday afternoon, a group of us, boys and girls, Pete included of course, had gathered at my house, planning a hike to the river at Dardanelle, a favorite outing. I had prepared sandwiches, and the others had brought desserts and drinks, and we were just about to leave when my father came out on the front porch where my friends and I were congregated, some sitting in the swings which were suspended on either side. I have relived that day many times in an effort to sort out and understand it, and it is yet a mystery. My father looked at me and suddenly declared, in a deafening roar, "What have you got on your fingernails—nail polish?" (I was never allowed to use cosmetics.) And with that, he got his razor strap and began striking me across my back, cutting blood out of my back, with all my friends watching in total shock. My mother attempted to intervene and he shoved her—the only time I ever saw him touch her in anger. She lost her balance and fell across the piano bench. Pete attempted to defend me, but that went nowhere. My guests scrambled to escape, and Pete took me to his house, where I remained for a day or two, sleeping with his step-sister and vowing never to go home again.

Of course, Mama was very upset and called me frequently, trying to get me to come home. I missed her very much, and my brother, too. I have given my father's behavior that day a great deal of thought, because he had not disciplined John and me in that manner very often, and he was not a mean man. On the contrary, he was a very kind man. He was familiar with the admonition in Proverbs which referred to "sparing the rod" and its effect on children, and I think he sincerely believed he was disciplining me "for my own good."

I never thought it gave him any pleasure, but he had many opinions that were contrary to mine. For instance, he would not allow either Mama or me to wear slacks. I remember trying to reason with him. "Chinese women wear pants," I argued, and "If I had on pants when I ride the bicycle, less of me would be exposed!" But my arguments fell on deaf ears.

I was not allowed to dance—it was a sin—nor to play cards. I remember Mama confiscating and burning cards that John and I had picked up in the street after political rallies at the courthouse. We put numbers on the back of them and converted them into playing cards. Daddy called all soft drinks "belly wash," and they were never allowed in our home. I probably am the only adult female in the world who has never drunk a Coca-Cola! I tasted one once, and I still remember the negative reaction I had from the carbonated drink.

I do not remember how long I remained at the Johansen residence, but I became homesick, and Pete took me home one night. When I entered the dark house, I remember stumbling over an object. Switching on the light, I saw a beautiful cedar chest, something that I had wanted for a long time. Cedar chests were a great fad at that time with teenagers. We called them "hope chests" and stocked them with embroidered napkins and tablecloths, and those who could afford it, silverware. All girls looked forward to the time when they would be married. I am sure Mama had a hand in Daddy's buying a "consolation" gift for me.

* * *

My father had one conviction that I am grateful for every day of my life. I have no idea how this relatively uneducated man came to the conclusion that cigarette smoking was bad for your health. To my knowledge, he had never studied chemistry and knew very little about substances like nicotine, but he hated cigars and cigarettes and made no bones about it. I remember being very ashamed of the enormous homemade sign that he had hanging in our living room: NO SMOKING. And he meant it. He requested guests and the people with whom he came in contact to extinguish their cigars and cigarettes in his presence, and if they did not, I have known him to knock it out of the offender's mouth! Shades of Carrie Nation!

I wish he could have lived long enough to see smoking barred in public places and businesses, and tobacco companies successfully sued and required to pay enormous amounts of damages. I obeyed my parents largely because I was taught that that was what children were supposed to do, and I never smoked a cigarette. It is very sad for me to see how difficult it is for most people to kick the habit of smoking, even those suffering from emphysema and other ailments exacerbated by the use of nicotine. Unfortunately, my beautiful daughter is in that category.

* * *

After my two-year stint at Arkansas Tech, I enrolled at the University of Arkansas in Fayetteville, as my brother had done earlier. After his graduation, John became a certified public accountant in St. Louis, Missouri, where he met and later married Dorothy Christensen. She and all her siblings were born in the United States, but her parents came from Denmark, and although her parents learned that they had lived only 10 miles apart in the old country, they did not meet until they each came separately to America.

John and Dorothy had a wonderful marriage, Dottie devoting her life entirely to being a wife and a mother, as did most women of that era. Wives were homemakers; husbands were breadwinners. It was not until World War II that women began to work outside the home. I remember a popular song entitled "Rosie the Riveter." My brother and Dottie had two daughters: Gaye and Shirley, both of whom graduated from Baylor University, the entire family being devout Baptists. John even volunteered to work in the Billy Graham revivals when they were held in the city where the family resided at the time, his career as a certified public account requiring different locations. My first trip to New Orleans was made to visit him and meet his first daughter, who was born there.

Dottie was a consummate housekeeper and an outstanding cook and seamstress. She made all of her children's clothes decorating them with intricate tatting, and she even ironed her sheets and pillowcases.

7

On December 8, 1941, I was gathered with the rest of the students attending the University when we heard the news on the radio that the Japanese had attacked Pearl Harbor, on December 7, "a day that will live in infamy," and heard Franklin D. Roosevelt state that he had asked Congress to declare that we were in a state of war since that date. Pete, who had gone to work after graduating from high school, was drafted and was stationed at an air base in New Mexico.

All the male students attending Arkansas Tech were drafted, leaving only female students, an event that made the national news at the time. Today's armed forces, with its great number of females, never ceases to amaze me. I remember when the WACs were created; I had a degree and could have been an officer, but my father would not hear of it. "No daughter of mine is going to be a camp follower," he declared, and although I was an adult, I capitulated.

The University had a rule that all freshmen had to live in the dormitory the first year, pledging their sororities their second year. Of course, pledging a sorority was entirely out of reach for me, but I was glad the University had that rule because Betty Brooks Hays, our congressman's daughter, was a good friend of mine, and she also lived in Carnell Hall. We remained friends after she was pledged Chi-Omega, one of the most coveted sororities. Of course, at that time there were dormitories for women and dormitories for men. We were able to run up and down the halls with very little or no clothing on. If by chance a male appeared to repair a leak or install a washing machine, we warned everyone by screaming "Man on Second," and doors were slammed everywhere as we scurried from sight.

Men were subtly treated differently from women—a situation that has improved somewhat, but still exists to a certain degree. I remember that Betty Brooks came in one evening, sobbing. She had gone out on a first date with a boy whom she had just met, and it seems that he had taken liberties to such an extent that she had to fight him off and run into the dorm to escape him. She immediately went to the House Mother and related the incident, furious and embarrassed. The House Mother's approach angered her even more. "What did you do that led him to behave in that manner?" she questioned, whereupon Betty Brooks tore into my room to be comforted. I think he was eventually reprimanded. I know he never had a chance to take Betty Brooks out again.

* * *

Graduation time was dawning, and I began to receive recognition by various organizations for achieving high grades. I remember that I was awarded an honorary membership in a journalism society, and there was a ceremonial dinner and installation held at Mary Maestri's in Tonitown, all of which required money. I wrote my parents that I needed $10, which arrived promptly. A few weeks later I had a similar honor, from my English courses, one of my essays having been sent to the *Atlantic Monthly*. (It wasn't printed of course, but my instructor thought it was good enough to be sent). There was the inevitable ceremony, dinner at the wonderful restaurant, with the necessary expenses, which the folks sent as soon as they received my request. And then, wonder of wonders, I was awarded Phi Beta Kappa, which required not only a ceremony and a dinner, but a key as well! I, jubilant and unbelieving, notified my parents. Imagine my consternation when I received my father's reply. He reluctantly sent 10 more dollars, but his letter was a stern one. "Sister," he wrote "stop joining them organizations; we can't afford it. Love Dad." I cried for hours. "A prophet is not without honor save in his own country."

My sojourn at the University at Fayetteville was spent working (grading papers), and studying. I had very little social life, not being able to attend dances in the beautiful Student Union building, and still holding on to my romantic fantasy with respect to Pete Kenney, who wrote to me regularly from his base, urging me to visit him. Once I had graduated and returned to Russellville, his efforts to get me to visit the base in New Mexico increased, and he even sent money for a train ticket. Of course I was flattered and I had traveled nowhere since the house car days. I had never been on a train, and in the end it was arranged.

I shall never forget that trip. I spent the entire time running from side to side looking out the train windows at the totally strange Zane Grey country side, with its tons of sand and blowing tumbleweeds.

Pete was overjoyed to see me and eager to show me around. It was a big base, housing the hero of World War II, the B-17, and Pete was a Sergeant who was trained to guide them in. I thoroughly enjoyed seeing everything and meeting everyone, but imagine my surprise when I learned Pete had told everyone that I had come to New Mexico to marry him! I really hadn't; I had been flattered by Pete's obvious infatuation, but I really did not want to be married. I also did not want to hurt him, or embarrass him in front of his friends. So I married him. I cried throughout the ceremony.

* * *

There was only a week-end, spent in Deming, New Mexico, and Pete was back on duty and I was being shown housing provided enlisted servicemen on base for the married servicemen. It was far from luxurious, but it was adequate, and we had fun fixing it up. Our neighbors were all servicemen and their wives—most of them, like us, newly wed. Before long, we were cooking out together and spending hours at the enlisted men's club. The Commander in charge was Colonel Hamrick, and when he learned that I knew shorthand and typing, I became his secretary.

I had read about Carlsbad Caverns as far back as the *Book of Knowledge*, and that was one of the first things I did—arranged a trip to Carlsbad. What an exciting trip that was. When I learned that my parents were coming to visit, I immediately planned to take them to view the caverns. I shall never forget that Daddy, upon learning the amount of the fare, decided that he would not go. "I've read all about it and seen pictures," he said, "and that's good enough for me."

I threw a crying fit, and he finally agreed to go. Once he took the elevator down and got his first glimpse of the caverns, he turned to me in awe. "Sister, I didn't know what I was talking about!" And he refused to take the elevator out, electing to walk so he could savor the awesome caverns longer. It was one of the few times I remember Daddy ever admitting that he had been totally wrong. "I didn't know what I was talking about, Sister!" he declared.

While the folks were in New Mexico, I arranged for Col. Hamrick to take them up in what then was an enormous airplane, and they both were thrilled to death. It was the treat of a lifetime. When we landed and exited the airplane, I remember Daddy pointing to the long black tracks left on the landing and remarking that that "certainly would wear off a lot of rubber and cost a lot of money to replace."

I still remember the look on Col. Hamrick's face. "Mr. Harkey, they are working on that problem right now in the lab. They are trying to design some kind of device that will start the wheels rotating before they hit the runway." I was really proud of my daddy, and you could see Col. Hamrick was amazed. The Arkansas "hick" was not dumb.

* * *

I can't remember when it was that Pete got his call to go overseas, but I do remember the day the long troop train rumbled through New Mexico, taking most of the servicemen stationed at Hobbs on the first leg of their journey. We all told everybody "good bye," and when the train pulled out, we ran along side, waving and throwing kisses.

I had kept up with Betty Brooks Hays from the time we were in Carnell Hall before she moved into the Chi-Omega House, and she had made plans for me to go with her to Washington, D.C., and work with her for her father, Congressman Brooks Hays. I was excited and really looking forward to that. It was all decided. I would go back to Russellville for a short visit with my parents, and then I would meet her in Washington.

I found Russellville greatly changed from the time I had lived there, but I had a wonderful visit with my folks, Pete's family, and many old friends, one of whom was Boyd Keathley, still court reporting.

I was eager to begin working in Washington. Betty Brooks was already there, and she was having a great time.

And then, a bomb dropped. It was the atomic bomb, dropped August 6, 1945, on Hiroshima. It changed the world. Mine and everyone else's. Pete was on a ship on his way to invade Japan. His ship was turned around in mid-ocean, and he was on his way home. I did not get to join Betty Brooks Hays in Washington, D.C. I was very disappointed.

Mama had converted her small garage into an apartment, and that was where Pete and I set up housekeeping. At my urging, Pete took advantage of the G.I. bill and unenthusiastically enrolled in college at Arkansas Tech. I got a job in a typing pool at the Forest Service. No couple was ever as mis-matched as we were, and without the excitement and activities of the air base, that fact became increasingly evident.

8

No account of one's life would be complete without dealing with the topic of sex, and that is a topic that I knew very little about. I had never heard the word mentioned in my home, and no sex education was taught in the schools at that time. I was totally unprepared for the onslaught of menstruation. I had been riding the bicycle and when I discovered blood on my underwear I assumed that I had accidentally hit the bar while pumping too vigorously. I remember entering the bathroom, dashing past my mother, who had set up her ironing board on the back porch, trying to catch a breeze on a hot summer day as she ironed mountains of shirts. When I emerged, I hastened to tell Mama I was bleeding. She continued to move the steaming iron back and forth as she lugubriously shook her head. "Oh, Sister, I hoped it would happen later." I was almost 12. It seems that her own periods had begun when she was 16, and she thought and hoped mine would occur then. She disconnected her iron, located a soft white piece of material, and folded it into layers to make a pad. There was no money for sanitary napkins, although I assume they were available at that time. The pads were carefully washed and re-used.

Mother explained what had taken place and what to expect, and why it was necessary. That's quite a revelation to absorb all at once, and I have never been at ease with the process. Why should menstruation take place for days, dribbling blood? Why could it not occur all at once and have it over, like a bowel movement? How I have enjoyed the cleanness I have had since my hysterectomy!

I was a virgin when I married Pete, and I suspect he was, too! Once, his mother jokingly told me that his penis was so small when he was a baby that she had difficulty getting hold of it! Needless to say I never experienced any wonderful sensations, and many times told Pete I had a headache, or I was very tired. Once, I simply said, "No, I don't want to!" and my guilt doubled when he kissed me and said "You can't help how you feel," then left the bedroom and walked, outside, until midnight.

* * *

One day when I was grimly typing in the typing pool at the Forestry Building, Boyd Keathley called me. It seems that he had agreed to go to Fort Smith to take a deposition in an interstate commerce case involving a shipment of spinach that had become overheated and ruined as an alleged result of improper shipping procedure, but his judge had set an emergency hearing in a case and he could not leave Russellville. "I'm going to tell them that you're going to come in my place," he said.

"I can't do that!" I answered.

"Of course you can," he said. And I went. I have never been as frightened, but I learned that most people really don't talk that fast, and if you are truly concentrating, you can carry a considerable amount of speaking in your head. At any rate, I filled several notebooks with my shorthand symbols, drove home and immediately transcribed it while it was still fresh in my mind, earning in excess of $200. The Forestry Service was paying me $300 a month!

When I learned that everything was fine and I had received money, I called Boyd to thank him and to tell him if he ever resigned or died, I wanted his job!

Sometime later I got a call from Fayetteville, from a Judge named Ted Coxsey. "Mr. Boyd Keathley tells me you are a court reporter, and I need one," he said.

"When do you need one?" I asked.

He said, "Monday." It was Friday! I can't remember the amount of money he said the job paid, but four counties contributed to it: Washington, Benton, Carroll, and Madison. It was not a staggering amount, but Judge Coxsey went on to say, "In addition, you get transcripts." While I was hesitating, Judge Coxsey said, "Why don't you come up and report the case Monday and then decide if you want to take the job or not." I agreed, and Monday found me driving from Russellville to Fayetteville, arriving at the courthouse apparently during a break of some kind, for there were people milling around in all directions in the lobby. I saw an elderly distinguished man and approached him. "Judge Coxsey?"

"No" the gentlemen said and pointed. "That's Judge Coxsey." I turned and saw the man he had identified. He was straight out of Hollywood! Ted Coxsey was six feet or more tall; he was wearing a handsome pin-striped suit, displaying a flat stomach, and I was drowning in his dark brown eyes as he reached for my hand.

"You made it," he said. "I really appreciate it. My court reporter has resigned, and I have a full docket."

I followed him, now in his robe, into the courtroom, found my place directly below the bench where he was sitting, and began to write shorthand frantically, as the jury had been sworn in, and the trial had begun.

It was a criminal case: incest. The defendant was charged with having intercourse with his daughter who was 13 years old! I was transfixed. His own daughter?

I could not believe it. I would take down a word or two and then stare at the unkempt, overalled man with the close-set eyes.

Of course he was convicted, and mercifully for me, the verdict was not appealed. I recorded one word in three of that entire transcript!

* * *

I took the job and became the official court reporter of the Fourth Judicial District, and preceded Pete's moving to Fayetteville by several months as he had to finish the semester at Tech. He also was trying to decide what course or courses he was going to pursue, having flunked out in engineering, his first choice.

It was 1946. All the veterans whose educations had been interrupted by World War II had returned. Fayetteville was engulfed; there was no place to live. The circuit clerk's mother had a spare bedroom in her basement, which she rented to me, and my career as a court reporter was launched. I lived in Washington County, but I traveled other counties: Benton, Carroll, and Madison. Carroll County had two county seats where court was held: Eureka Springs and Berryville, a situation that still exists. I received payment from all four counties, each paying varying amounts, determined by the legislature, and I never understood how my salary was determined. No county paid the same amount. It must have had something to do with population and/or the amount of litigation each had, but I do recall that Madison County paid the smallest amount. The judge, whom I regarded as my employer, paid nothing.

The basement apartment was damp and cold, and all my clothes molded. In addition, it was full of roaches and other creepy-crawlers, and my landlady would lock the door that led to her part of the house where the refrigerator was located, my only source of water. When my parents learned where I was living, they were appalled, particularly Mama. They had officially retired and were planning to take what Daddy referred to as a "delayed honeymoon," but they could not leave me living in that situation.

They located and purchased a wonderful, small two-bedroom house, which, although it was located directly across the street from the University's Student Union, sat back in the middle of the lot, with a long driveway from the street leading up to the house, the mailbox located at the beginning of the driveway.

Pete joined me when he left Russellville and enrolled in the University, this time seeking a degree in business administration.

I loved that house; it was charming. It had been furnished and decorated by a professor's wife who had apparently planned to live there, but had married and moved into her husband's house. It had a wonderful breakfast bar in the kitchen, a feature I liked so much that I put a breakfast bar like that in my present house. There was a clock shelf in the living room with a marvelous gingham ruffle that extended across the entire side of the room, with matching pillows on the couch. Both bedrooms were equally lovely.

I believe Mother and Dad paid cash for the little house. They prepared a note for me to sign. They did not demand monthly payments, but they wanted to be sure that the record showed they had given me a house, and that they had not given one to John!

They wanted to make sure that no partiality was displayed. I understood their theory, but in reality John was a very successful certified public accountant, making a great deal more money than I, and that condition prevailed throughout most of our lives. John and I never kept score; he was always the wonderful big brother of my childhood.

Daddy had retired and purchased a mobile home, which they modified, installing an oven in which Mama could bake cornbread and an innerspring mattress made to order. They set out on the "delayed honeymoon," going first through the Mayo Clinic to check on the status of their health, which proved to be excellent. It was two years before they returned to Russellville, traveling throughout the United States and Mexico, visiting each other's relatives and the many friends they had made through their business.

So close was our little house to the University campus that Pete walked to all of his classes. I was reporting cases all over the district, sometimes riding with the judge or the attorney whose case was being tried. One day I returned from such a day's work to find Pete and the car gone. There was a note on the breakfast bar that left me completely surprised.

"Dear Sunshine," it began with his pet name for me. "I am going to work for Pete [his brother] hanging sheetrock. I love you, but I will always be an albatross around your neck. You are ambitious, and I am not. As long as I have a clean shirt and a dollar in my pocket—that's enough for me. I don't want to go to school. I have taken the car, but I will pay you for it." And he did.

I think I cried, but not because I was going to be alone. I think I cried because Pete was going to hang sheetrock for the rest of his life.

* * *

I didn't bother to change my marital status. I was seeking no companion. If Ted Coxsey had been single, it might have been a different situation! Aside from his physical attraction, I was fascinated with the law and with his being a lawyer and a judge. We spent a great deal of time together, and I am sure that our associates thought we were having an affair, but outside of heavy petting, there was no sexual contact. Ted had been a professional baseball player, and quite a successful one, before he went to law school. He also had married the love of his life, Billie, who died on the operating table during a tonsillectomy. The doctor was Frank Riggal, who became one of my best friends. He also was Ted's friend, both before the tragic event occurred and afterward.

Ted remarried, and he hastened to tell me, over and over, that his new wife had been a wonderful mother to their children and companion to him, but that the little town of Berryville had put them together after Billie's death and he had very little choice in the matter. "You are like Billie," he used to whisper to me. "You are just like Billie," and I was deliciously happy and sad at the same time. I could never be "Mrs. Ted Coxsey," but we had many, many wonderful hours together investigating cases after he became prosecuting attorney.

9

So fascinated was I with the law that I enrolled in law school in the spring of 1948, attending classes in Waterman Hall, before the new law school building was built. Waterman Hall had no ladies' rest room; there was no need for one! Fortunately, I could walk across the street, when nature called, to my own home.

There was an unusual occurrence that year. The first African American (we called them "blacks" then, or "colored people") to attend a white southern university since Reconstruction, entered the law school program at Fayetteville. His name was Silas Hunt, and it is still hard for me to believe that a cage, more or less, was built around him in the classes, to separate him from the white students. It was torn down mysteriously, but to avoid trouble Silas's classes were held in the basement, at 7:00 a.m.

I was still working as a court reporter and very often had to be downtown at the courthouse by 9:00 in the morning, so I went to the dean of the law school, Dean Leflar, and asked him if I could attend classes with Silas in the basement at 7:00 a.m. so I could go to work afterward. I shall never forget that Dean Leflar listened to my request and then, averting his eyes from me, said: "Virginia, I can't tell you to do that, but I can look the other way while you do it." And so naïve was I that I did not understand what he meant. However, I soon found out. My employer at that time, Judge Cummings, was very upset and complained that he had received a lot of criticism because his reporter was attending classes with a black man. I even received threats from some members of a fraternity who were very racist. In fact, they "seceded from the Union" every year, reliving the Civil War, shouting "FORGET, HELL!"

I ignored all the criticism and continued to attend Silas's early morning classes. Several other students began to do so as well, because they had a chance to hear Dr. Leflar's lecture on torts again. It was a very difficult and important subject, and it helped to hear it a second time. In addition, the textbook method of teaching was relatively new, and in order for students to receive the maximum benefit from it, group discussion was necessary.

All of us enjoyed knowing and sharing our class with Silas Hunt. Sometimes after class, we would say, "Let's go to the Student Union and have a coke," and Silas would very quietly say, "I am not allowed to go there." At that time, some of us would go and get the refreshments, and return to the basement class where Silas was waiting. I remember being ashamed and angry, but there really was nothing we could do about the situation. Silas understood that and never made an issue of anything. He simply studied his assignments and participated in the discussions, absorbing as much information as he could, without any complaints or bitterness. I don't think I could have behaved in that manner.

* * *

During the time I was attending law school, I was privileged to participate in a very historic endeavor. I had become well known to Dean Leflar; at least he was familiar with the difficulties I encountered financially. It seems that the Ford Foundation had called him with the information that they were going to sponsor a study on the probable decision the United States Supreme Court was going to make on *Brown v. Topeka Board of Education*, which dealt with integration and was before them at that time. Understandably, a very controversial issue. The

University of Arkansas School of Law at Fayetteville had been selected to conduct the study.

Dean Leflar had assigned the research to Wiley Davis, a brilliant professor in the law school, and he and Dean Leflar chose me to help with the project. Officially, I typed up Wiley Davis' notes and opinions, but I did a great deal of research on all the cases which had been heard by the Court on the subject, an exercise that not only was extremely interesting but vastly important to my law school experienced. In addition, I was receiving payment from the money the Ford Foundation had given Dean Leflar. I cannot remember how much I was paid, but it was on an hourly basis, and I was instructed to keep up with my time.

Late one day, I went into Dean Leflar's office to receive my weekly paycheck, and when I submitted my figures to him, he looked at me and said, "Virginia, I think you were in the library much longer than that. I saw you here several evenings until quite late."

"No, sir," I said, "I think I have documented all the time I was there"—and I was astounded to hear the Dean exclaim, "*Virginia*, the Ford Foundation has allocated X-amount for secretarial help, and we are not going to penalize you because you are fast. Go back and re-figure your bill!"

Of course I did, and the enlarged check was extremely welcomed.

As it turned out, our analysis of the probable decision in that memorable case was entirely correct. The Court ruled that the segregation of students in the public schools violated the equal protection clause of the 14th Amendment, and that is exactly what Wiley Davis and I predicted the Court would rule.

* * *

I confess that Silas revealed to me, and perhaps some of the others, many aspects of the Jim Crow era that were totally unknown to me. For example, I remember once when we had completed our lesson and were talking together, I pointed out, rather condescendingly, that I was sure he and his family had fared better by living on a farm than had the blacks who had infiltrated the big cities. I remember saying, "At least you could have a garden, grow your food, and have plenty to eat." I knew his father had been a sharecropper.

His answer, delivered matter of factly to me, without anger or resentment, revealed something I had never heard before, and certainly had never thought about. "Well, not really," Silas said, and then went on. "There was cotton planted on every available inch of land, even under the front porch. We had no yard." The landlord wanted every possible bale of cotton that could be cultivated and apparently required the use of all the land. Silas' family had no garden.

If a black person were treated in that manner today, a lawsuit would be filed, but that didn't occur to Silas, or to the students who followed him. They sat, quietly absorbing whatever knowledge was available to them. All of us who knew Silas liked him very much, and as I said, he enlightened us a great deal about many, many things that we had never thought about. Silas did not get to finish his education. He became very ill and died in a veteran's hospital in Missouri. It was from tuberculosis, and I seem to remember that he suffered a hemorrhage once, in class.

I am glad that Silas has been recognized and honored somewhat. Silas H. Hunt Hall is located adjacent to the Robert A. Leflar Law Center in Fayetteville, and in addition, there is a historical marker in front of the law school. Also, in October of 2003 there was a Silas Hunt Scholarship established in his honor. Although it is not just for people of a minority race, the scholarship seeks to enhance diversity within the student body. That diversity includes, but is not limited to, being a member of an underrepresented ethnic or minority group, showing interest in a major that is untraditional for the student's ethnic group or gender, residing in an underrepresented county in Arkansas, or being a first generation college student.

It was a privilege for me to know Silas and to attend classes with him, and I wish he had been able to complete his legal education. In 2008, 60 years after he enrolled, Silas Hunt received a posthumous law degree in his name.

* * *

I was in the Student Union on one of my trips there to get doughnuts and coffee when I was introduced to Everett Ham by an old friend of mine, Smokey Stover. I learned from Smokey later that Ham had seen me somewhere and had asked Smokey to introduce me to him. I acknowledged the introduction and went back to class. I was not seeking male companionship. I was totally immersed in the law, both law school and the practice of law that I was encountering as a court reporter. Moreover, I had not filed for divorce, and, as far as I knew, neither had Pete. I took little notice of Everett, but noted that he had black hair, was very tall, and not bad looking.

I remember that at that time I was trying to complete a transcript of a criminal case that had been appealed, and I had handwritten shorthand to decipher, type, separate, and put together, after proofreading. I was leaving my law classes and typing on the small screened-in front porch of my wonderful house. It was quiet, and I was undisturbed, an atmosphere that was imperative when I was trying to meet a deadline.

It was nothing short of miraculous that I was able to function as a court reporter using shorthand that I had learned so many years before at the age of 12. Of course I had practiced writing it constantly from the time I learned it, taking down the preacher's sermons on Sundays, the words to the popular songs I heard on the radio, speeches—all were taken down and transcribed. Sometimes I got stuck on a passage in a transcript and spent hours sounding over and over the phonetic symbols until the correct words could be ascertained and recorded. I even had a doctor friend whom I called, trying to determine a medical term or condition by asking him if there was an "ith kay" located anywhere near the esophagus, and he would tell me the correct name and how to spell it. Court reporters before there was recording equipment really earned their money!

At that time, I had a "party" line telephone with my law school friends, Bill and Marion Penix, and Marion's mother was visiting her from Oklahoma. When my telephone rang, it rang in their house as well.

The night after Smokey introduced me to Everett Ham, my telephone rang very late. I was trying to finish my criminal transcript, or I would not have been awake. I picked up the phone and heard the voice of a man who had obviously been drinking. "I thought of who had the prettiest legs I had ever saw, and I thought of you," he said. I hung up.

He called back instantly. "This is Everett Ham," he said. "I met you today and I am coming over."

"No, you're not!" I said. And I hung up again, only to have him call again. I knew the Penixes and her mother would be awakened, but I really didn't know how to get rid of him.

"If I can't come now, when can I come?" he asked.

To get rid of him, I said, "Why don't you come in the morning?"

"I will," he said and hung up. I did not lack a great deal on my transcript, and I was very tired, so I went to bed.

The following morning, I had awakened early, made a pot of coffee, and resumed my typing, hoping to finish it that day. It was Sunday, and I had planned to work all day.

There was a knock on my door, and I opened it to see Everett Ham, still in the rumpled clothing he had had on when I saw him in the Student Union.

"Didn't you say I could come this morning?" he said, and I laughed in spite of myself.

"Well I guess I did!" I replied, opening the door. "Do you want some coffee? Come on in."

He followed me inside and then asked, "What are you doing?"

I explained that I was finishing up a transcript, and that it had to be done before my deadline. He began separating the three copies I had made, obviously interested in the process.

"Are you going to make breakfast?" he asked. "I can scramble eggs like Fanny Farmer," he said. Fanny Farmer had published a gourmet cookbook, and I was surprised at what he'd said until he added that his mother had Fanny's cookbook. Then he proceeded to volunteer to scramble the eggs, asking if I had a double boiler.

I have scrambled eggs in a double boiler that way ever since, and they are wonderful. I fried bacon and made toast, and we sat at the breakfast bar, eating and talking about everything.

He was majoring in agriculture and asked if he could pick the bugs out of the apple tree in my backyard; he had to make a bug collection. I told him I would be glad to be rid of them, and after washing the dishes I apologized, but I had to return to my typing. The deadline was upon me. I thought he would never leave, but he stretched out on my couch and turned the radio on to classical music, which made me take a second look at him. I had heard my first classical music when I enrolled in the university as an undergraduate and had loved it.

After awhile he came into my office, where I was typing away, and said "Why don't you take a break and let's go to a movie?"

The transcript was almost finished, and I welcomed the invitation, but I though I'd better explain to him my marital status.

"I really can't go to a movie with you unless you let me pay my own way," I said. "You see, I'm married."

"Where's your husband?" was his next question.

I replied, "I don't know; he left."

I had not "dated" or gone out since Pete had left. I went to church almost every Sunday, and I was working and taking classes. I did not miss social activities. And for some silly reason, it seemed all right to me to go with him to the movie, provided he did not pay for my ticket! I learned later that Ham was delighted not ever to pay for anything!

* * *

My cousin Louise, Aunt Vera's oldest daughter, had done the same thing I did. she went to Arkansas Tech when it was a two-year school, living with us. While I was living there in the little house so near the campus, she had finished her course in home economics at Fayetteville, married, and had become the house mother for the home economics house. I had always liked her. She and her husband visited me from time to time, and she had had me at the home economics house, where I learned a great deal about how to set a table—where the different forks, etc., went—for needless to say, Mama never had a set of silverware when I lived with her. I remember trying to show Mama what Louise had taught me, but Mama's reaction was totally surprising. She became indignant and screamed at me that I thought "I was better than her" and declared that she was sorry she ever sent me to college!

Several times, Louise and her husband and Ham and I went to the football games the "Hogs" played, sometimes in Fayetteville and sometimes in Little Rock. When we went to Little Rock, I met Mother Faisst, Ham's grandmother, whom I loved from the first time I saw her. I had always wanted a grandmother, and she fit the bill. She had a lovely home near the waterworks in Hillcrest. She was a devout Democrat and had worked hard to elect Governor Cherry. I was visiting her when she had a party, serving cherry pies, and was furious to learn that one of her guests had eaten her pie and "didn't even have a poll tax!," meaning that she could not vote, a poll tax being required at that time.

Mother Faisst's husband had been county judge at one time, but Lena, Ham's mother, had married Everett Ham, Sr., after meeting him while living in Boston, Mass. He was a rabid Republican. The Faisst family had migrated from the Black

Forest area of Germany and had acquired a substantial fortune in timber and sawmills, all of which had been dissipated, according to her, by her son-in-law's lack of judgment and laziness, sleeping every day until noon and not tending to business.

* * *

When Louise and her husband and Ham and I went to the Razorback games in Little Rock, we never spent the night, but drove back quite late. Louise and her husband would drive us to my little house, and then Ham would walk on to his dormitory, which was a block or so away.

On one such occasion, Louise and her husband drove to my little house as they always did, and I went into the house ahead of Ham to turn on the lamps, which were on either side of the couch in the living room. To my complete surprise and dismay, Ham shoved me down and fell on top of me. I have thought many, many times about the role one's undergarments play in one's life! Had we had pantyhose at that time, it could not have happened! The style then was loose "step-ins" with a garter belt holding up the hose. I could not push his weight off me, as he simply pulled my underwear aside.

"Ham! Ham!" I screamed, pushing him and trying to get up or away.

He said, "Shut up! I'm going to!" And he did. It was instantaneous, and he was gone.

The rest of that night was the worst night of my life, so far. I walked the floor, wondering what was going to happen. Could I possibly become pregnant? I was scheduled to be picked up by the judge the following morning for a case in Bentonville, 25 or 30 miles away. How could I possibly report a case? Should I call him and tell him I was sick? I couldn't call him this late, and he would be at my door early the next morning.

I have learned you do what has to be done. The judge and I drove to Bentonville, and I wrote shorthand for hours and was brought back to my house. When I walked in the back door,

Ham was sitting at my breakfast table. This was an era when nobody locked doors, particularly in that prestigious academic neighborhood.

"Get out of my house! Get out of my house!" I started screaming and pushing him.

He stood up and put his arms around me, me still pushing him away and crying. And then he said, "I knew this would be your reaction. I want to marry you."

Of course, before I could do that, I had to call Rex Perkins, a wonderful lawyer friend of mine, and file a divorce against Marble Woodroof Keeney, Jr.—"Pete"—and I didn't even have his address!

I think we advertised in the paper, for after Pete sent me the money for the car, I never heard from him again.

Ham had a lawyer friend, Tommy Russell, who became my friend, too, although what a checkered relationship that turned out to be! Tommy's father had worked on the railroad, and I think Tommy had, too, for awhile, an experience that made him realize he wanted a profession, so he enrolled in law school in Fayetteville.

At that time, it was the only law school in Arkansas, although there was a night school staffed by practicing lawyers and judges in the Little Rock area until its demise in the early 1960's. John Carmichael was a dominant force in legal education in Little Rock from 1900 until his death in 1950. That school was still functioning when I served as deputy prosecuting attorney, and I remember its location, which was just across the street from the courthouse.

When I met Tommy, his father was dead. However, his mother was still alive. She was a very talented pianist and served as choir director of her church. Tommy and his mother had a modest house in North Little Rock, in a community where all the railroad employees resided. Mrs. Russell organized a simple wedding ceremony for Ham and me, with Tommy as our only attendant. Afterwards, we then hitchhiked back to Fayetteville.

* * *

At the time I married Ham, I had never met his parents. Some time after we married, they sent us plane tickets to visit them in Chicago where they resided. Ham's father had a very lucrative (to me) job with a major air-conditioning company. They had three children, two girls, Eleanor and Carolyn, and Everett, Jr., whom they called "Boy." I liked Lena, his mother, instantly, but his father, the first Everett, was not a very likeable man. He was the most opinionated, egotistical individual I ever met; he knew everything!

It was useless to try to change his mind about anything. Mother Faisst didn't like him, either; he was a staunch Republican and ridiculed her for being a Democrat. Ham's mother had met and married him when she studied music in Boston, Massachusetts. He had been married before, and his wife had died in childbirth. The little girl's paternal grandparents had taken her, and Ham's father didn't have the heart to take the child away from them. Either that or he didn't want to be bothered with a child; the child was raised by her grandparents. When I met her, she still resided in Boston, comfortably, according to Ham. She inherited a great deal of money from her grandparents. I remember when her grandparents died, Ham borrowed some of it from her and never paid her back.

After Lena Faisst married, the couple lived in Arkansas, where Everett, Sr., managed her family's considerable lumber, sawmill, and timber business, her father having died and Mother Faisst having no ability to take care of it. According to her, Everett lost most of their fortune. It was never discussed, although Lena often said, almost offhand, "I could never get him up in the morning"—a trait that I found his son had inherited!

* * *

My honeymoon was spent lying in Mama Ham's guest room, wondering when the bridge game was going to end. Ham, his mother, his father, and his two sisters were competitive bridge players, and it seems that they had kept a running tab on the scores through the years. They grabbed Ham and chose up partners, with the girls taking turns, producing former scores, and taking turns with "Boy." My role was making coffee to be sure the players remained alert. Since I had never been allowed to play cards, I obviously had no knowledge about bridge, except that it looked very complicated. I finally gave up and went to bed—alone. Did that make me see any writing on the wall? Unfortunately, it did not.

Ham's parents showed me Chicago, taking us to a play and a wonderful restaurant, although the weather was incredibly bad and the highway on the lake front had to be closed.

I saw my first television set. It was in a bar, and I was soon to learn that bars were going to be my husband's hangout, wherever we went.

I disliked his sister Eleanor from the beginning. She was very beautiful and had been a beauty queen in her youth. To give you an example of her thinking, when she and her girlfriend made a trip abroad, they took lodging in the city's most expensive and prestigious hotel, for one night only, as they were on a very limited budget. They made a point of meeting every interesting patron, and then they moved into a non-descript hotel they could afford. Had they registered there in the beginning, they would have had no chance to meet the wealthy tourists they continued to associate with, arranging meetings with them at various museums and tourists attractions. Such a course of conduct would never have occurred to me!

Eleanor was married to a doctor who was an officer in the military during the war. However, when the war ended, he had been required to remain for some period of time to treat enlisted men who had contracted syphilis, and it had apparently affected him very adversely. Ham's mother told me that right after he had returned home, she was hanging a picture and injured her finger with the hammer she was using. It seems that Eleanor had called her doctor husband to look at her mother's finger, and he had declined and fainted when he saw the blood. In spite of that reaction, Eleanor had demanded that he return to his profession, and he had done so. One day when she came home from work, she found he had placed the telephone directory on the bed opened at the hospital's number and shot himself in the head. Eleanor claimed that his death was related to his service, traveled to Washington to fight for compensation, and eventually was successful in obtaining a substantial amount of money. He had been in the service almost from the beginning of World War II and had sent her many beautiful things—silverware, pictures, and linens—which he had looted when he participated in the invasion of Germany.

Carolyn had married a millworker, a marriage that had greatly upset Lena Ham, who used to say to me, "She will never have anything," and she didn't until he fell from a stairway and died. She was able to make a better second marriage.

* * *

Ham, of course, moved in with me in my wonderful little house and continued his education in agriculture. I never understood his interest in farming. No one in his family had ever lived on a farm. I remember that he used to look at the farms we would pass when driving in and around Fayetteville, and he would say, "Look at that. That crop needs fertilizing. He could produce three times as much."

I had seen farming first hand, and I would point out to Ham that the farmer might well be aware of his need for additional fertilizer and not be able to afford it. Not even to have credit enough to borrow the money necessary to obtain additional fertilizer. Like his father, Ham brushed aside anything and everything that I said, with the attitude, "what do you know about anything?"

I did not return to law school that year. It was years before I did, as a result of a completely unexpected occurrence.

In the meantime, Judge Cummings was hearing cases in all four counties during the fall and winter months. I had a steady stream of appeals, with transcripts to be typed, and I had wifely duties to perform—shopping for groceries, preparing meals, washing clothes, and cleaning house. I had no spare time at all. And Ham never lifted his hand. In fact, he was gone most of the time, attending classes during the day and spending a great deal of time in the evenings with his friend, my instructor in criminal law, Edwin Dunaway, a prominent attorney in Little Rock who taught criminal law in the law school at Fayetteville for a short period.

During this time, the rules of civil procedure were modified to allow a new procedure for trial lawyers: discovery. Prior to this development, lawyers went to trial without any idea what witnesses were going to be on the other side or what their testimony was going to be. It truly was trial by ambush. A plaintiff who was seeking damages for injuries he had received in an accident might be confronted with a witness who would testify that he, the plaintiff, had run a red light and was wholly responsible for his injuries himself. Under the provisions of the new rules allowing discovery, lawyers could send written interrogatories about the case, and indeed almost everything, requiring the opposition to answer and verify them prior to the case being set for trial.

There was a great deal of opposition to the new rules, some of the "old" attorneys simply declaring that they would not reveal their trial strategy to the opponent. They alleged it was their "work product," and the other side was not entitled to know about it beforehand.

As far as the rules of discovery initiated at that time, I have lived to see them abused and misused by many attorneys, submitting computerized questions simply to bill hours. I once represented a veteran who was very disabled from his military service. As a matter of fact, his condition was inoperable at that time, with several bullets still lodged in his spine. He, his wife, and numerous children were living in a mobile home, and when a new baby came, they purchased an old school bus, which they attached in some manner to the mobile home, making a nursery for the baby. Not unexpectedly, marital problems erupted, and there was a divorce filed. My client's opposing attorney sent mountains of interrogatories, asking inane and inappropriate questions in my opinion, like "Do you have any paintings or other collection of art? If so, please list the number of same and their value." And, "Please list your bank accounts, CD, etc."

My client had nothing, and I did not answer the interrogatories, planning to object to them at the temporary hearing. The judge did not agree with me. I was ordered to answer them immediately and was fined $100. I paid the fine, but I still think the attorney who asked all the ridiculous questions was abusing the interrogatory system. He had to know the man had no such assets. (In my opinion, the discovery provisions of the law should be limited in some manner with penalties or sanctions if proceedings are abused.)

A teaching seminar was held, and I was hired by Dean Leflar to record the proceedings. He also had a young man recording the seminar electronically. I remember that Ham and I were invited to dinner at Edwin Dunaway's house that evening, a dinner attended by several members of the Arkansas Supreme Court, as Edwin served as one of the youngest members of that court before he came to Fayetteville to teach.

Edwin was renting one of Fayetteville's "Faye Jones" houses—perched on the side of a mountain and made almost entirely of glass to capture the magnificent view. I vowed one day to have one like it, and I do.

After dinner, Peggy Smith, Judge George Rose Smith's wife, asked me what I was doing, sitting up there on the stage during the seminar. I replied that I had been hired to record the meeting, and I shall never forget her laughter and sarcastic response. "Oh, you were checking on the man who was recording it, were you?" I said nothing. As it turned out, however,

Dean Leflar had been very wise to have two records made. It seems that the young man with the recording machine accidentally erased a large part of his recording, and my transcribed shorthand record was the only complete record of the seminar. I never told Peggy Smith that, but I should have.

10

Edwin Dunaway and I were both Democrats, often accused of being "Yellow Dog" Democrats, so loyal that if a yellow dog ran as a Democrat we would support it. It is true that I have always embraced the philosophy of the Democratic Party, but during the Faubus days in Arkansas, I did not vote at all. He alone, in my opinion, was responsible for the terrible experience Little Rock had as a result of disobeying the law of the land, integration.

Ham, on the other hand, was a rabid Republican, like his father. I remember coming home one evening with a bag of groceries and simply remarking that I thought something I had purchased was inordinately expensive. Ham exploded. "It's your entire fault!" he screamed. "You voted for the s… of a b…!" I had no idea what he was talking about, but he quickly informed me. He was speaking about Franklin Delano Roosevelt. He hated the man and never missed a chance to criticize him and blame him for the ills of the world. Frankly, up until that time, I had been so busy studying and working that I had paid little attention to politics. Little did I know politics was destined to become a great part of my life.

Ham was nearing graduation, earning his degree in agriculture, and still wanting nothing more than a farm. I had grave misgivings, but he located some acreage that was for sale not too far from town. It seems that it was owned by a woman whose husband had died, and she was not able to manage the place alone. Ham thought it was a great bargain with a lot of potential. He contacted his sister Eleanor, who had a substantial amount of money. She had worked throughout the war, but lived at home, paying no room and board. Moreover, she had gained a significant settlement from the U.S. government by convincing the military that her husband's suicide after the war was service-connected. At any rate, before she would lend her brother the money to purchase his farm, she demanded security, and the only asset available was my house. Ham assured me that he could pay it back in short order, and the deal was made.

The house on the farm where the owner had lived was dilapidated and had no running water and no bathroom. I was firm in my demand that those facilities had to be present before I took up residence on the farm, so the early days of Ham's farming endeavor were limited to cutting brush and putting up fences. One day, Ham called me to tell me that he had written a check to have a pond dug on our property for the cattle we had purchased. We really needed one, he said, and the man who dug them had been digging another one in the "neighborhood," and it had been much cheaper to have him do it while he was there than to have to hire him to bring all the equipment back!

Ham had decided that there was money to be earned by having a dairy, and again, largely through my assets and income, we purchased a herd of dairy cows and installed electric milking equipment. Of course Ham could not do it alone, and he also had applied and had been accepted as an agent with the United States Agricultural Department. Eisenhower was president, and Ham was able to get a Republican appointment. His new duties required him to travel throughout Arkansas and to make frequent trips to Little Rock, so he hired a young man who lived nearby and who said he had had experience with running a dairy. His parents had just died, and he was caring for his younger brother and sister. In addition to allowing them to live in the house on the farm, Ham paid him a salary, and I contacted all my friends and church members, collecting clothing and other necessities for the young man and his siblings.

Imagine our surprise when Ham returned from Little Rock to find the entire family gone, the unmilked dairy cows scattered throughout the entire acreage, and all the items we had collected for the family taken. Our earnings for the entire year were gone.

And I was pregnant.

I was glad, because my biological clock was ticking away. I would be 30 when the child was born. There was no procedure at that time to learn the sex of the fetus, but I wanted a boy. My brother had two little girls, and Mother and Daddy both wanted a grandson, even though he would not be a "Harkey."

* * *

My doctor was Dr. Frank Riggall, who was both a doctor and a lawyer. At least he was taking law courses and working to become an attorney while maintaining his practice. He was also the mayor of Prairie Grove, Arkansas. I first encountered Dr. Frank when he testified as a witness in a lawsuit being heard by Judge Cummings. I, of course, was reporting the trial.

Dr. Frank was a tall, distinguished Britisher, who, despite the many years he had lived in America, still had an unmistakable British accent. He and his brother, also a doctor, had the Elizabeth Hospital, named for their mother, a small but very efficient and highly rated hospital located directly across from the historic battlefield where a major battle had occurred during the Civil War. Dr. Frank had come from England as a very young man and worked as a telegrapher on the railroad to pay for his medical education, which he received at an institution that turned out to be a "diploma mill." And while he was legitimately a doctor, his school was not recognized as being a good school, a distinction very foreign to Dr. Frank, who maintained that such a condition did not exist in his country. At any rate, Dr. Frank kept Elizabeth Hospital until his younger brother, whom he had sent to Tulane Medical School, graduated. Then

Dr. Frank repeated his entire medical training, but he did it in Canada, graduating with highest honor and a chest full of medals. He also studied in his native England, and related countries, becoming a member of the Royal College of Surgeons in Glasgow. None of his titles were honorary; he had studied and earned all of them.

I do not recall what type of action Dr. Frank was subpoenaed to attend as a witness, but I shall never forget his reply when the attorney asked him if he were a member of the Washington County Medical Society, which of course he was not. Dr. Frank turned in his chair to address the court. "Your Honor," he began "Are you a member of the Washington County Justice of the Peace Society?" Judge Cummings' gavel quieted the loud response of the spectators, and although Dr. Frank had to answer the question, I believe everyone got the idea of why he was not a member.

I had sought an appointment with him shortly after his appearance as a witness, as I had experienced some vaginal bleeding and was sure I had terminal cancer, putting off consulting a doctor until I mustered up enough courage to set up an appointment. I had read and re-read literature that set out certain symptoms of cancer, and I was sure the end was near.

Dr. Frank did an examination and immediately diagnosed a minor infection. I remember his observation that while the literature was necessary, it often unnecessarily caused people to be alarmed. He prescribed and filled the prescription from the pharmacy located in the hospital, and became my friend forever.

* * *

He and his wife had two sons, one of whom was a brilliant pre-med student and became a physician; the other was homosexual, and Dr. Frank could not and would not accept it. His wife did, and tried to make peace between the two, but Dr. Frank would not accept that the situation could not be altered. He sent his son to Menninger's, the famous psychiatric hospital, convinced that his son's aberration could be changed—all of which did nothing except create a deeper division between Dr. Frank and his younger son.

That division apparently was much deeper than I had realized, for many years later, after I had graduated from law school and was working in Little Rock, I received a call late one evening from Dr. Frank's gay son who had moved to Little Rock and set up a beauty shop. After I said hello, he went into a tirade about his father and ended up by saying, "If you ever want to see him again you better go see him," and hung up. I wrestled with the angel. Should I call Dr. Frank? Was I imagining anything? Dr. Frank had never told me any details about their relationship—or his son's "illness," as he called it. Finally, I decided to call Dr. Frank—thinking I don't want to be sorry that I didn't warn him if anything happened. So I dialed Prairie Grove and related to Dr. Frank what his son had said to me.

The doctor's next words struck cold fear into my heart. "How much time do I have?" Those were his only words. I told him what time I had received the call. He thanked me and hung up the phone.

I didn't hear anything else until the following morning when Dr. Frank called me to thank me. His son had indeed made the trip from Little Rock to Prairie Grove with the intent to kill his father, and maybe his mother. Dr. Frank was able to obtain lawmen that stopped the younger Riggall as he entered the area near Dr. Frank's residence. He was heavily armed, and without a doubt there would have been a violent episode. Dr. Frank thanked me profusely, and I was so glad that I had called him.

* * *

I had an uneventful pregnancy, working literally up until the day I went to the hospital. I was finishing up reporting a trial on that date, and another attorney came in to set a case for trial. Judge Cummings looked down where I was sitting and said "When is your baby due?" and I replied "Today," so the judge didn't give the attorney a trial date at that time. I went home and discovered that I was, indeed, in early labor.

Ham's father had visited us once when I was far advanced in my pregnancy, and an incident occurred that says it all about him—and Ham, also, for that matter. Mother raised a great crop of strawberries and had given me a lot of them. I had prepared them and put them in the freezer. I knew Ham's father loved strawberries, so when I got out of court, I scurried around to prepare our dinner: steaks, baked potatoes, salad, and strawberry shortcake. I was very pleased with the menu when I sat down along with Ham and his father for our evening meal.

All of a sudden Ham's father discovered the colorful paper napkins I had placed at each plate and exclaimed: "I don't use paper napkins." I was astonished at what I considered his rudeness, but my husband's reaction was even worse.

"Get my father a linen napkin!" he demanded. This to a woman in late pregnancy who had worked eight hours prior to preparing the meal! Why didn't I turn the plates upside down in their laps? I don't know. I didn't say a word. I struggled to pull my extended body up, walked to the linen closet, got one linen napkin, and handed it to Ham's father before I again sat down to eat my dinner.

I have never eaten very much beef, or any other kind of meat for that matter. I think my aversion to meat began when my grandfather lived with us. He had to have a great deal of milk, or thought he did, so our Jersey cow was always bred to make sure there was a milk supply. The baby calf was a great pet for me. I fed and watered it, and took it to and from the pasture. I remember that I was devastated when it was butchered and put on the table to be eaten. I remember crying and calling everyone "cannibals!" As I have grown older, I have recognized that I am a vegetarian, and I make no apologies for it. I do always let it be known that it is a preference, not a religion!

* * *

Although I wanted children, I must admit that I had a very unnatural fear of childbirth. Mother never failed to relate to me how very difficult her two pregnancies had been. Both of her children, my brother and me, were born in August, when the Arkansas weather is at its worse. It was almost unbearably hot and air conditioning was nonexistent, so far as I know. I do remember Daddy once rigged up a cooling system for us that consisted of water being poured over a window with a fan located in some manner to blow the water-cooled air into our bedroom, but it was a very inefficient device.

Both John and I were born at home. Mother had not seen a doctor until her "water broke" and delivery was imminent. She and Daddy had gone to Mount Magazine just prior to John's birth in an effort to find a cooler place for her to be when the baby was born, but Mother wanted to be closer to her doctor, and they did not remain there very long.

I had heard her description of her labor, how it lasted, how painful it had been, how enormous both John and I were (John nine pounds and me almost that) until I had to admit that I certainly was not looking forward to childbirth. I was amazed when my daughter and her husband, many years later, invited friends, and me, to attend the event, which she was going to accomplish without medication, all the while listening to classical music and videotaping the entire procedure! I declined, and by choice, did not meet my grandchild until she was cleaned up and dressed in a beautiful little gown.

Ham had insisted that I breast feed my child, and I agreed that I would, as Dr. Frank had said it was very good for the baby, guarding against various illnesses and so forth, so that was established.

We arrived at Elizabeth Hospital in Prairie Grove, and Ham was directed to the waiting room while the nurse helped me undress and get ready for Dr. Frank, who was on his way. Husbands were not allowed in the delivery room at that time, so far as I know. I did not ask that he not be present. I think for whatever reason it was a rule of the hospital. I was very glad that he was not.

Dr. Frank gave me Demerol almost immediately, and to tell you the truth, I don't remember anything after that until they brought a bundle to my beside and I got my first glimpse of my daughter. I do remember the nurse saying that "somebody had scared her to death." She did not elaborate, but I must have cried or complained, or something.

When I saw the baby, I remember exclaiming over and over, "She's beautiful," and she was. She had a lot of hair, and all her fingers and toes—for I checked them and counted them and fondled them over and over. Nobody could have been prouder and happier than I was.

And I was furious when my mother, who had arrived with my father shortly after Gretel was born, took one look at her and said, "Another little split-tail!" disappointed that she was not a boy. They had girl grandchildren—two of them, no grandsons.

The only problem I had with Gretel not being a boy was that we had not chosen a girl's name. John had two girls, and everyone had wanted a male baby, but I forgot all about that when I saw my beautiful little daughter and held her to my breast for her first meal. The hospital required that the child be named before we went home, and nobody had even thought about it, believe it or not. Ham came in with his *Victor's Book of Opera* and began reading of names. "Brunhilda," he said, "How about Brunhilda?" And he went on—until he came to Gretel. "I like that," I said. "I really do; and it's unusual."

To my surprise Ham liked it, too, and we decided to name her "Gretel." I remember saying that we should find a middle name that was not so far out in case she didn't like the first name, and after much discussion, each of us refusing many suggestions, we hit upon Christine. That's what we named her: Gretel Christine Ham.

* * *

Dr Frank kept new mothers a week, as I recall, and he also bound my breasts for some period of time.

I had prepared a nursery in my little house, with a baby bed and a wonderful device that had a canvas bathing basin with a lid that was heavy enough to support the baby's weight. It was to be used for dressing the child and changing diapers. It was tall enough that no stooping or bending was necessary. I don't know if that item exists today, but I could not have survived without it.

The day I went to the hospital, I learned that a criminal appeal had been filed and that I had 30 days to transcribe the record in one of my cases. Immediately upon my return home, I began typing, for the 30 days was running. Incidental, I received no extra money for criminal appeals; they were free.

I had called several friends and showed off my beautiful child, but I also was typing up the record and nursing Gretel, in addition to preparing meals and my usual household duties, as Ham was gone most of the time, coming home at all hours.

Shortly after I arrived at home, I was nursing my baby, which was quite painful, and there was a great rush of blood. I was terrified, thinking my baby was dying, but then I realized the blood was not hers, but mine! I called Dr. Frank, who told me to come to the hospital immediately, and I did, leaving a note for Ham as to where the baby and I were and what had happened.

Dr. Frank did not allow Gretel to be returned to the hospital nursery, but put her little bed next to mine, and immediately began treating what he said was a breast abscess. As a matter of fact, we decided to stop the breast feeding and put her on a bottle, for she had not been getting enough nourishment. When my mother learned that I had stopped breast feeding, she browbeat me and said, "God will take her away from you," which sent me into hysterics, requiring Dr. Frank to intervene, and administer medication. I made the 30-day deadline on my criminal transcript, despite the breast abscess and my return to the hospital.

* * *

Ham's new employment, with his use of the only vehicle we had, made it necessary for us to have a second vehicle. Again I called my folks. Daddy had bought a new car and had refused to trade in the old one because the dealer had offered such a small amount of money. He was using it to carry all sorts of equipment used on his various projects, saving the new car from such projects. I called to see if we could borrow the old one.

I can't remember the pet name we had for it, but I called and asked if we could use it, telling him that I would put new tires on it, and so on. The following Sunday, my parents drove to Fayetteville, Daddy driving their car and Mama driving what I thought was a new Chrysler. It wasn't new, but it was a late-model Chrysler.

"It's beautiful," I said. "When did you get it?"

"It's for you," Daddy said. "Old So-and-So isn't safe enough for you and the baby to ride in. Mama and I got this one for you. We didn't pay very much for it, and you can pay us. Just give us a mortgage on the house, and pay us when you can."

I was in shock.

"We can't afford it, Daddy," and we really couldn't. What a predicament! What was I going to do?

Telling the folks that we had to go to the farm, we left them watching baby Gretel. We went to the farm all right, but it was simply to get away from the folks while we tried to find Sister Eleanor, who had the mortgage on my house, to see if she would release it and take a mortgage on our livestock and equipment, which was paid for. I simply could not tell my parents that I had mortgaged the little house they had bought for me. I owed them the entire amount of its costs.

We finally located Eleanor; she was attending a Republican Convention in another state—I don't remember where we located her. We told her the situation. I shall never forget her reply. "No," she said. I won't release real estate for livestock. Cows die," she giggled.

And Ham? What did he say? "She's right," he said. "She had the right not to release her security."

I suppose she did. I told the folks we would have to think about it; that we really were in a financial bind, and although they were hurt, they did not argue about it at that time. They left the Chrysler for me to use, and I was to let them know when we decided. What I decided at that moment was to sell my beautiful little house, pay off Eleanor, and never set eyes upon her again!

Ham had not used his right to buy a house on the GI Bill. I had found a house on Louise Street perched on a very steep hill, with very little yard, but it was available with no down payment and rent-like monthly payments. My lovely little house sold almost immediately, I sent Eleanor her money, and told her never to contact me again for any reason, and I meant it.

I also paid my parents and kept the Chrysler.

11

My relationship with Judge Maupin Cummings was not good from the very beginning. He "inherited" me as a court reporter, and I believe that he regarded me as his personal secretary. I did not regard myself in that capacity, mainly because he did not pay any part of my salary.

The judge who first hired me was Ted Coxsey, who lived in Berryville. Judge Cummings lived in Fayetteville, with an office in the courthouse there. I believe he felt I should be there everyday, although he never made an issue of it. I had an office set up in my home and did all of my transcribing there, going to the courthouse only to report trials there or to file something. If Judge Cummings asked me to write a letter, I had no problem helping him, but I certainly did not want to have to go to the office every day. I was making substantially more by freelancing—reporting insurance adjusters' investigations, depositions, and any other proceedings that needed to be recorded—than Washington County was paying me.

Also I had been working as a reporter for years and had never had a raise. If I had not had transcripts and been able to freelance, I could not possibly have survived. When I discussed the issue with Judge Cummings, he told me he had no control over it at all, that it was up to the legislature. I knew that he had only to request a raise for me, and it would have happened.

Judge Cummings had married a widow who had a young son and whose husband had been a very wealthy developer. I think there was always trouble there, because I remember the judge complaining that his wife wanted to re-carpet the house, and that if she did, she could use her own money. He didn't intend to use his. In fact, on the long trips we had to make to Bentonville, Eureka Springs, and Berryville, I heard far more about the judge's marital problems than I wanted to hear. He even intimated that his wife was too interested in, and spending a lot of time in the presence of, a young male tenant she had rented to, her deceased husband having left her a substantial number of apartment houses. I remember once telling the judge that I was sorry, but I really didn't feel he should be telling me these things. However, for the most part, Judge Cummings paid no attention to me whatever. He would go ahead of me to court, allowing the swinging door to close, just as I, with all my recording gear, approached it. When I complained to Ham about how I was treated, he assured me I was overreacting and imagining things, that the judge was just absent-minded. Time proved otherwise.

* * *

One eventful day in late fall, the judge and I traveled to Berryville for a trial that turned out to be longer than expected and was not finished in one day, making it necessary to spend the night and return a second day.

Berryville had only one hotel, and it was antiquated, with only two bathrooms on each of the three floors, one for ladies and one for men. The judge suggested we drive over to Eureka Springs, the second county seat. Although Eureka Springs was not as developed then as it is now, it was a very picturesque place, with fine restaurants and hotels. We arrived at the Basin Park Hotel at dusk and registered for two adjoining rooms, separated by a bathroom.

The Basin Park Hotel was being re-modeled, and in walking to our rooms, it was necessary that we step over paint buckets and all kinds of debris. I remember remarking that if there were a fire, we would die in our beds. Whereupon the judge said to me, "Don't you know where the fire escapes are?"

"No, sir," I replied. "I have never been here before."

"Come on," he said. "I'll show you," and began walking down a long corridor toward a door.

The Basin Park is built on a mountain and advertises that each room is on the "ground floor."

The judge opened the door, allowing me to walk out first, and I gasped. It was so beautiful. We were high above the streets, with a magnificent view of the city, yet the building was against the mountain. "It's beautiful!" I exclaimed, and suddenly the judge grabbed me. I have never been so surprised—it was a truly unexpected experience. I protested—"Judge, Judge," putting up both hands to fend him off, "Judge, you are married!"

He said, "I know it. I can't help it! I have tried to get you out of my system! I've been mean to you!"

Well, he certainly had. And he was admitting it! His treatment of me had been deliberate!

And then he said, "You are the kind of woman who should be having my baby, not that god-damned Louise!"

I got away from him and ran as fast as I could to the safety of my room, where I locked the door and piled all the furniture up against the door that led to the shared bathroom. There was a sink in my room that had to suffice as a rest room. I was not going to use the connecting bathroom.

I didn't sleep a wink that night and somehow managed to get dressed the next morning and go downstairs to the cafeteria. The judge was already there ahead of me and said "Good Morning" as if nothing had transpired. In fact, he sat with me as we had our coffee and discussed the fact that he thought the trial would go to the jury before noon. He never referred to the incident, and a similar situation never took place. You can bet I didn't mention it.

***

On Christmas Eve of that year, I received a telephone call from an attorney in Tulsa, Oklahoma, expressing his need for a court reporter in the early part of the new year—January fourth, I believe. It seems that an Indian by the name of Wattie Turtle had blown himself up accidentally in some manner and was suing the manufacturer of the substance that had exploded. The attorney who was contacting me advised that Mr. Turtle was in the Veterans' Hospital in Fayetteville, and that he, the attorney, wanted to take his testimony as soon as possible, for he might die before it could be recorded. I told the attorney what I told all attorneys seeking my services. "I am the official court reporter for the Fourth Judicial District. If we have nothing scheduled on that date, I will be happy to help you. I will check with my judge, and if you do not hear back from me, I will be at the Veterans' Hospital on that date at 9:00."

Then I began searching for Judge Cummings. He was not at home; he was not at the courthouse. I finally located him at his farm. "Judge," I said, "I have a chance to make some money on January fourth next year if you don't have any court scheduled."

He hesitated ever so slightly, and then said, "Go ahead; that'll be fine." I thanked him and said, "Happy New Year."

Ham and I had been invited to a New Year's Eve party at the home of Faye Hill, and I had made arrangements for a babysitter to stay with baby Gretel, so when there was a knock at the door, I thought it was her.

It was the postman with a special delivery letter addressed to me. As I signed for it, I was a bit worried; a special delivery letter was not a regular occurrence at our house.

To my complete surprise, it was a letter from Judge Maupin Cummings notifying me that my contract as the official court reporter for the Fourth Judicial District would not be renewed.

I was fired! Effective January 1, 1953, the following morning—less than 24 hours—I was unemployed.

I could not believe it. I had just spoken with him earlier in the day when I had asked permission to take Wattie Turtle's testimony. Why had he not told me then? I immediately called him. "Judge, I just got your letter."

"You did?" he said. "Yes," I replied, "and I don't understand. Why didn't you tell me when I talked to you this morning?"

His answer was ridiculous. "I thought you would have received my letter," he said. Obviously, he couldn't think very well on his feet. Why, then, would I have called him to see if I could work for somebody else the earlier part of the New Year? My mind was going a mile a minute.

"Have you hired a replacement?" I asked. "Because if you haven't, I can work for two more weeks. I had planned to enroll in law school when the semester starts," I lied. "I was going to give you my notice."

I was saving face. I would receive two weeks' salary, and we certainly needed the money. I could clean out my desk at the courthouse without everyone knowing that I had been fired. Enrolling in law school was a dream, of course; one that was virtually impossible.

At that moment, Ham emerged from the shower with a towel wrapped around his waist. He had heard my conversation with the judge. "CRAWL!" he screamed. "Why don't you crawl to the son-of-a-b———!"

He was talking so loud that the judge heard him. "Well, that would cause trouble at home," he said. At that moment I didn't know which one of the two I was madder at—the judge or Ham.

"I think I can handle it!" I said, and the conversation ended.

The babysitter arrived. Ham and I went to the New Year's party. I never heard anything more from Judge Cummings.

* * *

"I'm going back to law school," I told Ham. "I really am."

"That's impossible," he said, giving me no encouragement. "Where would you get the money to do that?"

"I don't know," I told him, "but I am going to do it. I'll practice law in his court—or die in the attempt."

As soon as the holiday ended, I went to every attorney's office in Fayetteville and told each of them the story. Maupin Cummings had fired me. I was no longer the court reporter, but I was available to work at any job they had. The reaction of every one of them was actually quite gratifying. No one could believe it. I had been a conscientious, hard-working reporter, getting records out on time, and occasionally subtly reminding attorneys to "save their exceptions." Back then, if an attorney failed to say "save my exceptions" when inadmissible evidence had been allowed or the court had made an erroneous ruling, it was presumed that he waived his objection and he was barred from bringing the matter up at a later time. When an attorney, particularly one that I really liked, was about to forget to make his record, I had been known to clear my throat or cough loudly, at which time the attorney would hastily say, "Save my exceptions!" In fact, the attorneys used to laugh and say if they could keep the court reporter out of it, they could win their case!

* * *

My experience as a court reporter was extremely valuable to me with respect to my understanding of the law and court procedures. I made myself a notebook of jury instructions, except for the names of the parties. I had found that the instructions were all essentially the same in every case. I compiled the notebook for my own use in transcribing cases. The Uniform Instructions had not been compiled and published at that time. When Judge Cummings ascended to the bench, he took my notebook as his own and used it when he instructed his jurors.

Once, I was in Bentonville reporting a damage case that was quite long. There was a function I wanted to attend that evening, and I was hoping the trial would be over early and we would be back in Fayetteville; however, as it wore on and on, I began to give up hope. It seems that a man had negligently put his hand in a grinding machine of some kind, with disastrous results, and he was suing for damages. When the plaintiff rested, I went over to the defense attorney, Val Lindsay, a very prominent and capable attorney, and said, "Why don't you move for a directed verdict? Who put a gun to that man's head and made him stick his hand down in that hole? That was nobody's fault but his!"

"Do you think so?" he asked me.

"I certainly do!" I answered. "What have you got to lose?"

I really wanted to get back to Fayetteville early. Mr. Lindsey moved for a directed verdict, it was granted, and we were on our way home right after lunch.

The next day I received the biggest box of candy I have ever seen, addressed to "My co-counsel." As I said, all I really wanted was to go home early, but in retrospect I was learning a lot about law and trial tactic, and I felt pretty proud of the assessment I had made of the case.

* * *

One of the most interesting experiences I ever had was when I was appointed by the court to monitor the only female juror of the 12 finally accepted to sit on a death penalty case in the trial of a young man charged with killing his girlfriend. The defendant was the son of a man who was employed by the city water department, a highly respected member of city government. The selection of a jury took weeks, with prospective juror after juror being excused and scores of new potential jurors summoned. The problem was that the prosecuting attorney was seeking the death penalty if the defendant were found to be guilty, and no one wanted to assess that against their friend's son. I saw strong men gasping the rail of the jury box, tears rolling down their faces, begging, "Don't put me on this jury!" There were teachers who had taught the defendant, church members who taught him in Sunday school, people who had worked with his father. This list went on and on. Finally, we had 11 jurors. The 12th prospective juror was a woman, the wife of a local doctor. When she was asked if she could impose the death penalty if the State proved its case beyond a reasonable doubt and she found the defendant guilty, she replied, in a barely audible voice, "Yes." We had our jury, and they were sworn in.

Because it was a murder case, the jury was sequestered. How could we keep 11 men and one woman together for days, maybe even weeks? I was appointed to stay with the female juror. Jurors were together in one long hallway in the town's only hotel—the men on cots and the doctor's wife and I on beds in an adjoining room, with the door open at all times. She and I were sworn not to discuss anything about the case. We both almost burst, because the proof that was introduced was straight out of Hollywood. She and I swapped recipes, talked about clothes, vacation plans—anything but the only subject on our minds: the case that was being tried.

Of course the defendant was found guilty; the evidence was overwhelming. Everyone concluded that the defendant must have been on drugs, for he had been living in California. This was long before drugs had been introduced into Arkansas; they were unheard of anywhere but in California, which everyone knew as a den of iniquity. The defendant was executed and left his eyes to a blind man.

*   *   *

As soon as the New Year's holiday ended, I drove to Bentonville to the law office of one of the attorneys who had been a classmate when I was taking cases at the law school in 1948. He had just graduated, and I was sure he would still have his textbooks. I was right.

"You'll have to put some other books up there to impress your clients," I told him, "I'm borrowing these."

He selected those that he thought I'd need and helped me put them in the car. He knew that I had been a good student and a good court reporter, and thought that my firing had been unfair.

When it was time to enroll in law school for the second semester, I bravely went to the registrar's office and requested that I be allowed to enroll and pay the necessary fees at a later date.

"We don't do that," he told me.

"Well," I said, "you're going to this time. I think I will have the money very shortly, but I need to enroll now." I explained to him that I was a court reporter doing freelance work and that I had a number of jobs lined up, which was true. Wattie Turtle's statement was pending, as was a number of other legal proceedings promised by the attorneys I had contacted.

And that was how I began my second attendance at the University of Arkansas School of Law in Fayetteville, with borrowed books and postponed tuition.

Another important task was to find proper care for Gretel, who had grown into a beautiful little girl with drop-dead eyes and gorgeous curly hair. She was the light of my life, and I loved caring for her, but if I were going to be going full time to law school, plus working to pay for it, I needed a competent person to take care of my baby. I thought about all the kinfolks I had known from my earliest recollections of visiting in Harkey's Valley, and I remembered a pattern of behavior that may or may not be allowed now in hospitals. In those days when a member of a family was ill, the relatives—*all* of them—visited the ailing member, sometimes two or three together, sometimes more, and they stayed until the relative either died or went home. I went to the Veterans' Hospital and checked the veterans who were going through long-term hospitalization to see if any of their relatives were steady visitors. I found pay dirt! She was a grandmotherly looking woman, very quietly simply dressed. It was evident that she was not a wealthy woman. She was Mrs. Penny, and "Penny" she became to all of us, particularly little Gretel. Penny jumped at my proposal. I would give her free room and board in exchange for her helping with my housework and caring for Gretel during the day. When I came home, I took over, and she was free to visit her husband as long as the hospital allowed her to stay. The same thing was true of the weekends, and from the beginning it was a wonderful arrangement. Penny was a grandmother, but her grandchildren were no longer babies, and she fell in love with Gretel at first sight.

I fixed a room for Penny in the basement, with a very comfortable new mattress positioned on blocks. A dressing table and a spare rocker completed her room, except for a rug and a floor lamp.

General Eisenhower had been elected president, and Ham had graduated with a degree in agriculture. As I mentioned earlier, he was able, through his Republican connections, to get a job as an agricultural extension agent. The job required him to travel extensively, inspecting farms and farmland all over his considerable territory. It was necessary that he make frequent trips to Little Rock, and he had frequent contact with his friend Tommy Russell, who had finished his law course and was practicing law in the capital city. Ham's relationship with Tommy Russell, and my relationship with Tommy, through him, was a mixed blessing, as time would reveal.

* * *

Judge Cummings hired a young attorney named Lee Williams to replace me as official court reporter of the Fourth Judicial District. Lee was not a shorthand reporter. Indeed, I believe at that time he was beginning a trend of reporting electronically rather than by shorthand. I have often wondered exactly how much money was expended to fund the necessary equipment for Lee to function as a reporter. Possibly thousands, when I had never had a raise! However, as my mother used to say, the Lord moves in mysterious ways. Very shortly after Lee Williams replaced me as a court reporter, I received a call from him asking if he could talk with me. More out of curiosity than anything else I agreed, and he came to my home on Saturday afternoon. As a result of that conference, there developed a remarkable friendship between me and Lee which worked to the advantage of both—a friendship that exists today. Lee had married a beautiful German girl he had met during his service in World War II. Her father was a prominent man, I believe a judge. I could be wrong about his profession. I can't remember the details, but I know the family was uprooted and eventually ended up in the United States. When the war ended, Lee enrolled in law school at the University of Arkansas in Fayetteville, using his GI benefits. Money was tight. Because of her limited knowledge of English, it was difficult for Lee's wife to find employment. However, so eager to help, she took a job at Tyson Farms sexing chickens.

Lee had finished law school when he took the reporting job, but had no money to start a practice and had not been successful in obtaining employment with an established law firm. That eventful day we talked, Lee told me that he had no intention of remaining a court reporter—that he had simply taken the job because he had to have an income. He said he was beginning to get a few cases—traffic offenses, divorces—with prospects of more and better clients. He wanted to build a law practice. His proposition to me was simple and direct: with his new recording equipment, he would "take down" the cases, then bring the disc, or the records, to me and pay me to transcribe them. Was I interested?

Was I! It was an answer to prayer. I would have a sure income, rather than waiting and hoping for calls. I don't know if Judge Cummings ever knew that it was I who transcribed and prepared all the records that had to be transcribed or not. I never told anyone, and I don't know if Lee did or not. He certainly didn't remain a court reporter. He became administrative assistant to Senator William Fulbright and had a very illustrious position in Washington, D.C. I regard him as a life-long friend, and many, many years later he helped my son, who was working in the Clinton Administration.

12

My attendance at the University School of Law was, for me, the pursuit of happiness. Nothing was more interesting or exciting than the study of law and legal research. I was the only woman in law school that year, along with many World War II veterans. A young woman from Dumas, Arkansas, enrolled and began law school, but left to get married and live in Italy. It was many years before I saw her again. After I had moved to Little Rock and had become deputy prosecuting attorney of the Fourth Judicial District, I attended a lecture at the University of Arkansas at Little Rock, given by a federal judge, and afterwards at the reception I was walking behind a lady and waiting to fill my plate with the delicious hors d'oeuvres when I recognized her voice. It was her, back in Arkansas to obtain a divorce. With her was a handsome young man, obviously Italian. It was her adult son. I never inquired, but I assume she did not pursue a legal career.

I shall never forget the look on the faces of my fellow students when the grades from our first examination were posted. I received a six-point—all A's, which wasn't surprising considering that I had a degree (almost a master's) in English that certainly didn't impair my ability to write answers to test questions. Moreover, I had been in actual court trials for years, hearing legal discussions and arguments by some of the finest lawyers practicing at that time.

The attitude of my instructors was interesting. One of them called me in and said, very bluntly, "Now, you would do well to forget everything that you think you know and just listen to my lectures." I nodded respectfully. One of the others, specifically my civil procedure instructor, gave me an elaborate recitation of the way jurors were selected, after which he turned to me an inquired "Is that the way you do it, Miss Virginia?"

I was diplomatic enough to reply, "No, sir, we may be doing it wrong, but here's what we do," and proceeded to outline a totally different approach. I have always wondered why part of the law school curriculum did not include attendance at real trials when the school was located in the county seat where trials were routinely conducted. Some of the instructors had never witnessed an actual trial, let alone conducted or appeared in one.

* * *

I had a myriad of wonderful instructors in law school, with Dean Robert A. Leflar leading the pack. What a brilliant individual he was, and what an excellent instructor. He had the ability to unravel the most complicated set of facts in a case and make it understandable for all. He loved to embarrass me as the only female in the class, never failing to call upon me to discuss any case which involved sex. I remember a case where the wife had sued her husband for giving her herpes, and, ironically, when I started my practice I filed just such a case, with some success. A similar case had just been tried in Texas, and because the incident occurred at home, the wife was able to collect damages from her homeowners' insurance company. Needless to say, all the companies re-wrote their policies, and I was unable to recover from the insurance company.

One of Dr. Leflar's books, *Conflict of Laws*, is still the law, although he wrote it many years ago. Everyone liked and admired him, and those of us who danced with him knew to expect a playful pinch or squeeze. It became the territory and meant nothing.

Another great instructor was Wiley Davis, who went on to become dean of the law school for some period of time. He had a wonderful sense of humor. I remember his adding a paragraph to a social publication describing the activities of the students' wives' organization, noting the "the only female student's husband met and played with himself"!

Another wonderful, unforgettable instructor was Judge Pudge, whose real name was Judge Merriweather, but his girth was so large that "Judge Pudge" fit him much better than Judge Merriweather. He taught real estate law, and I shall never forget his use of "butcher paper" as a convenient way to read abstracts.

* * *

I guess it was by virtue of my grade point that I was placed on the *Law Review*—again the only woman. I became well known, and even sought after by other students, particularly if one assignment was difficult. Sometimes a group would meet me in the Student Union and discuss the subjects we were covering in our classes. I enjoyed the visible change in my male classmates' attitude toward me. For the most part, I was accepted. I was a potential attorney; I was one of them.

Although almost three years loomed before I would be eligible to take the bar examination, it passed like the twinkling of an eye. I have thought many times of something my father said when I discussed with him my plan to enter law school. "It'll take three, maybe four years," I moaned.

His reply, though simple, was astute. "Well, Sister," he said, "The time will go by whether you do anything with it or not."

So it would have; so it did.

* * *

One Christmas I had photographs made of Gretel for my family: Mother and Dad, and Dottie and John, and of course a copy for us. Money was scarce, and the photographs were not very big. I was walking down the Fayetteville Square shortly after the picture had been given to my family, and in the photographer's window was a 10x12 picture of my Gretel, with a beautiful 22-inch frame. I immediately stopped and checked again. I was not imagining it. It was a very large picture of Gretel—being shown by the photographer to the public.

Somehow I felt, from my limited legal training that something was not kosher! I had not ordered that picture; I could not have afforded it. I walked into the photographer's office. "That picture in the window is a picture of my daughter. I did not have it made, nor did I give you permission to put it on exhibit."

Without my saying another word, the photographer asked: "Would you like to have it?"

I could only nod. It was my proudest possession then, and has remained so through the years. I am sure the photographer's display of the picture resulted in his being hired to do similar pictures for his clients, so arresting was the image of the curly-haired baby in her little blue dress with matching shoes. I hope he made a fortune, for the picture is worth a fortune to me.

Gretel grew into a precocious, curly-haired little girl. I had set up an office in my basement where I transcribed Lee Williams' recordings at night. There was a playpen next to my desk, filled with Gretel's toys, a blanket, and a pillow. Night after night I typed away, pausing frequently to play with her—bouncing her ball, playing hide and seek, hugging and kissing her until she curled up in her blanket and fell asleep.

Not too long ago my adult Gretel was visiting at Querencia, my home. I was typing away on the typewriter I have on my desk there when I discovered that she was standing behind me listening intently to the swift clicking, almost in tears. I did not know that she had come into the room, and have no idea how long she had been there, but "Don't stop, Mama," she implored. "Don't stop! It's like a lullaby." We had never discussed my transcribing the cases after I was no longer the court reporter. The long hours of typing while she played and slept in her playpen had burned into her subconscious and remain there.

Ham, when he was not traveling for the Agriculture Department, continued to keep late hours almost every night, a great deal of the time in the company of Edwin Dunaway, who was teaching criminal law at the law school in Fayetteville.

* * *

One of the lawyers who frequently appeared in court while I was the court reporter was Irving Kitts. He was a municipal judge in Springdale, a few miles north of Fayetteville, but in the same legal area. Although he served in municipal court, he was allowed to practice law, as were a great many judges at that time, and a few even now.

By his own definition, he was a "gob"—meaning a sailor. I looked it up in Webster, and although the origin is unknown, a gob was a sailor. Irving took great delight in talking about his "gob" experience prior to going to law school, and about his plans for the future. He was divorced—and divorce was not as common then as it is today. He said that his former wife had had a hysterectomy, which freed her from fear of pregnancy, with the result that she had become promiscuous while he was away— which led to the divorce. Irving was very happily remarried, and he and his wife had adopted a little girl. He and his first wife had a son who was in college, and Irving made no bones about his future. He did not like the practice of law, nor, for that matter, being a judge. He and his wife planned literally to become beachcombers once the son finished school. When he learned that I was working on a degree, he talked to me one day at the courthouse and said simply, "Come see me when you graduate."

Of the many attorneys with whom I had associated for all the years I worked with the courts, Irving Kitts was the only one who approached me with a concrete proposal. I remember one particular sole practitioner in Fayetteville for whom I had done an enormous amount of work during the weeks and months that I was financing my law school education. I talked to him about my joining his law firm. He looked at me admiringly and said,

"Lord, wouldn't that be wonderful? But Marie would never let me do that!"

Marie?

That was his wife. I had met her at various functions, and I liked her.

"Marie?" I said. "What do you mean, she wouldn't let you?" I was totally and truly unaware of what he meant. He was serious; she would never allow him to take a female law partner, regardless of that person's ability.

And it got worse. I had never realized my sex would be a problem!

I was graduated from law school in 1955—top honor graduate, as the plaque hanging in the law school at Fayetteville even now reveals. I served on the *Law Review* and won a series of awards—books and money—all of which was greatly appreciated, for the family income was not enormous. So exhausted was I from studying, working, caring for Gretel, and pursuing a dozen other activities, that I found myself in Dr. Frank's Elizabeth Hospital for a while. He thought that he was going to have to perform a tracheotomy, or so he told me later, but after a few days of rest I was fine. Of course my family came to my rescue; Ham was still traveling, and I believe I was back at home before he was able to get back to Fayetteville.

* * *

After Mother and Dad returned from their extensive "belated honeymoon," they found that Russellville had experienced the greatest boom period in its history, and real estate was selling, as Daddy said, like "hot cakes." He still had his broker's license and Mama had obtained a salesman's license, and they set up a business. She proved to be the better of the two at selling real estate, particularly houses. They first rented a downtown office, but when the city placed parking meters in front of it, he moved. He purchased a brick house on highway 64, with a big yard that afforded adequate parking, and converted it into a spacious real estate office.

But prior to that project, my unbelievable parents built their dream house, a three-bedroom brick, on the two beautiful lots directly behind the wonderful antebellum home on Commerce Avenue, which they turned into a rooming house. They had used that space to maintain an oversized garden. My mother knew exactly when to plant everything—some in the dark of the moon and other interesting magic times, and her garden was the show place of the neighborhood. It was from this garden that my brother John had furnished the Weedins enough vegetables to learn bookkeeping to the extent that he went on to become a certified public accountant in four states! It was not necessary to buy very much foodstuff, only seasoning. Mother canned enough to carry us through the winter until the next growing season came around. She loved every minute of it and never seemed to tire. We didn't grow our own peaches. However, nearby Clarksville was the peach capital of Arkansas, and the orchard owners allowed you to pick the fruit for a nominal amount. The whole family participated in canning the delicious juicy fruit, although Daddy could not resist eating every other one after he had peeled it.

After my dad took out the building permit on February 1, 1949, there was no longer a garden, but what had been a dream through their 43 years of marriage at that time became a reality on April 22, 1950.

Ham had an uncle, Bernard Faisst, who lived in Little Rock and worked for a building company. I shall never forget him watching my dad measure and stake out the various rooms he planned to construct, stretching twine between the markers, and then later viewing the finished house in absolute disbelief. Except for the bricklaying and cabinet work, my father, with my mother's constant help, built the entire structure, including the wiring, the plumbing, and the hardwood floors. Mother papered each room in beautiful patterns and installed carpeting in the living room, which boasted a large picture window. She had her first matched living room furniture and state-of-the-art kitchen appliances. How she loved her dishwasher! And she had one before I did! She also got her first set of china, picking an exquisite flowered pattern that I treasure today. I think she stopped short of real silverware, but at least the cutlery, in addition to being serviceable, matched, though Daddy kept using his black-handled knife and fork.

About the time Mother and Dad built their "dream" house, the motion picture, *Mr. Blandings Builds His Dream House*, appeared, and I wrote an article about their astonishing accomplishment, titling it "The Harkeys Build Their Dream House." It was published in Russellville's *Courier Democrat* to Mother and Daddy's great gratification.

* * *

It was at the new house that Ham dropped Gretel and me, to remain there until I took the bar examination in Little Rock, with Mother taking care of both of us while I studied and prepared for the three-day examination.

I organized the subjects on which I was to be tested, putting the ones I had taken back in 1948, along with Silas Hunt, first, and then those I had studied next, and so on—ending up with ones I had just finished—some 37 subjects. I took over Mother's front bedroom, stacking my textbooks and notes on a writing table made from a converted bread tray, an arrangement that allowed me to sit up in bed, with the pillows behind me, and read and study far into the night.

I started early in the morning, right after breakfast, and did not stop until noon, when Mother told me "dinner" was ready. My mother had three meals: breakfast, dinner, and supper, and all three were regular and bountiful. I shall never forget finding my little girl curled up on the rug, which connected all three bedrooms, ready to see and talk to her mother, a position she adopted every day at noon. The rest of the time my parents entertained her, and she was not allowed to interrupt me.

I can't remember exactly how long I studied and reviewed, but I remember the last day before I was scheduled to ride the bus to Little Rock and take the three-day examination. About midnight the night before, my dad opened the door and said, "Sister, you need to get some sleep." I slammed the book shut that I had in my hand and said, "That's it! I've reviewed everything. Can you believe it, Dad? Thirty-seven subjects."

And his reply will always ring in my ears: "I don't think you can do it, Sister. It's too big an undertaking."

My immediate reaction was defiance and anger. "Well, you hide and watch!" I said.

* * *

The examination was one of the most grueling experiences of my life, but I passed it, making next to the highest score, the winner making one point more than I. The test was administered at the Lafayette Hotel, which had only pay toilets, and in addition it occurred at the wrong time of the month for me. I remember thinking that none of the young men who were being tested with me had that particular handicap, but to resent it was a waste of time and energy. I simply thought and wrote as fast and as hard as I could, and miraculously, the three days passed and I was on the bus, returning to Russellville. After the test was completed, I had gone with a group of fellow sufferers to a wonderful restaurant, Bruno's Little Italy, which at that time was located on Roosevelt Road in Little Rock and the first Bruno was alive. He was a very stout Italian man who wore his chef's cap and tossed pizzas into the air, catching them deftly and serving them up, almost red hot, singing Italian arias all the while. The restaurant's walls were covered with pictures of celebrities who had dined at Bruno's. It is still a wonderful place to eat, with Bruno's sons continuing the tradition, although it has been re-located to Bowman Road in West Little Rock.

Mother, Dad, and little Gretel picked me up at the bus station, and the next day, Gretel and I left for Fayetteville, making the whole trip a celebration. We stopped at a gift shop and bought her a memorial gift. I can still feel the immense relief and excitement I had experienced.

Some time later, I received the official notification that I had passed the examination and all that was left to be done was to be sworn in. In those days, there were no case coordinators with the duty of setting the dates when cases were to be tried. A certain day was set aside, and all attorneys who needed to set cases gathered at the courthouse where the sitting judge would "sound the docket." He would announce each case, and the attorney, or attorneys, who represented the litigants and wanted the matter set for trial would stand, their calendars in hand, prepared to set cases, after learning what date or dates were available.

When I came into the courtroom, I was greeted by all of the attorneys I knew from the court reporting days, and Judge Butt, who was a chancery judge at that time. He was an old friend and member of a very prominent family who resided in Eureka Springs. His father was a legislator with a very colorful past, which included a short time in the penitentiary as a result of a feud with another legislator. His brother was a doctor employed by the University of Arkansas. His sister was also a prominent person, and all of them were identifiable as being members of the family. Judge Butt laughingly told me a wonderful story about an incident that occurred when he was very young. He was skating down the steep hills of Eureka Springs and ran into a man, knocking him down. Quickly, the well-mannered boy hurried to help the man up and apologize. After dusting himself off and determining that he was uninjured, the man studied the boy intently and then said, "Young man, I don't know your name, but your face looks like a Butt!"

Judge Butt saw me and knew why I was there. "Virginia," he said, gesturing for me to walk over to where he was sitting, "I can swear you in."

To which I replied, "Oh, no you can't!" And of course he knew why. His offer was a joke; he knew that I would not allow anyone to administer the oath that cinched my being an attorney except the judge who had treated me so unfairly!

One of the older lawyers extended his arm to escort me to the bench, and in a forgiving gesture, I accepted it. I well remember when I was pregnant, reporting cases up to the very day Gretel was born, this particular man was puffing on a very potent cigar.

"Would you mind not smoking that cigar?" I had asked, trying desperately not to up chuck.

I was totally unprepared for his reply: "You put yourself in this man's world," he had replied and continued to smoke his cigar, even blowing some in my direction.

But at this time, he led me to the bench and addressed the judge: "Your Honor, I have the pleasure of presenting the newest member of the Arkansas Bar, Mrs. Virginia Ham," and the room burst into applause. I took my oath of office. I was a bona-fide Attorney-at-Law!

According to my licenses, which hang on the wall in my office, I received my bachelor of laws degree, with honors, in the "Year of Our Lord Nineteen Hundred and Fifty-Five, and the Eighty-Fourth Year of the University." My name was Virginia Harkey Ham.

In the Year of Our Lord Nineteen Hundred and Sixty-Nine, and the Ninety-Eighth Year of the University, I received my juris doctor degree, with honors.

There certainly were many changes in the 14 years that had transpired, not the least of which was my name. I was Virginia "Ginger" Atkinson. I still am—what a relief not to be Virginia Ham!

13

When I saw that I was going to graduate, I decided to have another baby. I wanted Gretel to have a sibling, hopefully a brother. To have a grandson would make my parents very happy, even though the Harkey name would not be carried on. And I wanted the experience of having a child of each sex, and I certainly didn't want to have more than two children! I can't imagine why the Dugger family here in Arkansas has 18 children and are expecting another child as I write this.

Ham said "I'm glad," when I told him that I was "with child"—but that's about all he said. He was still traveling with his government job. I contacted the only lawyer who had asked me to come and see him when I graduated—Irving Kitts—then I would need to be living in Springdale, not Fayetteville. So I set about trying to sell the house on Louise Street and find living quarters in Springdale.

My first and only interview with Irving Kitts was unbelievably wonderful. He was aware of the money I had received for having made high grades, and he suggested that I deposit that in the bank with him as joint owner as my first payment on his law office. We would be partners and each would receive 50 percent of the income each month, with this arrangement lasting only until his term as municipal judge expired and his son graduated from college. Then I would be able to borrow enough to pay him off for the office, if I wanted to continue with it, and if I did not, then I could simply withdraw my money and go elsewhere. I remember asking him what was in the deal for him. And his reply was, "I need you to run my office now, while I am on the bench. And I have my pension. I'm fine." He went on to tell me intended to work only until his son graduated, which was near at hand as I recall. Then he planned to retire and move with his new family to Florida and be a beachcomber!

Of course I took him up on the deal, and the partnership of Kitts and Ham was launched. His office was upstairs in one of the older buildings in downtown Springdale, on the main street, Emma Avenue. And believe it or not, I found a great house on the opposite end of Emma Avenue. I have jokingly said that that's when I learned to live like a millionaire, because the owner was a very successful man, and very rich. He and his wife had built a magnificent new home, and the one they had lived in on Emma Street was up for sale. They had left a lot of wonderful things, like a dining room suite with chair seat covers matching the draperies on the windows, and a clothes dryer, which was a relatively new appliance at that time and which almost nobody had. The dryer proved to be a godsend when I had a new baby born on December 31st that year in the midst of a snowstorm.

I was able to sell the Fayetteville Louise Street house and put the money on the Emma Avenue house in Springdale, making the deal and the move before Ham ever saw the place.

There was a long back porch that stretched across the entire back of the house. I turned it into an apartment, which was quite pretty and very efficient when I finished it. I then offered it, rent free, to a middle-aged couple in exchange for their watching Gretel while I was at work. I also enrolled her in a wonderful kindergarten that was in walking distance of the house. I took my child there every morning before I walked to the Kitts and Ham law office. Everything fell into place, almost miraculously. Mother said it was the hand of the Lord, which she saw in everything favorable that occurred, and I certainly wouldn't argue the point!

* * *

Irving Kitts' practice consisted of relatively poor clients with routine legal problems—wills, traffic offenses, divorces, and bankruptcy. I recognized early on that we probably were not going to be handling million-dollar personal-injury suits, but I loved every minute of our practice. One morning, I had just reached the office when a bib-overalled man lumbered up the stairs and stood, spradle-legged, in front of my desk, saying nothing—just standing there looking at me. I said good morning to him and then asked, "May I help you?" His reply was unexpected, to say the very least. Shaking his head from side to side, he replied, "No ma'am. I just wanted to see what a female lawyer looked like." With that he turned and retreated down the stairs without a backward glance. I have often wondered what he expected and whether or not I measured up.

I had located the shopping area, which was also close by, and I went one evening after work to replenish the pantry and the refrigerator. Hamburger meat was a staple. Gretel loved hamburgers, and it was cheap. I spoke to the owner at one of the stores, who scooped out a generous amount of ground meat, wrapped it, and put its cost on a sticker before he handed it to me, then he said questioningly, "I understand you are a lawyer?"

"Yes, sir," I replied.

He went on: "Do you know Courtney Crouch?"

"Oh, yes, of course!" I replied. Courtney Crouch was a very well known, prominent attorney who had a number of attorneys in his firm and practiced in a luxurious office building.

Well, "he's my lawyer," the store man said. "I'll tell you right now, he's the finest lawyer in this country!"

I agreed "Oh, yes, I know. I have seen him try many cases; I was formerly a court reporter."

That didn't stop Mr. Crouch's client. "I'll tell you right now, he's the only lawyer that I'd ever trust to do anything for me; he's a really a smart lawyer."

I had not disputed Mr. Crouch's ability or his popularity, nor had I attempted to undermine him. I suppose I revealed my resentment when I very quietly said, "It's too damned bad he doesn't sell hamburger meat!" And I turned on my heel, paid my bill, and exited the store.

Not long after that episode, I received a letter from the grocer containing a large number of over-due bills, asking me if I could collect them for him! I guess he got the point. I had my first client in Springdale.

* * *

Shortly after moving there, I had a frightening experience that turned out in an interesting, if not fully satisfactory, way. I had taken Gretel to kindergarten, to be picked up at lunch time by my tenants, and continued walking toward to the office of Kitts and Ham, enjoying the beautiful late fall weather and the exercise I was getting as my pregnancy advanced. Suddenly I noticed that I was being followed very closely by a very strange-looking man.

Well, he had a right to walk on the public street, I told myself. Don't be imagining things. However, when I slowed down, he slowed down; when I speeded up, walking swiftly, he speeded up. There was no doubt I was being followed. No one else was on the street, and there were no cars in sight. Frantically, I dashed up on the porch of one of the houses on my route, but he joined me there, looking strangely at me and literally drooling. I heard him ask a weird question: "How high are your heels?" At that moment a police car appeared, and before I could do or say anything, the officer took my follower's arm, and with no explanation to me, addressed the obviously mentally retarded young man, "Come on—get in the car," and drove away. The phone was ringing when I, totally bewildered and still shaky, arrived at the office. It was Irving Kitts, just about to begin his duties as municipal judge. "Virginia, I hear you've met old So-and-so. Don't worry about him. He's harmless. He's a shoe freak. We have to lock him up every time the shoestore sets up their new stock of shoes. He stands in front of the store doing things you don't need to see in public. I'm sorry he scared you. His Mama will take care of him! She puts the fear of God in him." And with that he hung up. I am sure that the "Stuff" he was talking about was masturbation, and I wondered at the strangeness of what triggered such a reaction—three-inch heels? And his mother did take care of the situation, calling me and apologizing, assuring me that he wouldn't do that again! I was shocked that the authorities, including Judge Kitts, had not tried to get some kind of help for the man. Apparently, everyone considered the problem to be his mother's, and as long as I lived in Springdale I never saw him again.

* * *

I thoroughly enjoyed practicing with Irving Kitts, and knowing and visiting with his family—his wife and their little adopted daughter. Everyone liked him, and my association with him helped me, although the overalled man who had climbed the stairs to inspect a female attorney was not by himself. The general public reacted to me in the same manner, but little by little they began to accept me. We had to drive from Springdale to Fayetteville to attend court, and I learned to schedule cases which Kitts and Ham were handling on the same day, eliminating having to make extra trips, which even then were expensive and time consuming.

I was appointed by one of the judges in Fayetteville to handle the estate of an elderly man who had died without any next of kin. He had a burial policy provided by a local funeral home on which he had paid for several years, but allocated only $250 for a burial, which included the coffin. He owed some utility and other small bills, plus some taxes, and I auctioned off his personal belongings, which were not very many nor very valuable, to gain enough money to pay the outstanding bills, plus a very modest attorney's fee for me. There was not enough money to pay the $3,000 the funeral home charged. I denied their claim, informing the court that the deceased had paid burial insurance for a considerable length of time, and the funeral home should accept the allocated amount of $250, in full settlement. Otherwise, it could be argued that the only purpose of the burial insurance was to insure that the body was brought to that particular funeral home. To my great satisfaction, the court agreed with me, and the funeral home received nothing more than the amount of the policy.

Among the old man's belongings was an inexpensive, but quite pretty picture of a peaceful landscape, complete with trees, flowers, and grazing cattle. However, on the other side was a picture of a very beautiful, scantily clad female. I knew my father would get a kick out of it, so I bid on it and won, using most of the fee I had just earned. How much fun my father had relating the history of how the landscape picture had been acquired, and always laughing heartily as he exposed the nearly-naked beauty on its reverse side!

* * *

Late in the fall of that year—1955—Irving was talking to me about a case we were going to try to set for trial, and I looked at him and said, "Well, I'm not going to be able to do that about that time, because my baby is due," and he looked as if I had just stepped off the moon.

"A baby? You're going to have a baby?"

It is true that I had not discussed my pregnancy with him. I thought my increased girth was a dead giveaway, but apparently Irving had paid no attention to it. He declared that he had no idea, but he and his wife were delighted, and everything we did after that conversation centered around the new baby.

I had also been warned by Dr. Frank not to tell Gretel until the baby's arrival. He pointed out that she could not understand time and would run me crazy asking when the baby was coming if she knew very far ahead of time, and he was absolutely correct.

Despite his instruction, and the fact that I waited quite some time before I told her about her little brother or sister, it was much too soon, as I learned to my sorrow.

* * *

On New Year's Eve, I had been invited to a party, and had made plans to go, as I was expecting Ham home from Little Rock. As it happened, he did not return until well after dark, and I didn't feel very well. My back had begun to ache, which reminded me that it had felt like that on my first onset of childbirth.

"Ham," I said, "I really think we need to go now." Dr. Frank's Elizabeth Hospital was in Prairie Grove, 22 miles from Springdale, on a very hilly road with light snow falling.

"I just drove 200 miles!" Ham yelled at me. "Hell I'm tired." He left me standing in the living room and went to bed. I had fed Gretel and put her down in her room before he arrived, so I lay on the couch and tried to determine if my labor had begun or was imminent. It was not very long before I knew the answer to that question. It had begun, we were miles from the hospital, and it was snowing!

I remember timidly shaking Ham awake. "Ham, I really think we had better go."

"O.K., O.K., I'll get you there," he vowed when he got a good look at me, pulling on his pants and a heavy coat. Meantime, I did the same thing and woke up the tenants, opening the door to Gretel's room which connected to the tenants' apartment.

"Gretel's asleep, and we're on the way to the hospital," I told them as I climbed into Ham's truck.

I was, indeed, in the beginning stage of labor. Searing pain grabbed me periodically—I was too rattled to keep count. Ham was speeding through falling snow, and I was hurting too much to be frightened. In fact, I put my head down between the seats and closed my eyes.

Suddenly, I realized the movement had stopped. Raising my head, I asked, "Are we there? Are we there?" I was trying to look out the window, but all I could see were lights and falling snow.

"No," Ham said. "I'm out of cigarettes, and this may take all night," and I lay in early labor while he entered an all-night cafe to get cigarettes!

When we arrived at Elizabeth Hospital, I was in advanced labor—there was no time to prep me. When my son appeared the umbilical cord was around his neck, requiring quick work on the part of Dr. Frank and his assistants. Sometime along the way, I got a shot of Demerol, and the grinding pain subsided. When I awoke, I had a girl and a new boy.

* * *

There was a small problem with naming the child. I wanted his name to be John Everett, after my father and brother, as well as my husband. Ham would not even consider that name, nor discuss it. The child was to be Everett Ham, the third, and no other name was to be considered.

And that was not the greatest disappointment I had. Ham and I discussed that we did not need additional children. I was 36 years old and had just embarked on my legal career. I wanted the doctor to tie my tubes, and Dr. Frank had told me that if it were going to be done, it was very easy to do directly after childbirth. At that time it was necessary for a husband to agree and sign the necessary papers, which Dr. Frank told me Ham had refused to do. When I spoke with him, to see what was wrong, he told me that he was not going to sign the papers. "But, Ham you told me you would—that you agreed with me that we didn't need or want additional children, particularly since the new baby was a boy. You told me it was O.K.," I was crying.

"As long as you were making the decisions I wanted," he said "I had no trouble agreeing with you." The operation did not take place. I had the problem of birth control until a hysterectomy became necessary several years later. Fortunately, however, exposure was not very often.

In those days, doctors kept maternity patients at least a week, and since I wasn't nursing the baby, the nurses were busily administering the formula that Dr. Frank had ordered for the little boy. He was born needing a haircut, and there was a large boil on one of his little legs, making it necessary to postpone circumcision.

My mother had planned to come to Springdale to take care of Gretel and to help me with the new baby, but I didn't know exactly when to expect her. The morning after I had my son, Dr. Frank came into my room, which was a double room, and asked, "Do you feel well enough to have a roommate?"

I replied that I surely did, and then almost fainted when the nurse pushed a wheelchair into the room with my mother sitting in it.

She had arrived in Springdale to take care of Gretel, but had fallen out on the floor from an attack of vertigo. My smart little girl had called my law partner. I had taught her his telephone number, and she called him, telling him that her grandmother had "fallen down." Irving Kitts brought Gretel and her grandmother to Elizabeth Hospital, and then took Gretel to his home until Mother and I got out of the hospital.

Ham missed all this; he had gone back to Little Rock.

* * *

Not long after Everett was born, Ham had a training session in Florida. He had the option of flying or driving his own vehicle and bringing his wife, and being reimbursed for the travel expenses. So it was decided that we would drive down for the event and stay at a cabin on the beach. I had never been to Florida, and I was eager to replace my maternity wardrobe, so I did my first shopping in Springdale, buying a couple of really nice things to wear to the functions that were planned for the participants and their wives.

We drove to Russellville to leave the children with my parents, who were living in their new home, and against my mother's wishes, Ham elected to drive some distance after dark before stopping for the evening. As we were eating our dinner with my parents, Ham asked me if I had any money, because he had not received his check. "How much do you need, Son?" my father asked, as Ham knew he would, and upon learning the amount, my father handed him the money.

Once we had told everyone goodbye and started on the trip, Ham acknowledged that he had not told us the truth; that he really had received his check, but he and one of his friends had purchased a piece of real estate, and Ham's half of the payment was due. He spent a great deal of time telling me how valuable the land was and how much money we were going to make, and about how his friend had offered him a half interest and it was destined to be a profitable resort. With his check and what my father had given him, he almost had enough for the payment, but he needed more. Did I have money? Of course he knew I had the account with Mr. Kitts, and he asked me about it. "I would have to call Mr. Kitts," I told him.

We were nearing Little Rock, and Ham drove directly to the Western Union Office for me to use the telephone. Of course Irving Kitts told me to write a check for whatever I needed or wanted; he had no objection. I can't remember how much I wrote a check for, but it was a substantial amount, which Ham put with the money he had and wired it off to his friend.

When we left the building, Ham held the door for me to get in on the passenger side of the car, which was parked directly in front, and I was speechless. My clothing, all of it, was missing! We had put a tape across the back seat and hung my new clothes on it, rather than put them in a suitcase. "My clothes," I kept saying. I could not get into the car. Ham then saw what had happened and drove immediately to the police station, which at that time was located in City Hall.

The police wrote a report and assured us they would try to find my clothes. One officer said he thought they might be pawned since they were new, and he sent an officer to investigate, taking down all the necessary information about us—where we lived, where we were going, and so on. Of course we never recovered anything, and when I asked Ham if he could retrieve the money I had written a check for, he was furious. "Of course not!" he yelled. "That's been sent already." I spent the entire vacation time in the cabin we had rented on the beach, wearing my dirty jeans and crying. The ocean was beautiful, but it rained every day, either in the morning or in the afternoon. Needless to say, Florida is not one of my favorite places to go!

I never heard anything further about my clothes, except to fight with my insurance company. I remember the lady with whom I had registered the loss calling me and telling me that she was denying the claim. "In the first place," she said, "you could not possibly have had that many garments in a suitcase." That's when I realized that I had not informed her of the fact that they were not in a suitcase. I hung them across the entire back seat on a rod, making it very easy for the thieves to snatch them! I believe I collected a small amount of money, but I know that the first weeks after our return from Florida were very lean. And of course, I never received any of my money back. The million-dollar project, like all of Ham's schemes, did not materialize.

PHOTOGRAPHS 119

(Left) My mother, Amanda Parks (Harkey) on the left, with Aunt Vera and Uncle Wiley Parks (1901). (Below) Me, my mother, and big brother John in front of the "house car" my father had built in Illinois so we could all travel together with him on his job.

(Top left and right) Me with Pete Keeney. (Lower left) Me right after Pete. (Lower right) Me and my brother, John, in front of a rent house in Russellville.

(Top left) My brother, John, and his wife, Dorothy in 1940. *(Top right)* Me with big brother John. *(Lower left)* Daddy, Gretel, me, and Mother in 1956. *(Lower right)* Mother and Daddy in 1970.

(Top left) My parents in their yard in Danville. *(Top right)* Daddy and Mother on their 50th wedding anniversary in 1956 in Russellville. *(Lower left)* My father, John Henry Harkey, in Russellville (1962). *(Lower right)* My mother and her cocker spaniel, "Honey," in a photo Everett took at her home on Ohio Street in Little Rock in 1976.

(Top left) Me with Gretel and Everett in Springdale (1956). (Top right) Gretel and Everett in their surrey in North Little Rock. (Lower left) Gretel and Everett. (Lower right) Everett A. Ham, III, in 1961.

(Top) Gretel, me, Everett, and Mother in our Sunday go-to-meeting clothes (1964). *(Lower right)* Everett, me, and Gretel on vacation at Knott's Berry Farm around 1962.

14

One day while I was living in Springdale, Tommy Russell called me and asked if he and his girlfriend could spend the night at my house. It seems that they were en route to a country music affair in Missouri, and they were going to stop in Springdale. I told him of course he could; I would be glad to see him and meet his friend. He told me that she had been on the Grand Old Opry and that she had composed the song "Looking Back To See." And I shall never forget his next remark. "She murders the King's English, but hell, she can afford me!"

It turned out that his girl friend was Maxine Brown, one of THE BROWNS—Maxine, Bonnie, and Jim Ed—a trio that became popular in the 1950's. They were members of the Louisiana Hayride and went on to join Red Foley as featured regulars on the Ozark Jubilee in 1955. Maxine and Tommy Russell were married and had three children, but the marriage was not a happy one and ended in divorce. Maxine claimed that Russell had, in one way or another, taken all her money, and it certainly would not have surprised me. Jim Ed served time in the service, but the group got back together after he was discharged, and in 1959 they recorded "The Three Bells," which sold over a million copies and created a sensation as the first number one country song ever to cross over to number one on the top rhythm and blues charts, as well. In 1962, they joined the Grand Old Opry. Bonnie had married a doctor and Maxine was caring for her family, and they had retired from the group, leaving Jim Ed to carry on alone. He is still with the Grand Old Opry, as well as performing a number of shows on the road.

* * *

One night while I was living in Springdale, Edwin Dunaway called me. He was no longer teaching criminal law at the Fayetteville law school, but was practicing law in Little Rock and was to become the lawyer for Winthrop Rockefeller when Mr. Rockefeller came to Little Rock.

"Can you still write shorthand?" Edwin asked when I answered the telephone.

I replied, "Of course! Why do you ask?"

He went on to make me an astounding proposition. It seems that Dr. Frances Brennache, a female doctor who had been working for the State, had been fired to make a place for a prominent doctor who had just completed his drug rehabilitation program and needed his job back. Edwin was representing her and contesting her firing. He explained to me that he could get no clear information from the agency concerning the hearing he had requested, not even whether or not it was going to be recorded. "I am going to have my client hire you as co-counsel with me, and I know of no reason why an attorney could not take copious notes! I want you to write down every word the witnesses utter!"

And that's what we did. I joined Edwin the day of the hearing and sat at the council table with him. When the hearing began, I recorded every word, and it was hilarious when the opposition discovered what was going on.

"Who is that and what is she writing down?" the opposing attorney asked.

Then Dr. Brennache rose to her feet and proudly announced: "I have the pleasure of introducing my co-counsel, Ms. Virginia Ham of Springdale, Arkansas," The potential witnesses said nothing after that. Edwin's client stated her position, and we adjourned.

Shortly after the hearing, Edwin's client was reimbursed for the lost time, which she had spent on Petit Jean Mountain with Winthrop Rockefeller, who knew of her wrongful firing and was letting her live in one of his cabins and attend to his herd of Santa Gretrudis. She had asked to be re-hired, but in the interim had been offered a much higher-paying position in Washington, D.C., so she accepted the offer and left Arkansas.

* * *

On the 13th of August 1960, I was admitted to practice before the United States Supreme Court. At that time, it was necessary to appear in person before the Court, although I understand that now it can be done by mail. Our congressman, John L. McClellan, introduced the Arkansas lawyers, and I took Gretel to Washington with me. While we were there, Dr. Brennache gave Gretel and me a wonderful time, showing us all the sights and taking us to a wonderful restaurant for dinner. While the doctor and I drank our cocktails, Gretel had her first "Shirley Temple"—a delicious non-alcoholic drink for children. She remembers everything we did on that momentous occasion, as do I!

* * *

Ham was spending more and more time in Little Rock, not only because of his job but because of the various projects he and his lawyer friend, Tommy Russell, were involved in, including the acquisition of graveyards, which required him to be there rather than in Springdale. For all practical purposes, the children and I were alone. It was decided that we would sell the Springdale property and move to Little Rock. In fact, Tommy Russell had found a piece of property on the highway in North Little Rock that was renamed John F. Kennedy Boulevard, which he urged us to buy. I looked at it and was unimpressed. It was located on a very busy highway, with a deep ditch in front full of water. It seemed hazardous for the children to me. Also, although it had an enormous living room with a wood-burning fireplace and hardwood floors, there were only two bedrooms and one bath. The kitchen was abominable. The counters were covered with dirty scrappy linoleum, and apparently additions had been added later, making the entire kitchen so dark that no activity could take place without the lights on.

Ham and Tommy Russell thought it was a tremendous bargain, and again we went to my faithful parents. A $10,000 down payment had to be made, and of course Ham and I did not have that much money. Neither did my father have it in hand, but he had unlimited credit; he borrowed the money and gave it to us, for which Ham and I signed a note, and off we went to close the deal.

It was not to be. When we arrived in Little Rock, with the movers and all our worldly possessions, we found that the sellers had not yet moved. We also found that the purchase price, which had been quoted to us and which we had accepted, was the correct amount, but the only problem was that it was two different loans, and one was in foreclosure!

We stored all our belongings in the garage, covered everything with visqueen to keep it dry, took the children to Russellville to stay with their grandparents, and called Tommy Russell.

Tommy filed a complaint and obtained an emergency hearing before the sitting chancellor. When Tommy finished presenting his case, the judge roared out his decision. "You'll get no pound of flesh in *my* court!" he stammered out to the person who was trying to foreclose. "How much time do you need?" he asked. I don't remember how much time he gave us, but it was sufficient. Tommy worked out the details of who got what of the money we had paid, and there was no foreclosure.

As for the seller's failure to give us possession, my dad took care of that situation. He brought the children back to me, and we all knocked on the front door.

"Oh," said Daddy, feigning surprise. "You're not out yet? Well, that's all right. There's plenty of room for us, too." And he set up my bed in the front room and went back to the garage for another load. I saw the recalcitrant former owner take down from the attic some large boxes, then climbed up and began removing spices and staples from her pantry. She was out of the house before dark, leaving us the chore of cleaning up everything.

* * *

When I told Dr. Frank Riggall that we were moving to Little Rock, he told me he had an attorney there who was a good friend and had a large law office: Ed Wright, of Wright, Lindsey and Jennings. He gave me the address and told me to write him. "Be sure to give him your credentials—honor graduate and all that. I'll bet he puts you to work!"

I spent a great deal of time on that letter, referring, of course, to the fact that Dr. Frank Riggall had given me his name. I carefully outlined my enviable scholastic record and my work on the *Law Review*, as well as my trial experience with Judge Irving Kitts.

Mr. Wright's rely was prompt, and I could hardly wait to open it. I am sure that I still have that letter somewhere, but I do not need it to know what Dr. Frank's friend wrote. Every word is burned into my brain.

"Dear Mrs. Ham. Your scholastic achievements are well known and greatly to be admired, but there is no place for a woman in our firm. I hope you find your niche."

Ed Wright went on to be president of the American Bar Association. His position with respect to women was not unique. I had encountered the glass ceiling.

I have thought long and hard about that response, and I have concluded that I was glad Ed Wright had been honest, rather than making some lame excuse about not needing any additional lawyers at the time. There was no place for me—a woman.

Discrimination. What an ugly word. What an ugly practice. I have always rejected the treatment the black members of our society experienced.

* * *

I had a law degree, but I was unemployed. The children were with their grandparents in Russellville, and I set out to see if I could be a lawyer—somewhere. One of the judges whom I knew in Fayetteville had been appointed to the Supreme Court, and I thought I would contact him and see if he knew of anyone who would hire me. I had no vehicle at that time; we were a one-car family and Ham had to have it, as he traveled throughout his territory. I rode the bus to Little Rock and a city bus to the Supreme Court building, only to learn that my friend was on vacation. His secretary told me, however, that he had a son who practiced law in the Pyramid Building; perhaps he would know when his father would return. Or he might know someone who would be interested in expanding his law office and hiring an attorney.

I walked from the Supreme Court building to the Pyramid building, noting that it was directly across the street from the courthouse, and took the elevator to the judge's son's office.

It was a very small office, and I had no trouble getting an audience with the son, who told me his father was on vacation and would not be back until the Supreme Court convened, which was a couple of weeks away.

I told him I was looking for a job—giving him some information about my credentials and my experience in Springdale. He said that he didn't need anyone, but he went on to say, "Now, H. B. Stubblefield in this building—his secretary is going to have a baby and he might need you. Why don't you contact him?"

I took the elevator to the next floor and went into the office of H. B. Stubblefield. It was a bit larger than the first office I went in—in fact, it was three rooms; there was a waiting room, with a secretary's desk, and offices on either side. There was no secretary in the waiting room, and Mr. Stubblefield emerged from one of the offices.

I told him that I had received my law degree and had practiced briefly with Irving Kitts in Springdale, and that I had moved, with my family, to Little Rock and was seeking employment.

"Well, I certainly do need someone." My secretary is on maternity leave, and I really need someone."

"Mr. Stubblefield," I said firmly, "I have been a secretary. But I am an attorney now, and until my children are hungrier than they are now, I am not going to be a secretary." And I stood up to leave.

To my complete surprise, Mr. Stubblefield asked, "When could you start to work?"

I replied, "Today."

"And how much a month are you expecting, or requiring?" he asked. I had no idea!

It was lunchtime and I thought quickly. I could call Tommy Russell and find out what the going rate was. "It's lunchtime, Mr. Stubblefield. I will call you right after lunch."

He agreed and I found the nearest telephone booth. I called the only attorney I knew in Little Rock, Tommy Russell. "What is the going monthly rate, Tommy?" I asked. "What should I ask for?"

"Two hundred and fifty," he said, "at least. And he's a good attorney, Mr. Stubblefield is."

I called Mr. Stubblefield and quoted that amount; he hesitated for a moment and then said, "I won't quibble over $50. I had in mind $200, but $250 it is. I'll see you in the morning."

When I got off the bus at the Pyramid Building the next morning, rode the elevator to the third floor, and stood in front of Mr. Stubblefield's office, I was elated to see my name, along with his, painted on the door: "H. B. STUBBLEFIELD AND VIRGINIA HARKEY HAM, ATTORNEYS-AT-LAW."

He had hired a secretary, who became a good friend and a great helper for me, as she had worked for Mr. Stubblefield before and knew a great deal about him and his practice. I was assigned to the office on the other side of the reception room, and I eagerly waited for a client or an assignment from Mr. Stubblefield.

* * *

It was tremendously exciting and interesting to be practicing law in the capital city. Mr. Stubblefield was highly regarded by his clients and his fellow attorneys. The Pyramid building housed most of Little Rock's practicing attorneys at that time, and it was very convenient simply to walk across the street to file documents or to attend court. The practice of specialization with respect to the practice of law was not as widespread at that time as it is now, or so it seems. Mr. Stubblefield handled all kinds of cases, but the greater number of them dealt with real estate. I read my share of abstracts! Thank heaven for Judge Pudge—our joking name for Judge Merriweather. He certainly gave us a sound foundation in reading abstracts. Who could forget his suggestion that we write abstracts out on "butcher paper"?

I did all of Mr. Stubblefield's filings and so forth, making dozens of trips across the street to the courthouse daily. I also spent a great deal of time in the law library, researching questions that arose in his various cases. I also did a certain amount of consultation with various clients when Mr. Stubblefield was busy with other clients or tied up in court, but the clients seemed always to end up checking with him to be sure that the advice I had suggested or recommended was the best course to pursue. In my defense, it almost always was sound and correct, and Mr. Stubblefield made few changes. Gradually, I began to be accepted.

One morning, after I had been with Mr. Stubblefield about a year, he called me into his office late one evening after the offices had closed and everyone had begun the journey to their respective homes. When I went into his office, he was on the telephone, so I sat down in one of the chairs used by his clients and waited for him to get through with his conversation. He did so very quickly and turned to speak with me. "Miss Virginia," he said, "You are a luxury. I have enjoyed having you in my office, but I simply cannot afford to have more than one employee." I sat very still, because I knew what was coming. I was not going to be working in his office. I was totally unprepared, however, for the manner in which I was released. "The manner in which you leave this office is going to be very important to your career, and for that reason your name will remain on the door and I will continue to pay you until you find another job."

I was near tears. What a smart, thoughtful, generous, kind man.

"How long, Mr. Stubblefield? How long?" I asked. His incredible answer was "As long as is necessary."

I did cry at that time—at least I teared up. "But Mr. Stubblefield, I couldn't possibly take your money and do nothing!"

"It won't be too long. You'll find something," he said. "Just do it as quickly as you can and don't worry about it, O.K.? This is between you and me. Let's go now."

The conference was at an end.

I was devastated. I had no idea what I was going to do, and I really did not know where to start. I certainly didn't want to take a great deal of money from Mr. Stubblefield when I was not earning it or helping him in any manner. When I told Ham about this development, he called Edwin Dunaway, who had returned to Little Rock after he no longer was teaching at the law school in Fayetteville and continued his practice of law. He was a very successful attorney and was actively involved in politics. He and Ham had continued to spend a great deal of time together, frequenting "The Gar Hole" at the Marion Hotel almost every evening.

Shortly after Ham had called Edwin Dunaway, I received a call from Edwin. He told me that Frank Holt, the prosecuting attorney, had an opening in his office, and that he, Edwin, had called him and he had agreed to hire me. He said that Mr. Holt needed me to record the grand jury if he ever convened it, and I probably would have to handle the indictments, but he said my office would be in the courthouse, and that all attorneys who worked as deputy prosecutors were allowed to practice law on the side. I would be paid $300 per month.

Of course I accepted the position and was sworn in as deputy prosecuting attorney for the Sixth Judicial District, which consisted of Pulaski and Perry Counties.

I was so happy that I could notify the generous Mr. Stubblefield that he need not pay me any more money; I had a job! I truly feel that I could never thank him enough for the experience he had provided for me, and his wisdom with respect to how and why I left his office.

15

There was never a nicer person than my new boss—Frank Holt, who went on to serve as attorney general. The Holts were from Harrison, and all of them were very active in politics. Frank Holt's brother, Jack Holt, ran unsuccessfully for governor, but he ran and was elected municipal court judge and served in that capacity for many, many years. John Jernigan was assistant prosecuting attorney at the same time as I, and went on to be chancery judge for many years. Frank's nephew, Jack Holt, Jr., was a deputy prosecuting attorney at the same time I was, and he went on to become chief justice of the Arkansas Supreme Court. Many other illustrious attorneys served as deputy prosecuting attorneys along with me, including Phillip Dixon, Rodney Parham, and Buddy Sutton. Frank Holt had a reputation of "training" young attorneys. Many came straight from law school to his office, and then left to go to very successful careers with prestigious law firms.

Mr. Holt had a group of very capable court reporters and legal secretaries, and all became fast friends of mine, although I did most of my own secretarial work, so busy were they helping the many male employees who were handling the prosecuting attorney's business, plus the paperwork that resulted from the lawyers' "practicing on the side."

Although I was sworn in as a deputy prosecuting attorney, as were all the attorneys who came to work for Frank Holt, the only thing I was allowed to do was type up the indictments and report the grand jury sessions, if any. The prosecuting attorney was authorized to file charges against individuals, and the use of a grand jury to lodge criminal charges against individuals, a tedious and laborious system, was used only if the situation involved a controversial or political offense or individual. However, when I began my duties as a deputy prosecuting attorney, I remember that there were many cases that involved the calling of grand jurors to investigate suspected wrong-doing and to file criminal charges if same were warranted. It has been many years since Pulaski County has utilized grand jurors, and I suspect many young lawyers have no knowledge of the procedure, but I have a very vivid recollection of some long, drawn-out investigations, with each of the 12 jurors having a different opinion! And I spent many, many hours recording what each of the jurors thought or believed, and finally how each of them voted for a certain action to be taken.

One of the individuals who worked for Frank Holt was Jean McDermont, although McDermont was her married name, she having met and married McDermont, an airplane pilot, in a Catholic wedding that all of us at the prosecutor's office attended. Jean's mother had worked in Washington, D.C., for J. William Fulbright, and Jean had married a man from a prominent well-to-do family and had had a son before it became necessary, because of his alcoholism, for her to divorce her husband and put her son in a military school. Jean worked more or less to have something to do and somewhere to go. She and I became fast friends. Whenever people came into the prosecuting attorney's office seeking legal counsel, Jean would steer them into my office, and before long I was filing divorces, drawing wills, collecting debts, and getting to be known as an attorney. Little Rock's black community was largely separated from the white population, and certainly the schools were. I saw a great deal of inequity and discrimination, which was new to me because I had had limited exposure to blacks in my lifetime.

* * *

I don't know how long I had been at the prosecutor's office when Mr. Holt called me into his office one evening as we were all getting ready to leave for the day.

"Virginia," he said, "I want you to take morning court next week."

I do not know where I got the courage to make the reply I made. I was a Phi Beta Kappa. I was the top honor graduate of the University of Arkansas' Fayetteville law school. I was on the *Law Review*. I had been in the courts, observing the state's finest lawyers for years, and he was going to have me REPORT MORNING court—write down what evidence the young lawyers who were conducting the trial were presenting to the judge!

I said, "Yes, Mr. Holt. I'll take morning court, but I want to ask you a question. If one of the boys in the office had been a brick mason before he fought, bled, and died to become an attorney, and the end of the courthouse fell off, would you send him out there with a trowel?"

And I jumped up and ran out of the office. I had no vehicle, but I was driving my mother's car, and I cried all the way home.

The next morning, Mrs. Dunkle, one of the secretaries on duty, said, as I entered the office, "Mr. Holt wants to see you."

OmiGod, it has happened. He is going to fire me. I was in debt. I had remodeled the awful house on JFK, turning part of the living room into a bedroom to make a room for Gretel, making the dark kitchen into another bathroom, and incorporating the enormous back porch into a kitchen and dining area, with beautiful cabinets and a fireplace. Once, when I had written shorthand all day during a grand jury investigation, arriving home well after darkness of an early fall evening, suffering from cramps and exhaustion, Ham vetoed my attempt to lie down before making dinner. "You got yourself in debt. Work and get yourself out," he declared. What would I do?

Slowly I traveled from the front desk to Mr. Holt's office, located at the very back of the courthouse. When I entered, Mr. Holt was sitting at his desk, pressing his fingers together—a thoughtful mannerism which he often exhibited.

"Pick you out an office down the hall, Virginia. I have hired another attorney to take morning court. I never thought about it."

I couldn't believe my ears! I screamed, "Oh, Mr. Holt!" And ran, crying to him, putting both my arms around him, sobbing. Of court people came running from every direction, and I don't known what they thought, because my relationship with Frank Holt had been totally at arm's length, and I was here hugging him and crying!

From that time on, I was truly a deputy prosecuting attorney! Major criminal cases were assigned to me, and I could count on most of the courthouse tenants being present to hear my closing arguments. We had only one judge who handled criminal cases as that time, Bill Kirby, and he used to tell Frank Holt, "You better send your lawyer on this one," referring to me, if the case was particularly difficult or sensational.

* * *

Child care was a problem for working mothers in that era. There were very few, if any, "Day Care Centers." If a working mother were lucky, there was a grandmother available, but my parents, although they loved the children, particularly the "BOY," they did not live in Little Rock and both were still actively engaged in their real estate business in Russellville. I hired one young woman after another without success. In fact, I purchased my first television set because no one would work for me unless I had television! It seemed to me that the material which I had seen on the television stations of the day was not really the best thing children could be watching for any length of time, and I am still of that opinion. In fact, I left instructions and attempted to regulate what my children could watch, but I recognized that my efforts were unsuccessful.

Since I needed child care every day except Sundays, and the North Little Rock house was not on a bus stop, I encountered constant problems. I had a wonderful friend named Evangeline Legg who had children almost Gretel and Everett's age. She and her husband had elected that she would stay home with the children at least until they reached school age. We had met in Fayetteville, and renewed our relationship when we found each other again in Little Rock, living in the same subdivision. Van, as we called her, loved my children and would keep them any time I needed her, reluctantly taking any compensation and always remarking upon how smart and well mannered they were. I was grateful, because working mothers were not universally loved and admired. I remember once when I was bragging about how much my small Gretel knew and the things she could recite, my female audience said, "Well, who taught her all that? You're gone all the time!" I have to admit that I grew very weary of receiving no credit for the amount of time I worked very hard to be able to spend time with my daughter. Once, I got annoyed at a woman who knew I was an attorney asking me what I did with my daughter when I went to work. I told her that I tied her to the bed post, what did she think I did with her? And walked away, leaving her open mouthed. It's a wonder the authorities were not notified and an investigation begun.

I finally converted my basement into a bed and bath apartment, offering room and board plus a small salary for child care. I was lucky enough to find our wonderful Rosie Barton, a black woman from Okolona, Arkansas, who answered my advertisement and lived with us for a good many years, going home to Okolona on weekends, when I took over the care of my children and the house. I did all the shopping and meal planning, but Rosie put together our dinners and cleaned up afterwards, which was a wonderful luxury for me. But before Rosie came I had one very scary experience which I shall never forget. I had placed an ad in the newspaper seeking child care, which was answered by a woman who said she was a registered nurse and would like to have the job of taking care of my children. I remember saying, "Ma'am, I can't afford to pay a nurse to take care of my children, although I certainly would like to be able to do so," and at that time she said, "I have very bad feet, and I am no longer able to stand on my feet and work as a nurse. I really need a job, and I would be happy to accept room and board as part of my pay."

I should have known better, but she came to my office in the courthouse, and appeared to be exactly what she had represented herself to be: a registered nurse with very bad feet! She convinced me that she could no longer continue her nursing career.

I hired her. She moved in, and she was too good to be true. The children loved her, particularly Gretel, whom she taught to make a bed so tight that coins could be bounced on it. At that time nurses wore the traditional white caps, and she was never without hers, which delighted Gretel even more. She decided that she was going to be a nurse when she grew up, and for several weeks my child care problem was over.

Not too long after my nurse moved in, however, she called me at work and told me that she had a doctor's appointment, and asked what she could do with the children. I told her to bring them to the courthouse, to my office. The children loved coming there; everybody "made" over them; they read and colored happily until it was time for me to leave, when we would walk through the tunnel which led to the parking lot to the jail, where the other attorneys and I parked our cars. I had purchased a car by this time.

The next week I was working away at my office, and received the same telephone call from the nurse. "I have to go to the doctor," she announced. "What can I do with the children?" This time, I told her that the practice of dumping the children at my office every week could not continue, that often I was in trial and could not manage the children, that she would have to make other arrangements, but to get them to me one last time. She did so, and before it was time to go home, I received a call from the manager of one of Little Rock's finest hotels.

"Mrs. Ham," he began, "Do you have a Ms. So-and-so working for you?"

To which I replied, "Yes. Why do you ask?"

"Well," he said, "She has charged her room to you, and she has been drinking all afternoon and running up and down the halls naked. We cannot continue to have her here."

I called the police immediately, all of whom knew me in my capacity as a deputy prosecuting attorney, but before they were able to get to the hotel and pick her up, she called my office and got me on the telephone. "You have made me cry," she said "And I don't like people who make me cry! I will never cry again until I go to your children's funeral."

Of course I panicked, and I was very grateful that the children were with me. The police arrested her and somehow managed to get her dressed and incarcerated in the Pulaski County jail.

Once she was gone, the hotel manager called me again and told me that he thought she had taken some of my personal property which she had left in the room she had occupied. As soon as I took the children home to Rosie, I went to the hotel, where I found most of my children's pictures torn from the albums they had been in—smeared with ink and some of them torn in two. I was able to salvage a disappointing few of the priceless photographs.

The police contacted her relatives, who resided in a nearby town, and her brother paid her fine and took her to his home, after apologizing profusely to me. She truly was unable to continue to work as a nurse, but it was not only because of bad feet. She had a drug problem, and her family had helped her many times over the years. Obviously they had not been entirely successful.

What a blessing Rosie Barton was. She loved the children and me, and she saw and understood the situation that existed between me, the children, and their father, although it was never discussed. She knew that I spent many hours alone, after I had bathed the children and put them to bed. Once she overheard me talking on the telephone and sobbing, and without saying a word she handed me a cup of coffee and gave me a quick hug before she went back to the kitchen.

When Everett graduated from high school, he sent an announcement to "his" Rosie at Okolona, Arkansas. It came back, unknown.

16

When John F. Kennedy was elected, Ham lost his government job and for a time was unemployed. However, an unusual and unexpected series of events occurred. Winthrop Rockefeller had come to Little Rock, Arkansas, in 1953. He had met and become great friends with Frank Newell, an Arkansas lawyer, when the two served in World War II, and Frank Newell invited him, actually persuaded him to come to Arkansas. It was everyone's belief that Rockefeller intended to obtain an Arkansas divorce from "Bobo" Rockefeller, from whom he had separated in 1950, as Arkansas had less stringent grounds, or requirements, to obtain a divorce. In fact, he hired his friend and former law school teacher Edwin Dunaway, who represented him in many areas and who eventually did help him work out a divorce and a property settlement, but it did not take place in Arkansas. An egregious legal racket was found to be taking place in Hot Springs, and a number of attorneys and judges were disbarred. At that time, it was discovered that hundreds of clients were coming from other states to Hot Springs to attend the races, filing for divorces on the grounds of "general indignities," obtaining their Arkansas divorces within 30 days, and returning to their home states, never having been a resident (or a taxpayer) of Arkansas! A large number of the offending individuals were from New York, a predominantly Catholic state where the only ground for divorce was adultery, an offense which is very difficult to prove unless it is admitted. A large number of Arkansas divorces were set aside, an occurrence which resulted in mass confusion. Many new marriages had taken place by individuals who were not legally divorced, making those marriages invalid. It took a long time to get everything straightened out. I believe that was when the statute was enacted requiring the plaintiff in a divorce action to prove, in addition to a legal cause for divorce, a residence in the state either by the plaintiff or the defendant for 60 days before the commencement of the action and a residence in the state for three full months before the final judgment granting the decree of divorce. Edwin Dunaway, therefore, advised Rockefeller not to file for divorce in Arkansas.

In 1961, Rockefeller was named National Republican Committeeman. The state of Arkansas was overwhelmingly Democratic, and Rockefeller, believing that the Democrats needed competition, formed a "Committee for Two Parties." It was true that the state of Arkansas was taken for granted and received very few political benefits, it being a foregone conclusion that the population would vote Democratic. I never knew how Ham came to be associated with and/or connected to Winthrop Rockefeller, but it was due to his fanatic Republicanism in some manner, for the Republican Party hired him to assist Rockefeller in his duties as the Republican National Committeeman from Arkansas. Since the Republican Party had very little, if any money, Ham was paid by Winthrop Rockefeller, and when Rockefeller stumped the state with his idea that it would be beneficial for the Democrats to have competition, Ham was his most dedicated assistant.

* * *

Very soon after Ham's new job had begun, Rockefeller sponsored an elaborate "Party for Two Parties" at his spectacular mountain-top home on Petit Jean Mountain. I was understandably concerned. I was a Democrat appointee; should I attend such a function? Should I endorse or reject the project? I sought, and obtained, a session with my boss, Frank Holt.

After I had told him about the elaborate party, something he already knew about, of course, because Rockefeller had been able to advertise the event to the extent that the entire population of the state was aware of the occurrence, Mr. Holt asked the question.

"You're a Democrat, aren't you?"

"I have always been a Democrat," I answered, truthfully.

"I don't think anyone could blame you for something your husband does. Of course you should go. And be sure to let us know exactly what goes on."

And so I went, taking the children, because it was something to see. Rockefeller had spared no expense, even flying in a number of elephants, the symbol of the Grand Old Party, and in 1962 the Republicans ran 150 candidates—more than ever before—for state offices.

To celebrate his 10th anniversary as an Arkansan, Rockefeller gave a mammoth party. Nelson Rockefeller, Governor of New York, came with his wife, "Happy," for the 6,000-guest banquet that started things off, followed three days later by a carnival of ferris wheels, pony rides, free hamburgers, soft drinks, and cotton candy. That event was featured in the September 6, 1963, edition of *Life* magazine, in which photos of Ham and Little Everett appeared. The magazine article ended with the comment: "Many observers think that some time in this decade Arkansas will have its first Republican governor since 1874—and they are betting Rockefeller will be the man."

That observation turned out to be true.

* * *

Even after I more or less remodeled the house on JFK Boulevard, I hated the place. First, it was very dangerous for the children. There was an enormous ditch with a bridge in the front yard that we had to cross to get to the house, and when it rained, it was almost impossible to get across. I had read that it was necessary to get permission to make any changes when one lives on a highway, so one day I went to the county judge's office to ask him how I should go about changing the highway in the front of my house.

County Judge Arch Campbell had become a friend of mine, because he sat every Friday to determine paternity cases, and since he was not an attorney, an attorney for the prosecutor's office was provided to advise him. It was a thankless task, and I was usually designated to attend. Judge Campbell had a "sure" way to determine whether or not the child belonged to the man the mother of the child or children had named as the father: he compared that party's ears with the child or children's ears. He was convinced that he could determine paternity in this manner and took a great deal of time examining and comparing the ears of the child with the ears of the putative father. I shall never forget a set of triplets that a young black mother brought to court dressed in identical suits, differing only in color; one red, one blue, and one yellow. The putative father was a good deal older than the mother, but he was beaming and eager to admit his paternity. Imagine his dismay when Judge Campbell, after examining everybody's ears, informed him that he was not the father! I have often wondered what happened to the group after they left the courthouse.

At any rate, Judge Campbell listened to my question about how I should go about getting rid of that deep ditch in my front yard. Looking back, I remember that he was very careful to determine my exact address, but he did not tell me what branch of the highway department I needed to contact and gave me no information. Several weeks later I was at home one Saturday morning, and Everett, who was only about five years old, came running into the house to tell me that there was a group of black men in our yard and "a lot of men with guns!"

Judge Campbell had sent a group of prisoners to fill in the ditch and change the access to my front yard! I had no inkling of his intent to do so until the crew swarmed into my front yard! It was a great improvement, however, and I appreciated it.

17

I have had plastic surgery. Like everything else that has ever happened to me, it occurred almost accidentally. All of my life, I had been extremely sensitive about my profile. I was as chinless as Eleanor Roosevelt! It was a combination of a small chin, crooked teeth, and a large slanting forehead. My parents had never heard of an orthodontist, and had they known about one, they could never afford one. Moreover, beauty shops did not exist for my mother and me, although she once gave me a permanent for Christmas, doing housework to pay for it. What a painful procedure the old permanents used to be!

After I graduated from college, I sought out an orthodontist, who told me, sadly, that I was too old for any meaningful corrections to take place. That was the verdict at that time; dentistry has come a long way. But back to my experience with plastic surgery.

It occurred while I was still a deputy prosecuting attorney, and it absolutely transformed my life. Of course I never would have gotten around to it if little Everett had not fallen on a friend's glass-topped coffee table, almost cutting off his nose. Holding a bloody bandage on the cut, I rushed him to the doctor's office, which at that time was in the downtown Donaghey building—along with all the other doctors in the city. Quickly the doctor sterilized the bleeding child's nose and stitched it up, instructing me to bring him back in a very short period of time—a couple of days or so to have the stitches removed. Of course I did take him back, making a great adventure of the event, with ice cream or popcorn, only to find a note on the doctor's door, informing us that he was out of town, but that the doctor next door was taking his cases.

Holding Everett's hand, I gingerly opened the door of the office next door, because the sign on the door said "Dr. Jim Stuckey, Plastic Surgery." When we got inside I thought we had entered a head-hunter's cave! Small plastic heads were everywhere, but we were in the right place. Dr. Stuckey acknowledged that he was seeing his next-door friend's patients and promptly lifted Everett on to the heightened examining chair, escorting me to a stool behind my son, so I could watch the procedure and comfort the child, if necessary.

"You're a plastic surgeon!" I asked, rhetorically. Dr. Stuckey acknowledged that I was correct.

"One of these days, I am going to have you cut off my nose," I said, as he was lifting stitches carefully from Everett's little nose.

The doctor looked briefly at my nose and observed: "It's a man's nose."

"That's right," I said. "It's my dad's nose, and it looks like hell on him!"

Dr. Stuckey continued to work on Everett, but from his next statement I knew he had assessed the situation.

"What you really need is a chin," he said, still assiduously removing stitches from Everett's nose.

I was glad the doctor was not looking at me at the time, for tears had filled my eyes. For years I had told myself that it was not too bad, that people really didn't notice it very much, but I knew better. I avoided hats, for they inevitably accentuate an ugly profile, and I never allowed my picture to be made except with a full frontal exposure.

"And that's quite an operation," the doctor went on, referring to his statement about a chin.

"Why?" I asked.

"Well, you have to have bone from somewhere," he explained. And then, either because he had finished removing Everett's stitches or because he "smelled" business, he said, rather quizzically: "You're serious, aren't you."

"Yes," I said, without even thinking. "Where do you get the bone?"

"You can buy it," he replied, "but if I were you, I'd use my own. There's less likelihood of rejection. We'd take it off your hip."

"Take it off my hip? I'm an attorney, and if a man came into my office and said he had lost a big hunk of his hip, I'd think he had been injured," I said.

"Well, we do it in a sanitary situation," he said. And then, because another patient was waiting, he said, "Why don't you come back tomorrow and let's make a mask, so I can show you the difference."

And Everett and I left to pursue our ice cream adventure before we went home.

The next day, I returned to Dr. Stuckey' office and had a most interesting experience. Nowadays, of course, it is all done differently, I am sure, but on that occasion Dr. Stuckey put me on a table and completely covered my face and head with plaster of Paris. It did not take very long, but I remember complete darkness, as the material covered my entire face, head, and eyes, for a short period of time. Then it was removed. The following day I held my entire head in my hands. The doctor moved it from side to side. On one side he had left my face and head as it was; on the other side he had carved my nose down and added a chin, using children's modeling clay. I was gorgeous; I was glamorous. I was excited.

"When can you start?" Was my only question, except, of course, and "how much?"

I arranged to have time off from the prosecutor's office without telling anyone why I was taking off. I told nobody about my operation. Of course Ham and the children knew, because my nose and chin were bandaged up, with a protective cover over them that had to be removed by Dr. Stuckey. Everett and I spent a great deal of time watching the construction of the interstate highway from Little Rock to Jacksonville. The time finally came when I looked in the mirror at a totally different face. I did not believe Dr. Stuckey when he said nobody would notice it if I didn't tell them, and he was exactly right. Even my parents did not notice anything until I showed them the before and after pictures. When I returned to work there were many comments about how good I looked, but everyone assumed that I was rested or had changed my hairdo. When I think about it, one would hardly ask if I'd had my nose cut off and a chin built from a piece of my hip!

* * *

One extremely interesting episode transpired, however, that I could never have dreamed would happen. A potential client was routed to my office by my friend Jean McDermont, and after the introduction and before I had questioned the charming young wife who wanted a divorce about anything, she suddenly looked at me searchingly, and then asked, "Has Dr. Stuckey worked on you?"

I was speechless. Not only had this complete stranger noticed that I had had plastic surgery; she knew who had performed it! Of course I later learned that she was a nurse who had worked for Dr. Stuckey, but at that time I knew nothing except that this young woman wanted a divorce! "Yes," I answered.

"Oh," she said scornfully, "he puts that nose on everybody." My gorgeous new nose! I still love it. I did, though, call up Dr. Stuckey, who was my good friend, and tell him that for the price I paid, I really thought I deserved a unique nose! Not the "same nose he put on everyone."

* * *

One of the first things I did was purchase a beautiful hat from a hat shop that I had not patronized before. Before long I had quite a collection, and I enjoyed wearing them on Sunday mornings, along with gloves and a matching purse. I continued to wear them until my daughter made fun of the practice, since nobody was wearing hats, except, of course, Willie Oates, Little Rock's famous "Hat Lady."

I dressed up each Sunday and took the children to the Baptist Church in North Little Rock. Ham never attended, usually being still asleep from having been out most of the night. I stopped asking him to go with us, as I knew he wouldn't. The congregation at the church thought I was a widow.

Gretel was in the children's choir and really enjoyed her participation in special events at the church. The young singers had matching costumes and a surprising repertoire for their age. I shall never forget one Sunday morning when Ham stumbled in while I was fixing breakfast for the children and Gretel asked him if he was coming to hear her sing. Without replying, Ham threw me an accusatory dirty look, which infuriated me. I had long since stopped asking him to participate in anything the children and I did, and I had not asked him this time. I was really angry.

"I didn't ask her to invite you!" I said. "Look at her and tell her you are not going to hear her sing!"

Gretel began to cry. "Mama didn't tell me to ask you, Daddy," she said. "I wanted you to come."

At that Ham went directly to the bathroom, showered, dressed, and then as I put the dishes in the dishwasher, dressed myself, and helped both children get ready, he got into the car and blew the horn for us to join him! When we got to church, a cheery greeter welcomed us, and Ham learned from her that the children's performance was not until after Sunday school. He turned on his heel and walked toward a nearby drugstore, with a curt "I'll be back."

I escorted Everett to his class, and Gretel went to hers. I went to a secluded part of the building and wept silently. I was angry, embarrassed, and sad—all at the same time.

Return he did, and the performance of the children's choir was great. Ham never attended again. The loss was his.

As were many other priceless moments.

* * *

One Saturday morning, I had taken little Everett to the North Little Rock Boy's Club while I went to my office at the courthouse to work until about noon in an effort to catch up. I had just settled down when I was summoned by the Boys' Choir Director. Everett had fallen while running up the stairs, knocking all his front teeth out. Of course I took him as fast as I could gather him up and drove him to our Doctor Don, in the Heights, where we were relieved, somewhat, to learn that the teeth were "baby teeth"; they were about to fall out anyway, and would soon be replaced. Dr. Don didn't think they even needed spacing or anything. Relieved, I lectured the toothless little boy unmercifully. "Now, Everett," I said, "God gives us two sets of teeth. You have used up one set. You will get some more before very long, and you must be very, very careful not to fall and knock them out, because no more will grow back in. O.K.?"

With his usual, wide-eyed demeanor, he listened, saying nothing.

The following Sunday morning, the children and I, running a little late, were ushered into the balcony at church, the sanctuary being full. We were alone, and the children, especially Everett, were intrigued with their view of the congregation sitting so far down from the balcony. Everett walked back and forth several times, looking down on the worshippers. And then while the collection was being gathered and only very soft music being played, Everett whispered in his loudest whisper: "Mama, how many sets of hair does God give us?" He was obviously remembering my lecture about his teeth.

I looked over the balcony, and it was evident why the child wondered about extra sets of hair. There was not a full head of hair in the entire male congregation.

I could not control my laughter. The children and I exited first the balcony and then the building. It was obvious that most of the male members of that congregation had used up their first set of hair!

* * *

Edwin Dunaway represented Mr. Rockefeller when the divorce from Bobo took place. He never told me the amount of money that Bobo received. But he knew, because he later delivered it personally to her. According to information I read later, she received a $5.5 million settlement composed of $2 million in cash and a $3.5 million trust fund set up for her and her son.

Edwin detested her and told us that she had taunted Winthrop Rockefeller, saying that the child she had seven months after her wedding to him might not have been his. She also attempted to take the boy once when he was visiting Rockefeller in Arkansas, and the notorious Marlin Hawkins, Sheriff of Perry County, Arkansas, appeared and escorted her off the premises. Rockefeller appreciated the sheriff's action so much that he never joined in the criticism of him that prevailed at a later date.

Mr. Rockefeller's divorce was final in 1954, and two years later, in 1956, he married his second wife, Jeanette Edris, whose father was an attorney and a very wealthy man who had dealt exclusively in timber. Edwin joked that Mr. Rockefeller had married her for her money. She had been married before several times: once to a pro American football player, once to a lawyer, and once to a stockbroker. She had two children, Anne and Bruce Bartley, who came with her to Arkansas.

* * *

Little Rock had no tall buildings downtown at that time, and Mr. Rockefeller, together with R. A. Lile and two investors from Dallas, Trammel Crow and M. E. Moore, built The Tower

Building, 17 stories high, a virtual "skyscraper." I took little Everett frequently to watch the construction of Little Rock's first tall building. The first lease, dated September 24, 1959, was signed by Merrill, Lynch, Pierce, Fenner and Smith, Inc., with a rental of $1,218.75. By 1960 the building was full. My friend H. B. Stubblefield left the Pyramid Building and paid $174 a month, along with other lawyers Gayle Windsor, William P. Bowen, McMath, Leatherman, Woods and Youngdahl, and my nemesis, Edward L. Wright, senior partner of Wright, Harrison, Lindsey & Upton. The tenants were banks, beauty salons, life insurance companies, and travel agencies. Jeanette Rockefeller had her Mental Health Association there, Rockefeller had a beautiful office on the 17th floor, and Ham's office was located on another floor.

The top floor accommodated the Top of the Rock Club with its magnificent view, a wonderful restaurant, bar, and other amenities. Ham apparently had unlimited access to the club, for he entertained dignitaries there and ate most of his meals there. It used to really irritate me, for he would call home to check on the menu for our evening meal, and if it was something he did not like, he would stay at the Tower Building, eat his dinner at the Top of the Rock, and then come home to his family, usually after the children had gone to bed.

I remember taking my cousins, who were visiting from Santa Fe, New Mexico, to the Top of the Rock for lunch, and Ham sent me a bill. I paid Winthrop Rockefeller for the lunch my cousins and I had eaten. I don't know what Ham's arrangement was concerning the meals he ate, but there were only a few evenings when he did not consume a top-grade fillet mignon. The kids and I ate macaroni and cheese.

* * *

As I said before, Winthrop Rockefeller was one of the most generous, kindest individuals I have ever known. Once, he was flying to Denver, Colorado, with several individuals and remembered that my brother lived there. He called to see if I could get away and go with them. Frank Holt told me he was glad I could go, and I have never enjoyed a trip more, despite Ham's attitude. Just as I was about to step onto Mr. Rockefeller's plane, Ham gripped my hand in a hammer lock and commanded, "Now, you keep your mouth shut on this trip."

Well, of course I didn't, and that was largely because Mr. Rockefeller conversed with me from the time he helped me aboard until we landed. I was the only female on board, and he wanted to show me the literature about the new and bigger plane he was going to purchase to replace the little one we were in. He was laughing because he had been able to get to Little Rock with some personal property that Bobo did not know about. "I really ought to name my new plane 'Bobo,'" he chuckled. "I got by with enough to pay for it!" Part of the property he had brought into Little Rock was his wine collection, which was housed in an underground room at his Petit Jean Mountain home and included some priceless bottles of wine from the opening of famous restaurants and skyscrapers and the launching of illustrious ships. Some of his collection was confiscated by the police because taxes had not been paid, but Edwin Dunaway was able to get everything worked out.

When we landed in Denver, I remember that someone at the hotel had made a mistake and Mr. Rockefeller's suite was taken. He had to sit in the lobby while the hotel people scurried around and found new quarters for the illustrious client, and while we were waiting, my brother, who had come to pick me up, asked Ham if he could meet Mr. Rockefeller. At the time, John was connected with the California Oil Company, and I believe that was part of the Rockefeller holdings.

"Oh, no!" Ham told my brother. "He's very tired, and now somebody has taken his suite."

Mr. Rockefeller heard him and immediately looked around for John. "Of course I want to meet Virginia's brother!" he told

Ham, and when he located him, outstretched his hand. He and John were immediately compatible. John was amazed at how much Mr. Rockefeller knew about the operation and the employees, and they visited until Mr. Rockefeller was notified that the suite the hotel had finally arranged for him had been cooled off.

And I didn't "keep my mouth shut," either.

Mr. Rockefeller and I discovered that we both had been reared by Baptists, and he and his brothers carried suitcases and worked when the family was on vacation. A wonderful lunch had been prepared for us by Mr. Rockefeller's staff when we left, but on the return trip Mr. Rockefeller was calling the hotel for another meal when he heard me whisper, "I like peanut butter and bananas."

"Me, too!" he declared adding peanut butter and bananas to his order. Despite Ham's admonition, I thoroughly enjoyed the trip, thanks to Mr. Rockefeller.

* * *

On one occasion, Mr. Rockefeller called me and invited us to spend the weekend in one of the guest houses on Petit Jean, but I had other things on my mind. Everett had just been released from the hospital after colliding with a car while riding his bicycle, My father, ever the money-saver, had bought Everett a bicycle that was really too big for him, but "he would grow into it," and he could ride it longer. Everett could barely reach the pedals, but as long as he stayed in the yard he was fine. Although he didn't actually get on the highway, he went down a side street which had an incline and was unable to stop.

I was on the way home, and as I came into sight, I saw several cars in the driveway. With my heart in my mouth, I parked and ran into the house, finding Everett lying on my bed, surrounded by Rosie and the frightened lady whose car had hit the bicycle.

"I'm all right, Mama," Everett assured me. Ham was right behind me, and we loaded Everett into the car and drove straight to the hospital. There were no broken bones, and apparently no serious injuries. The lady had been able to stop when she hit the bicycle, and she had not been driving very fast. The doctor told us to put him to bed and watch him carefully. If he had any swelling or other difficulties, we were to bring him back to the hospital.

Back at home, Everett was in his bed, and Ham had gone off without saying where he was going. Later, he called the house. "I'm on my way," he told me, and Rosie and I were uneasily waiting, wondering what, if anything, we needed to do.

Ham strode into the room, and noted that both Rosie and I were in attendance at Everett's bedside, one on each side. "He's just spoiled!" Ham concluded, "Here! Drink this!" he commanded, handing Everett the orange juice he had not been able to drink.

Wide-eyed Ev' obediently swallowed the juice, but no sooner than it went down it came back up. I was scared and furious. All I said was "Are you satisfied?"

At that time, Ham told me that he was "fighting for his life"—no other explanation—and couldn't go with me to the hospital. I said "That's O.K. I think he needs to go back to the hospital, and I am going to take him."

Ham left to go back to his office. Rosie helped me put Everett in the car, saying, "No, ma'am! My baby ain't spoiled! Look here," and she raised Everett's shirt to show me an extended stomach.

When I got to St. Vincent's Infirmary, the doctors immediately began giving Everett saline solution intravenously. He was severely dehydrated. I made plans to spend the night with him. It was Friday and Rosie would ordinarily be leaving for Okolona, but she volunteered to stay until Sunday morning to take care of Gretel.

The next morning, Ham called to see how Everett was feeling. "Oh, he's much better," I was happy to report. "He ate a good breakfast."

And then Ham said, "I know I ought to be there with you, but Win wants me to go to the game with him, and he has seats on the 50-yard line. Do you want to go?"

Wild horses could not have dragged me to a football game when Everett was recovering and still in the hospital. "No," I said, and the conversation ended.

That evening when the doctor made his rounds, he told us Everett could go home the following morning. What a relief. I slept much more comfortably on the roll-away bed the hospital furnished. After breakfast Sunday morning, I called home, waking Ham up. "We're coming home," I told him. "Let me talk to Gret-Gret."

I waited for him to wake her up or to call her if she was already awake. That didn't happen. He came back and said, "She's not here."

"Not there? Where is she?" I almost shouted, fighting panic. Gretel was still a little girl.

"I don't know," he admitted. Rosie had gone home.

"Well, find her!" I demanded and hung up, for I had to complete the process of getting Everett ready to go home.

Imagine my relief when Gretel called me herself, shortly afterward, although it seemed a lifetime.

"I couldn't wake Daddy up," she said, "so I called Aunt Liz and asked her to take me to Sunday School." That was a friend of mine. I had taught the children to call my adult friends "Aunt." "I'm fine, Mama. And Everett's coming home?" The children were very close, in spite of the difference in their age and sex. We were all relieved that Everett was all right and going home.

18

Obviously, my second marriage did not seem to have been made in heaven, either. Ham's neglect and verbal abuse continued.

All my life I wanted a diamond ring, and despite two marriages I had never had one. I understood that when Ham was a student and we married there was no money for a ring, but when he began to be paid by Rockefeller, I thought he might remember that I wanted one. One Christmas, Marion Burton, who worked for Mr. Rockefeller as a pilot, gave his wife a beautiful diamond ring. We were all at a function together, and I remember seeing the diamond, congratulating her, and showing the shining beauty to Ham.

"Oh, women just like to brag about having a diamond," Ham sneered, in the presence of the Burtons. "It's no big deal. A diamond is just a piece of carbon that stuck to its job." I think I received a can opener for Christmas that year.

Sometime after that (I have forgotten the occasion, although I believe it was on my birthday), I had fallen asleep reading a book after putting the children down, and had not gotten ready for bed. Ham came in very late. As usual, he had been drinking, and his first words were: "I brought you something."

With that, using his index finger, he pitched a box across the room. Of course I picked it up and upon opening it almost expired. It was a beautiful diamond ring. Although not huge, it was a very nice size. I burst into tears. He remembered! He bought me a diamond ring!

I wish I could say that the marital situation improved. Just the reverse. From that day forward, Ham would say to me monthly: "You'll have to pay the mortgage this month. I have to pay on that goddamned ring!" "I can't pay Everett's kindergarten this month; I'm paying on that goddamned ring!" I heard that over and over until all the joy of owning the diamond was gone.

And then came the *pièce de résistance*. One night Ham came home particularly angry about something. I remember that he was still making trips out of town and was quite late in getting started. I have forgotten why he was irritated at me, but he suddenly grabbed my hand and took the diamond off my finger. "Give me that goddamned ring!" he demanded. Of course I was crying, and Ham was preparing to leave. Just before he left, he went into the bathroom, and I heard the commode flush. As he went out the door, he told me: "I flushed that goddamned ring down the drain! That's what I think of you and this goddamn marriage!" And he was gone.

I lay sleepless the rest of the night, and somehow managed to help Rosie get the children up, dressed, and off to school and kindergarten the next morning. Then I called Mr. Holt to tell him that I was unable to come in. I then called my plumber, who was a friend, and told him what had happened. He dug up the drain and most of the yard, taking the greater part of the day, with no results.

"I don't believe he flushed it down the drain," I remember him saying. "Has he been gambling at Tunica and lost a lot of money, or anything?"

"Not that I know of," I replied, feeling very sad at our failure to discover the ring.

I went back to work, and somehow the time passed until Ham returned the next weekend. I acknowledged his return, but said very little of anything to him. He went into the bedroom, opened his wardroom drawer, and took out a packet of matches. Behind the matches was my beautiful ring.

"I guess a woman who has two children ought to have a wedding ring," he said, handing me the ring.

I put it on my finger silently. There was really nothing to say.

* * *

The relationship I had with Mr. Rockefeller, and later with his wife Jeanette, was one of the most delightful experiences I have ever had. Neither of them ever flaunted or abused their obvious wealth. Only once, when a group of us were having a discussion and someone complained about "hating Arkansas," did the fact that they were wealthy ever come up. Upon hearing the comment, Jeanette said, "Why don't you move somewhere else?" And I broke in to say that she did not understand that ordinary working people could not afford to move indiscriminately from place to place.

I was totally unprepared for Jeanette's angry retort. "That," she almost shouted, "was below the belt!" Of course, I apologized, but I still think it was an obvious observation.

Jeanette was almost as active as Mr. Rockefeller in various pursuits. She was very engaged with Mental Health Association, and greatly improved the facilities that existed in Arkansas for the mentally ill at that time. I did a small amount of volunteer work in that field, as I had very little spare time, but I became well acquainted with the doctor in charge of the State Hospital. I remember once seeking an appointment with him to relieve the anxiety my husband had installed, wrongfully, as it turned out. I had cuddled and kissed both my children from time to time as I had bathed and dressed them, and once, when I was engaged in that activity with my son, Ham had charged into the room, demanding that I stop such behavior. "Cut it out!" he yelled. "Do you want to make a gay out of him?"

Was that possible? I had to know. When I questioned the doctor, he looked at me as if I had suddenly lost my mind. "For heaven's sake, NO! Your husband said *that*? I think he needs help! You keep on loving your son! You won't hurt him by showing him love and affection."

I knew that in reason, but was relieved to hear it from an expert.

* * *

My first trip to New York was an invitation from the Rockefellers to stay in their apartment at Number One East End Avenue, one of the many residences they maintained in different parts of the country. The day we left for New York was a bleak cold, rainy morning in Arkansas, and my first flight on a big airplane. I have never forgotten the beautiful sunshine and the huge fluffy clouds that appeared once we reached the plane's flying altitude! It was truly miraculous.

And that was only the beginning. I had seen pictures of the big city and attended movies exploiting it, but upon stepping out of the bus that brought us from the airport to Number One East End Avenue, I could hardly take in what my eyes were seeing. The buildings literally touched the heavens, and it was impossible to count their number. And the apartment! It was several stories high and beautiful beyond description. The first floor housed the music room, with a baby grand piano and carpets so thick they were difficult to walk on. The second floor was an enormous living area, with a fireplace, soft couches, and of course entertainment centers and a bar. The kitchen was beautiful with an adjoining room that was really an icebox, with two entries, one from the kitchen and the other from a gorgeous dining area. Further up were the bedrooms and the wonderful bathrooms.

I could hardly believe my eyes. In the room that was really an ice box was everything one could think of to eat: rare cheeses, all kinds of deserts, meat, and vegetables. The bathroom next to the master bedroom had glass shelves from the floor to the ceiling, with elegant and expensive perfumes on each shelf. I sampled them all!

* * *

I was eager to explore New York City—maybe to see a play—but Ham cut that short. "If you want to see New York," he said. "Give me your wallet. There's plenty of everything here." And he retreated to the bar, much as I had retreated to the perfume shelves.

This was the era of live television shows, and I learned that *Name That Tune* was being filmed at a nearby studio. I took a cab to that destination and had a wonderful time watching the contestants and laughing at their performance. Imagine my surprise when, after the show, a man came up to me and said, "We would like you to be on the show. Would you like that?" Me, a contestant, "Of course I would like that," I answered. He gave me a pamphlet, with the address that I was to be at the following morning. I went back to Number One East End Avenue and learned that Ham had gone to meet Rockefeller in Chicago.

There were clean sheets on the bed every day, and when the maid learned that I would be alone each night, I found the bed turned down and the telephone book on the pillow opened at the number for the police!

The next day I took a cab again to the address that had been given to me, but I was hours early. I stayed on the same block, so I wouldn't get lost, but I visited several shops, getting trinkets for Gretel and Everett. And then I saw a leopard coat in the next window, and all the movie magazines that I had secretly read in our tenants' apartments flashed before my eyes. Every movie star had a leopard coat, and I had envied them and wanted one all my life.

I walked into the store and tried it on. "How much is it?" I asked, and when the sales lady told me the price, I knew something was not right. It was not very much money. "Is that all?" I asked, innocently, and the woman gave me a funny look. "Don't you know where you are?" she asked. I almost said "I'm in New York," but I simply looked at her and shook my head. "You're in a thrift store," she said. "These garments are used—second hand."

My time was running out, so I took off the coat, thanked her, and almost ran to the address where I was supposed to be. I had my various purchases in my arms, and while I was waiting for the elevator, a lady who was sitting on a bench nearby stood up and asked me if I would like to sit down. "Oh, no honey. Thank you. I'm fixin' to go upstairs," I replied, and she shrieked in surprise.

"Honey! Fixin'! Where are you from?"

"Little Rock, Arkansas," I answered.

And did she shriek then! "Hot Springs," she exclaimed, hugging me in excitement. "Hot Springs, Arkansas."

About that time the elevator arrived, and we went happily to our destination. It seems that she was employed by the company who sponsored *Name That Tune*, with the job of picking out persons to appear on the various sessions. I learned that there was a great deal more to being on the show than just walking out on stage! I was required to sing, and their live orchestra had tuned itself to my voice. I sounded wonderful—like a professional singer. I understood when they explained that they couldn't have terrible, off-key singing on the air.

After my practice session was over, my new friend from Hot Springs and I went to get a bite to eat, and she told me her story. She had come from Hot Springs to participate in one of the big game shows and had made lots of money, all of which she spent instantly, ending up broke and unable to even go back to Hot Springs. She said that she was in a bar and met one of the game show people; she said she'd had too much to drink and lit in on him, telling him the least he could do was put her to work, and he did! She had to pick people, as I had been picked, to appear on the show.

I wanted to know more about "thrift stores"—so I asked her about the leopard coat. "Do I dare buy it?" I asked. "I don't know," she replied. "Some of those things are fine and some come apart the first time you put them on." And then she said, handing me a card, "I may get in trouble, but meet me at this place in the morning." And then she waved good-bye as she left on a bus.

I got up early, doused myself with a different bottle of perfume, and took the bus to the address my Hot Springs friend had given me. Once there I had misgivings. There were people pushing racks of garments and furs down the streets and into various buildings. My friend appeared, and we went inside one of the big buildings, where I saw rows and rows of workers sitting at sewing machines, with no air conditioning, carefully separating furs. She took me into an adjourning air-conditioned office, where I met a man who went into a vault and brought out three beautiful furs. Of course the one I picked was the most expensive one—a leopard exactly like the ones I had seen in the movie magazines.

I have forgotten how much they were asking for it, but I dumped out all the money I had, and told them I wanted it. I said "I'll put this as a down payment, and when I get to Little Rock, I will send the rest," I told him. I had to have that magnificent coat.

"Is this all the money you have?" The little Jewish man asked me. I nodded my head. And then he scooped all the money up and pressed it back into my hand. "Dear, you can't give me all the money you have!"

"Why not?" I asked. "I'm staying at the Rockefellers' apartment, and I have my ticket home. I won't need any money."

He took the beautiful coat back, but marked it sold. "Give me your address and when you get home and get ready for it, I will send it to you."

And that's how I came to own a real Somali leopard coat. I still have a leopard coat, but that's another story and will be addressed in a later chapter.

I was able to be on *Name That Tune* and sing it successfully for two episodes of the show, and, thanks to the skill of the orchestra and since they had tuned their instruments to my voice, I sounded like Jo Stafford! When I picked a number that was from the World War I era, I knew only the chorus, not the verse: "We have no bananas." During the training given us prior to our appearance, all contestants were told to answer quickly, whether or not we knew the correct answer, for there could be no "dead" time on live television. So, when Bert Parks gave me a clue: "This is a vegetable," he said, "that you would not eat if you were going out in polite society," and I—remembering that we had to answer quickly—immediately said: "Beans!"

The correct answer, gentle reader, is "Onions," and my answer brought the house down. The members of the orchestra collapsed, with mirth, as did Burt Parks. That ended my appearance on *Name That Tune*. I don't remember how much money I received, but I put all of it on the beautiful leopard coat.

I also saw my first Broadway show: *A Funny Thing Happened on the Way to the Forum*, starring Zero Mostel. I took a cab to the theatre and had a wonderful seat, very near the stage. Next to my seat was a vacant seat, and then a party of three had the next three seats: an older man, a young man, and a young woman. Of course, I struck up a conversation and learned that the vacant seat belonged to the older man's wife, who was not feeling well and had decided not to attend. The younger couple were their son and his wife, whom they did not want to disappoint. It also turned out that the older man had been stationed at the Little Rock Air Force Base many years before, and of course we became new friends. In fact they drove me to Number One East End Avenue after the show! I had violated every rule in the book: I had talked to complete strangers and climbed trustingly into a vehicle driven by newfound friends.

* * *

My first trip to the magnificent city of New York was a thrilling adventure, as has been every visit since then. I love New York! For many years, I went every year with my friends Gene and Marilyn Weinstein, who sponsored annual trips to

New York that included sight-seeing and theatre performances. Also, my friend Bonnell Rice's very talented son resided there, playing his grand piano and performing in various musical events, including one off-Broadway show that he wrote and directed. We had a wonderful time walking up to the fifth floor! There was no elevator. That's where we stayed when we went to the Democratic Convention in 1976.

The best time I ever had in New York was when I visited Gretel there when she and Allen, her husband, had rented an apartment on the 26th floor of the Gershwin building for several months while Allen was doing lighting in that area. They decided to locate there temporarily rather than travel back and forth from their home in Jackson Hole, Wyoming. It was a beautiful apartment, although it was totally impossible to sit on the spacious deck because of the strong winds that sent any furniture not attached to the floor flying in all directions. At that time, the rent was $6,000 a month, unfurnished! It was located in the theatre district directly across from where *Good Morning, America* is broadcast now. Gretel feels about New York as I do, and has not entirely relinquished her dream of having a residence there. If that occurs, she can count on my being a frequent visitor.

19

I have not documented a shameful era I lived through, although I have related one ridiculous episode when Silas Hunt, a black man, tried to enroll in law school at Fayetteville. I think I understand why the Supreme Court ruled that schools could be "separate and equal," for if it had not so ruled, there probably would have been a revolution at that time. And had the black schools been truly "equal," there might have been nothing for them to complain about. But everybody knows the condition of most, maybe all, black schools and the terrible lack of books and equipment that existed. Also, I remember when I came to Little Rock blacks were not allowed to eat in certain restaurants and cafes in downtown Little Rock, and there were no restrooms available for them. Drinking fountains, even in the courthouse, were designate for "white" or "colored," and, unbelievably, nobody thought of not complying with the ridiculous distinction.

I was never comfortable with the "Jim Crow" rules, but I was powerless to change them. I remember an incident involving Charlie Bussey, a black man who was an investigator for the prosecuting attorney's office. Charlie went on to be mayor of Little Rock, and I believe there is a street named for him, but I remember a shameful episode that occurred when both he and I had been sent to Fayetteville to investigate a crime. We arrived about sundown and went to the Mountain Inn Hotel to make arrangements to spend the night. The clerk, to my astonishment, declared I could rent a room, but Charlie could not. I was shocked and embarrassed, and we certainly had money, for it had been provided to us by the prosecuting attorney. I was furious and told the clerk that if Charlie couldn't stay, I wasn't going to stay, either, although I didn't have a clue as to where we could go, or stay. Charlie Bussey saved the day, being used to that kind of treatment, I assume. Very quietly, Charlie said, "That's perfectly all right. I have friends here," he told the clerk. And then to me, "I'll see you in the morning." I watched him go down the street behind the courthouse where the black community resided, and he really did have friends there, fortunately. I stayed at the Mountain Inn, but I certainly was not comfortable with the entire event.

* * *

I am truly surprised that there was not a violent rebellion in America during that time. I suppose the black ministers and leaders like Martin Luther King, Jr., are to be thanked for the uneasy peace we enjoyed.

I remember a white woman who came to the prosecuting attorney's office when I was working there. Her complaint was that a young black man had viciously attacked her, reaching across the counter of the photography shop she operated in his effort to strike her. A co-worker had been able to intervene and put the young man out of the business, but the woman was very shaken and angry, and had come to the prosecuting attorney's office to obtain a warrant for his arrest.

I do not know why I asked the question, but I wondered why a young black man would try to attack a woman, and I asked "What did you do to him?"

"I just told him that we didn't take pictures of blacks," she replied, "And we don't!"

Then the situation became clear. The young black man had won a certificate for a free 8x12 photograph, in color, by identifying the name of the song in a contest sponsored by a television station. Imagine the disappointment a high school student, particularly a young black man whose family probably was unable to pay for a graduation picture, would feel. It would be natural for him to want to do something to the person who refused to honor his certificate for such a treasure!

I didn't issue an arrest for the boy, but I came very close to issuing one for the television station! I called the station and spoke with the person who knew about the contest. I told him who I was and why I was calling. I told him what had happened and that I was going to give him enough time to obtain a picture for that young man, wherever he had to go to obtain it; otherwise, he might find himself with a real problem. Of course, the television station took care of the young man, and that particular contest disappeared from the station's programs. Knowing that he was going to get his picture, the young man had no problem with apologizing to the lady at the photography shop for refusing to honor his certificate. Justice triumphed—all the way around!

* * *

During the time that *Brown v. Board of Education* was being heard, most people in Little Rock knew that segregation was going to be outlawed and that integration was inevitable. An attorney named Upton had run for a position on the school board, and he had run on the platform that he would integrate the schools. When the decision came down, Virgil Blossom, the superintendent of schools, had already made plans to integrate Little Rock Central High and had chosen the students who were to attend. It was Orval Faubus, seemingly the eternal Governor of Arkansas, who openly defied the federal court order, kowtowing to the segregationists in the Delta, with no motive at all except to seek re-election.

I stood in my office at the courthouse in Little Rock in utter disbelief as the members of the 101st Airborne Division came across the Broadway Bridge and proceeded to Central High

School. On September 5, 1957, nine black students were escorted by the troops to school at Central High.

All of the "Little Rock Nine" have now been recognized and honored, and all have been remarkable successful, despite the incredible treatment they received for simply trying to attend school. It was particularly sad to me, because most of my friends felt, as I did, that Faubus had done a stupid, illegal thing, and continued to do so, closing all the high schools in Little Rock in September of 1958. Although Central High closed, football went on! What an incredible decision as to what was important!

Almost every one who lived through that era had stories to tell about how disruptive it had been for them and their families. I surreptitiously joined an organization of women who were working to re-open the schools. I believe it was begun by Adolphine Terry, widow of Congressman Terry, a woman whom I admired tremendously and with whom I became very close. Another woman who belonged to the group and worked very hard to get the schools reopened, at a great financial loss to her doctor husband, was my friend Margaret Kalb.

The whole world knew about Little Rock's disastrous effort to disobey the federal court's order to integrate the schools. I shall never forget that I went to Europe in 1960, and immediately upon learning that I was from Little Rock, I was bombarded with questions and a certain amount of ridicule, despite the fact that I had never voted for Oval Faubus and certainly did not endorse his actions.

I am glad that I have lived long enough to see a dark-skinned bi-racial man become president of the United States, and to have had a hand in so doing. I do not think that the American people will ever be sorry, and I predict he will have a second term! I hope I am still here to vote for him.

20

I thoroughly enjoyed the entire time Ham worked for Republicans because of my relationship and contact with Winthrop Rockefeller. He was a most generous, delightful man; although he was nominally a Republican, his personality was far more Democratic! He bought 24,000 acres and built a mountaintop home on Petit Jean Mountain, actually converting an existing dwelling into a beautiful residence. The formal dining room had a waterfall from the ceiling to the floor, a delightful feature that I had never seen before. The living room had an enormous fireplace, and Mr. Rockefeller's grandfather's card table with chairs was set up near the fireplace.

The children loved going to Mr. Rockefeller's house. After dark, Ham would drive to the gate of the fence that surrounded the dwelling, and a voice would say: "Who approaches?" or something like that. Once Ham identified himself, the monstrous gates swung wide, and we proceeded forward. I remember one evening while little Everett was bouncing on the enormous couch in the living room, some armed men appeared on both sides of the room!

When we visited on weekends, we were housed in one of the many guest houses, but the children still had the run of the main house, particularly the kitchen, where the black cook always had a treat for them. Meals were often served outside by the pool, in enormous silver servers. We often had to look for Mr.

Rockefeller, who might be trimming one of his trees, perched high among the branches, which were dangerously close to the edge of the mountain.

One of the articles written about Mr. Rockefeller stated that he had "sprayed money over the state like water from a fountain," and that analogy was true. He once told me that he liked being able to see the difference his endeavors had made—schools, hospitals, an art center, an automobile museum. He also established Winrock Enterprises and Winrock Farms with his famous Santa Gretrudis cattle and zoyza grass. In 1955, Governor Orval Faubus named him chairman of the Arkansas Industrial Development Commission, and he was able to bring many thriving businesses to Arkansas.

When I moved to Little Rock, there was no Arkansas Art Center, and although all 75 of Arkansas' counties donated money, our wonderful Art Center would never have been possible without the Winthrop Rockefellers. The three-day celebration that took place at its opening was a spectacular event. It was recorded in the August 1, 1963, issue of *Vogue* magazine, and believe it or not, among the celebrities—James Rorimer, director of New York's Metropolitan Museum, Ms. William Moore Clark of the Junior League, Mr. and Mrs. Winthrop Rockefeller—was a picture of Mrs. Everett Ham, junior deputy prosecuting attorney for Pulaski County, Arkansas! I did not pose for the picture and did not know it had been taken until I saw a copy of *Vogue*! Female prosecuting attorneys were rare at the time.

Vogue's relating description of the celebration and the facility bears repeating. "From all over the U.S., Arkansas travelers, artists, museum directors, stars of the performing arts gathered for the opening of Little Rock's many pronged, ambitious new Arkansas Arts Center. Three days of celebration included a loan exhibition from New York's Metropolitan Museum; private dinners and suppers all over town; a beaux-arts Arts Ball for six hundred, in a great tent on the Art Center's beautiful grounds.

Every night fountains changed colors and the lights brought out the green of the cedars. At the Bar, Japanese lanterns hung from tent tops, fresh flowers embraced tent poles, and candlelight illuminated dresses that veered toward full length, simple lines, and pale colors."

I shall never forget the beautiful fountain whose water changed colors, for I had taken a very young Everett to watch them one evening when he had been in bed for several days and was recuperating. While we sat silently in the early dusk, Everett looked up at me and said, "Mama, aren't you glad our eyes are in technicolor and not black and white?" What a joy Everett was, from the time he entered the world!

Vogue continued its description: "The Center comprises, in addition to handsome exhibition galleries, a splendid theatre, classrooms (students range from age two), sculpture courts, working studios and a dining court. Among the services that reach out through the State are an Artmobile that has rolled seventeenth century Dutch paintings through thirty-two towns. An Art Lending Purchase Service rents paintings to adults; a Children's Corner has good, full-size reproductions for, top price, 50 cents a month."

As great as the facility was then, it is even better now, and the Artmobile is still rolling!

I specifically remember the celebration, because Winthrop Rockefeller had engaged a big-name dance band, and I sat with him throughout their performance. Winthrop Rockefeller had "fallen off the wagon" and was drinking again, after having abstained for quite some time. I remember that I made it a point to stand up and clap if he were standing up, clapping, and to do whatever he did in an effort to conceal or minimize his condition. I remember Jeanette coming to pick him up and thanking me profusely—she even said, "I love you."

It was an evening, when he had had several drinks, that Mr. Rockefeller told me that there was a great deal of dissatisfaction among the Republicans for Everett Ham, and Mr. Rockefeller was doing his best to smooth things over. It was the first authentic complaint I had heard about, but I remember being at a function at the Top of the Rock once with Ham. I walked away from his group to the opposite side of the room, and I saw a lot of people whom I recognized as Republicans. I started over to talk to them, and Ham came dashing from the other group to intercept me. I remember asking him why they were not with the others, and I remember his reply: "Because I didn't invite them, that's why!"

As I mentioned earlier, I remember Ham telling me he was "fighting for his life" when Everett had to go back to the hospital, and I took him alone.

I do not think Mr. Rockefeller would have divulged anything to me, or even discussed it with me, if he had not been drinking, but it seems that Ham had led everyone to believe that it was necessary to contact him before they attempted to see Mr. Rockefeller. Eventually, Ham was fired, something he never admitted, and when Mr. Rockefeller was successfully elected governor, he did not take Ham with him to the state house.

* * *

It was evident to everyone that Mr. Rockefeller was interested in politics, but he moved very slowly. He spent two years developing his own farm before starting in on the state. As head of the newly formed Arkansas Industrial Development Commission, he made speeches to businessmen all over the country, plugging Arkansas.

In 1960, Rockefeller did not seek the governorship, but instead raised funds for the Republican nominee, Henry M. Britt, a lawyer from Hot Springs, Garland County, Arkansas, who still lost to Faubus. In 1962, Rockefeller similarly supported Willis Ricketts, a former pharmacist from Fayetteville and another in a long line of failed Republican candidates who sought to topple Faubus, with no success.

Mr. Rockefeller hired a number of people to help Ricketts in his race for governor. I was a dinner guest at Mr. Rockefeller's once when they were rehearsing and complaining about how difficult their job was when the candidate's name was "Bubbs"!

On July 13th through the 16th in 1964, there was a Republican National Convention at the Cow Palace in San Francisco, with Barry N. Goldwater of Arizona as the presidential nominee. Of course, Mr. Rockefeller and his wife were going, and Ham was going with them. I took the children to Disney World and made arrangements to visit my brother and his wife, who lived in the suburbs of San Francisco. I planned to join Ham only for the ceremonies at the Cow Palace and the Rockefellers' party.

The children and I were in a motel near Disney World, seeing all the sights, riding all the rides, eating all the junk food—having a wonderful time, when I received a call from Jeanette Rockefeller. She knew I was at Disney World with the children and knew in reason that I had not taken any formal or "dress up" clothing. She told me that she and Mr. Rockefeller were having a party for his brother Nelson Rockefeller and his wife, Happy, and I remember her saying "and you can't wear your formal if it's hanging in your closet in Little Rock."

I thanked her, but told her not to bother—that I was going to visit with my sister-in-law at my Brother John's home, and that I was sure we could put something together, which we did.

I purchased a long black skirt, and Dottie had a gorgeous white blouse and pearl jewelry. I drove to the hotel where Ham was staying, dressed very tastefully for the party. When I came in, Ham took one look at me and said, "Oh, I have not taken my tux out of the suitcase!" Of course it was Sunday night—he had been there three days—and he tore upstairs and unpacked a very rumpled tux. I was waiting in his hotel room while he scurried around to get his formal clothes together. I think he thought he might steam the garment—I don't know what he thought or was doing—but I heard a "goddamn it!" and then he emerged holding a very wet tuxedo. He tried to steam it and dropped it. It was dripping wet. It was almost time to meet Jeanette and Winthrop Rockefeller to go to the party. Ham tried to find someone in the hotel who could dry out his tux and press it, but there was no one available to do it. Ham went in his wrinkled suit—probably the same one he had worn all week. Jeannette was furious. I was glad that I had been able to dress properly.

That was quite a party. Ham and I sat with the Rockefellers and their guests; the food and the orchestra and other entertainment were wonderful, but Ham was the only man who was not in a tuxedo. The thing I remember the most is that Winthrop Rockefeller was "on the wagon; attempting to slow down, if not stop, drinking, and Mr. Rockefeller and I were the only ones not drinking alcohol. It took all of Rockefeller's prestige to get each of us a glass of water!

* * *

Mr. Rockefeller rewarded Ham and his efforts to elect him governor by sending us abroad—with all expenses paid. Ham invited a male friend of his who had also worked in the campaign to go with us, and the three of us flew first to Germany, on Lufthansa Airlines, and then rented a car and went all over, tracing down Ham's family, who were still in the Black Forest area of Germany and were friends of the Finkbeiners.

My friend Faye Hill and her daughter moved into our house to be with Gretel and Everett while we were gone, and Rosie stayed there, except on weekends.

This was in 1965, and we flew "the corridor" into Germany. What an exciting piece of history! But, I confess that I flew all the way, white-knuckled, clutching my seat and holding my breath. The airport, which has just been closed, was right down town! We flew in over the tall buildings—and, again, I held my breath.

On the flight, I met a lovely woman whose military husband was stationed in Berlin, and she gave me a list of wonderful places to eat and places that I should see. The highlight of the trip was our journey to East Germany, through Check Point Charlie—what a disgraceful, terrible slice of history. I witnessed a very sad and distressing episode when hundreds of elderly people were allowed to leave East Germany, their relatives embracing them, some of them sobbing, and none of them carrying any belongings. As tourists, we were allowed to board a bus to be transported through East Germany, but before the bus left, the driver came around to each of us holding a bag into which we dumped our possessions, including money. To my surprise, it was all returned when we finished our tour and left the bus, but I certainly would not have been surprised if we had not had anything returned.

* * *

The difference between West Germany and East Germany was so dramatic that it is hard to describe. Everywhere in East Germany were enormous piles of rubble—stones and bricks from destroyed buildings and houses, and great empty patches where everything had been torn down and demolished. We went to a graveyard that was like none I had ever seen before: great mounds of graves with soldiers buried standing up. While I was at the graveyard, I asked if I could go to the restroom, and I was escorted to the door, which I entered. There was no one there, and I really needed to use the restroom, so I entered a booth. When I came out, there was a true witch standing outside the booth I had entered, holding out her hand and talking a mile a minute in a language I couldn't understand. There was no doubt about what she wanted—was demanding: money! I had put most of my money in the bag the driver had held before the bus took off, but I had a small make-up kit, which had some change in it. I dumped it all out into the old woman's hand and literally ran to the bus, for it was about to leave on the return journey to West Germany. The old woman pocketed the money and didn't follow me, so I assume she was satisfied.

That was one of the saddest things I have ever witnessed. The wall went through houses and cemeteries. The people of West Germany had plastered flowers outside of the wall for their dead who were in graveyards that were no longer accessible to them because of the wall. In fact, the difference between the two Germanys was startling. The people in West Germany were cleaning up, re-building, and getting ready to celebrate Christmas, while the East Germans were noticeably stymied and discouraged.

We had planned to visit Hitler's Eagle's Nest, and even started up the steep road, but it was snowing very hard, and we had to turn around. We did get to Zugspitzplatt, the highest ski resort of Germany, taking the cog railway from Garmisch-Partenkichen to the peak. It was incredibly beautiful, and crowded with tourists and skiers. There were two cable cars that went to the peak, one ascending from the German side of the mountain and the other from the Austrian side.

We drove all over Germany and were able to locate Ham's relatives still living in the Black Forest, in a wonderful house that was attached to the dairy where the milk cows lived. The house was spotless, with enormous beds covered with beautiful snow-white linens and countless pillows.

* * *

Paris, France, was our next destination, and as we drove through the beautiful countryside of Germany, I was struck by its cleanliness. There were no trashy houses with broken-down refrigerators sitting on the front porch, like we have encountered in rural America. Wood was stacked neatly, and the surrounding grounds looked as if they had been swept with a broom. And that was true of all we saw there, not just a few.

I loved Paris and went everywhere, wearing my hush puppies. (The day before we were scheduled to leave Little Rock for our trip, I had dashed out of the house to get the newspaper and had broken a toe. There was nothing they could do about a broken toe. I could wear none of my shoes. So I bought an oversized pair of hush puppies, which I wore all over Paris—even a snazzy nightclub where the dancers were topless!) I saw all the beautiful cathedrals, particularly Notre Dame, while Ham and his friend spent the greater part of their time in French bars. They didn't care where I went or what I did, so I tried not to miss anything. I spent hours in the Louvre. It is, after all, the largest museum in the world. The Grand Gallery had the world-famous paintings of the *Mona Lisa*, and the masterpieces on the first floor included the sculpture *Venus de Milo* and the *Winged Victory of Samothrace*. I could have spent a lifetime there. It was impossible to see it all. There are eight miles of galleries!

I rode the elevator up the Eiffel Tower, went shopping in a beautiful mall, and sampled some wonderful food.

* * *

Mr. Rockefeller ran again for governor in 1966, and this time he won. He had energized and reformed the Republican Party, but only a few Arkansans considered themselves Republicans. However, everybody was tired of Oral Faubus, who had had six terms as governor and, in my opinion, had been totally responsible for the disgraceful disobedience of the Supreme Court's integration order, the closing of the schools, and the presence of federal troops in Little Rock.

I remember one night I was a dinner guest at the Rockefellers when he was running for governor the second time. I had driven myself directly from my office in the courthouse, to Petit Jean, Ham having flown up with Mr. Rockefeller.

All of the other guests had noticed the car with no "Rockefeller for Governor" signs on it, and when they had identified it as belonging to me, they immediately got together a batch of political signs and started out the door to place them on my vehicle.

"Sit down!" Mr. Rockefeller commanded. "That's Virginia's car, and she's a Democrat. We are not going to embarrass her."

And I said: "That's right, Mr. Rockefeller. It's going to take us to elect you. There's not enough of those b——!"

And that's exactly how he was elected. There was a large group of "Democrats for Rockefeller" and an odd coalition of Republican and Democratic reform voters who catapulted Rockefeller into the governor's office. He defeated a conservative Democratic Arkansas Supreme Court Justice, "Justice Jim" Johnson of Conway, and his running mate for lieutenant governor was Maurice Britt, a decorated World War II veteran and a former professional football player.

* * *

In the meantime, my marriage continued to deteriorate. There was constant disagreement about everything. For instance, I noticed that one of Everett's eyes seemed to be crossed. I was concerned and pointed it out to Ham. He stormed out at me. "Well, it sure must be from your side of the family. Mine never had anything like that!"

I was furious. "What difference does it make? I'm going to take him to an optometrist!" And I did. I shall never forget what he said, after he examined the little boy.

"He has 'lazy eye,' and he may have lost his eyesight in that eye. We will know in a minute," and he continued testing. I held my breath. When the doctor returned, he told me we were lucky and that he was going to put corrective glasses on Ev.

I made a big thing about my "scholar" and how intelligent the glasses made him look, and Everett has worn glasses all his life. I did have a problem with my father, who kept saying the boy would "outgrow" the problem. In fact I had to replace glasses often because Grandpa told him to throw "them things away!"—and of course he did. Sometimes we found them and sometimes we didn't.

* * *

Everything came to a head unexpectedly one night. Ham and one of his friends had bought a boat that they planned to remodel and put a new engine in. However, like most of Ham's projects, the boat had been lying in the same spot in our backyard untouched for a year or two. It had been placed on the picnic table, and its weight had broken the table down. Grass had grown up under it, providing a haven for snakes, and it was a dangerous and unsightly hazard for children who ran through the backyard—not only our children, but also those of our neighbors. I had repeatedly questioned Ham about when he and his friend intended to complete the project, but I received no satisfactory answers, and no activity had taken place.

I had made arrangements for a yardman to come the following morning to cut the grass, and whatever action was going to be taken with respect to the boat needed to be addressed. Ham came in quite late, as usual, and it was evident that he had been drinking. I had fallen asleep on the couch after I put Ev to bed, and Gretel was spending the night with a girlfriend. I asked Ham if he thought he and his friend might be able to move the boat, and I guess vodka took over.

"I'll move that boat when I get God-damned good and ready!" he said, and I lost it! I have heard all my life about the "straw that broke the camel's back," but that night I experienced it.

The first thing I knew, I had pulled off one of my spike-heeled shoes and was hitting Ham over the head with it, screaming at the top of my lungs, "You'll move it now, now, now!"

Ham was a great deal taller than I am, but I can still see him ducking and dodging as I relentlessly struck him over the head with my spike heels. And then I opened his closet door, took all of his clothes that I could reach, opened the front door, and threw them as far as I could throw them. When Ham almost instinctively went out to retrieve them, I slammed the door and pulled the lock. He must have gathered up the garments, put them in his car, and left, because I heard the car start, and he made no attempt to come back in. I really don't know what I would have done if he had tried to do so.

I called his uncle Bernard Faisst. "I have put Ham out of the house," I told him and was astounded to hear Bernard say: "Well, he can't come here!"

I pulled on my pajamas and lay down on the bed. I have never felt better. The next morning, before Rosie left for the weekend, she told me that she had fixed Everett's breakfast for him before I woke up, and he had told her that "Mama and Daddy had a fight, and Mama won," and Rosie was chuckling.

I broke into tears. "Oh, I said, "I didn't want him to hear that."

But Rosie still chuckling. "Don't you worry; he's fine," she said. So it was never mentioned. I think the yardman and his helpers pulled the boat off, and I didn't ask what became of it.

21

When Edwin Dunaway called Frank Holt and more or less told him to put me to work, Mr. Holt's chief deputy, John Jernigan, who went on to be prosecuting attorney himself, threw his hat on the floor and jumped on it, so opposed was he to having a female deputy (or so Frank's nephew, Jack Holt, Jr., who went on to be chief justice of the Arkansas Supreme Court, told me). I do not know if that occurred or not—Jack may have exaggerated things a bit—because John Jernigan was always courteous to me. However, I never realized what a remarkable skill my being able to type a hundred words a minute was. It was a situation that John Jernigan had gotten himself into that made me realize that typing was an extremely important skill.

As I said before, all deputy prosecutors were allowed to practice law on the side, and John Jernigan had a very important client for whom he did a great deal of work. I am sure the client, who was a prominent construction company, paid John handsomely. The client had performed a large remodeling job for which he had not been paid, and it was the last day for a workmen's lien to be filed John Jernigan had realized it and dashed into my office in a panic. It was almost closing time; the secretaries were gone. The legal description of the property, which had been improved, was a half-dozen pages of "the northwest quarter of the southwest quarters"! Poor John was beside himself. And he did not know how to type.

Quickly, I rolled a sheet of paper into my typewriter—right after I called the circuit clerk and asked if he could hold the office open for a minute or two, that I was on the way down with a very important document that had to be filed on this date.

If John had not wanted me when I was hired, he certainly wanted me that day, and every day thereafter. He and his wife were wonderful friends for many years. I shall never forget that they had three darling daughters and a new baby was on the way. Of course all of us were hoping this baby would be a boy, but it was not to be. The fourth little girl appeared, and so often it is the case, she is the one who proved to be the greatest comfort to all the family. "I'm set up for girls," John told us that morning, and he undoubtedly was.

* * *

Prosecutor Frank Holt allowed me to function as a real deputy prosecuting attorney; I handled some extremely interesting cases. One in particular comes to mind, because it was very difficult to convince the prosecutor that the case should have been filed, and I was not successful in obtaining conviction.

The penalty for rape at that time was death in the electric chair or life imprisonment. It was almost impossible to obtain convictions in a rape case unless the victim had been severely wounded or killed. What we usually did was to make the charge "attempted rape" even when actual rape had occurred; in this way at least we were able to obtain some kind of punishment for the illegal act. I do not think the victim in the case I am remembering was injured except psychologically, but I have no doubt that she was atrociously raped, and I really thought that the perpetrator should not have been allowed to behave in the manner in which I am sure he behaved and go scot free. A very disturbed single black mother brought her teen-aged daughter in, and the embarrassed young woman told a hair-raising story that no young woman should have to endure. It seems that the perpetrator was a white bread salesman who serviced all the schools in the area, including the all black one the victim was attending. The bread salesman's wife had had a baby, and he contacted the principal of the school to see if there was a student who participated in a program that allowed students to go to school and work part time, as he would be interested in hiring one to help him and his wife. When I was researching the facts of the case I talked to the principal, and she specifically remembered that the bread salesman had been adamant that she recommend a student who had a good record and was not involved in the use of drugs or any type of deviate behavior.

According to the girl, she had accepted the job offer, leaving school about 2:00 and working at the man's home until 5:00, and the wife had been able to resume her employment. Everyone was pleased with the arrangement for some period of time. Then it seems the salesman contacted the young woman one weekend and asked if she could babysit while he and his wife went to a movie that evening. She agreed, and he picked her up, ostensibly to babysit for the evening. However, instead of driving to his home, he drove down the unfinished highway that was being constructed from Little Rock to Jacksonville, found a remote spot, and proceeded to rape her. I inspected the location, and she had torn up the area, trying to escape. When he had accomplished his goal, and after the length of time her mother expected her to return, he drove her to her home. Before he allowed her to get out of the car he handed her a five-dollar bill, stating that her mother "expected her to receive compensation for babysitting." The devastated young woman took the money until she was safely out of his car, and then she threw the money back through the car's open window as she ran to the hooked screen door of her home, tearing it open as he drove out of sight.

Upon seeing her daughter and hearing the story, the mother lost no time in taking her for an examination. The evidence was all too telling. She had, in fact, been raped.

Once the man was charged, he immediately left the state of Arkansas. It was evident that it was going to be a long, hard case. He was finally discovered in a neighboring state, I think it was Louisiana, but he had to be brought back, which took time and is a complicated procedure. He was placed in jail, and either bond was denied or he did not have enough money to make bond. I remember that he spent quite some time in jail awaiting trial.

I don't know where the money to obtain counsel came from, but he had hired Max Howell, a very prominent and capable attorney, a former state legislator. While I was working on this case, I met a retired attorney from another state who had recently moved to Little Rock and had become extremely interested in the case because he had had a similar one, so of course I was happy to talk to him and benefit from his knowledge and experience. Imagine my surprise when Max Howell filed a motion alleging that the gentleman was a representative of the National Association of Colored People, and that I had wrongfully engaged him to help prosecute the action—all of which was patently incorrect. I was able to establish that, but the newspapers and the rumor mill went crazy for several days, which of course did not help my case.

The day finally came. It was a jury trial. I had done my homework, getting whatever information was available about what this group of jurors had done in earlier trials in which they had participated, but unfortunately there had been no rape cases. Mr. Howell had the right to excuse a certain number of jurors, and I worried he might include one that I really wanted! At any rate, I was comfortable with the jurors who were chosen to sit on the case, and I certainly was familiar with my facts. I had talked to witnesses and rehearsed the facts with the young victim. Except for the difficulty of convicting a rapist who did no obvious physical damage—something about which I had been warned—the trial went well. Of course, the defendant said that the sex, which he admitted, was consensual; that in fact the young woman had been very enticing when he and she were together before his wife came home from work; that sexual intercourse between them had happened on a regular basis, and he had no idea why she made up the rape story. He thought maybe it was to try to cover herself with her mother, who was working very hard to be sure her daughter got an education.

In short, the man was not convicted of rape.

To say I was disappointed is putting it mildly. I had been warned, but I still could not understand how he could do such a drastic act against an innocent girl and receive no punishment.

The black spectators who had so faithfully attended every session from their segregated seats made it a point to shake my hand and thank me, a gesture which only added to my disappointment. But at least they realized that I had done my best, and I was grateful for their understanding and appreciation. But what I learned through the grapevine was that because the defendant had spent quite some time in jail, he had lost his job, and his wife had divorced him, the jurors felt that was punishment enough for raping a black woman! I could not believe it. Mr. Holt had tried to warn me that we could not get a conviction, which was the major reason he was reluctant to file the charge.

Fortunately, the law has changed. Rape is now a class Y felony, carrying a penalty of not less than 10 nor more than 30 years. It is, of course, a very serious crime, but it no longer carries a life sentence or death in the electric chair.

* * *

Another memorable case, which I handled on the side as defense attorney, involved a battered wife, a mother of two young children who shot and killed her husband, although I truly don't think she knew that she did. I was contacted by the woman's pastor, and I have no idea how he came to call me, but I think that the woman's parents lived in a neighboring state, and they had their daughter's pastor contact me. At any rate, the minister and I went to the Pulaski County jail late the evening it all happened, where we found the woman covered in blood and not entirely coherent. "You mean he's dead?" she kept saying, referring to her husband. And then she would sob. "My children's father is dead? And it's almost Christmas?"

It had been a miserable marriage. Her husband had repeatedly abused her physically, having choked her earlier on the same day. He had left before the police arrived, but she had called them; they had responded and made pictures of her neck and throat which still bore his fingerprints. He returned that evening, very drunk and brandishing a pistol. She had taken it from him. It was a shot from that weapon that ended his life. I do not think she intended to kill him; it was a very old pistol, and she knew nothing about guns.

The family lived in Meadowcliff a lovely little subdivision peppered with small houses and beautifully kept lawns and gardens. I once owned a house there. A client had given me his equity in it as payment on his fee, and both my children resided there at various times. We fondly referred to it as "the goose house," reminiscent of my parents' first residence after their marriage.

At any rate, I contacted Dub Bentley, who was the prosecuting attorney at that time, and discussed my client's predicament with him. She was employed as a receptionist and secretary for two prominent doctors. They knew of the abuse she had encountered, and both indicated that she was a very efficient and competent employee; they were willing to keep her.

"Dub," I said, "she isn't going to kill anybody else! She has a job and two little kids. Why don't I plead her guilty to manslaughter, pay a fine, and let's get on with our lives. It's Christmas!"

"Sounds good to me," Dub said. And so it was settled. I was making arrangements to get a hearing when Dub called back.

"You're not going to believe this," he said. "There's a bunch of women picketing the courthouse on your case!"

"You're kidding," I said. "Why? What's going on?"

"The victim's mother has all her buddies marching around with signs, saying that if a man had shot his wife like this woman shot her son, they'd put him in the penitentiary! So I guess we'll have to try your client."

I was dumfounded. "Well, I'll walk her!" I bragged, but secretly, I was worried sick. She had indeed shot and killed him, whether she intended to do it or not. I had no alibi; I couldn't say she was visiting her mother in Tennessee when he was shot! And the fact that he was an abuser didn't give her the right to kill him. But the thing that bothered me the most was that she had a little boy and a little girl, both old enough to know what was going on, particularly the boy. Of course, I demanded a jury trial, and I did something that I had never done before. I hired a psychiatrist to help me pick the jury. So far as I know, there were no individuals engaged in helping attorneys pick jurors at that time as there is now. I have no idea how much time or money I spent in that endeavor, but I obtained the list of potential jurors, and the psychiatrist and I obtained everything available about each of them: their age and occupation, their religion, their records with respect to decisions in other cases they had served on as jurors, and anything else about them we could discover.

When the case began, I requested and was allowed to question each juror individually. I believe we had scheduled a four-day trial, two days for me and two days for the prosecutor, and the greater part of the first day was consumed by jury selection. Of course, each side had its right of excusing a certain number of jurors, but we tried to have them excused by the court for cause, if possible, saving our arbitrary right to excuse a juror for the persons we really didn't want to sit in judgment on our client. I remember that the expert and I agreed on each of the jurors selected except one, and you can bet that I bowed to his opinion. When the panel was accepted and sworn in by the court, I felt very comfortable about them.

We tried that case all one day and all the following day, until quite late at night. I had exhibits one and two, my client's little boy and little girl, sitting with me, and the doctors who were her employers testified. We also were able to show that her husband was an abuser and had actually abused her on the day he was killed. It was his gun that she had been able to wrestle out of his hand, or she might have been the victim.

The jurors were not out very long. The unanimous verdict was "Not guilty." My client and the children were crying, I was crying, and the judge was clearing his throat. My closing argument was a tear-jerker, but so sincere! I don't know what I would have done had she been convicted.

My client, the children, and I had to be escorted to our vehicles by the police, for the disgruntled and disappointed demonstrators were even more militant, following us and shouting, "MURDERER, MURDERER, MURDERER!" over and over. I have often wondered if the mother-in-law ever had any contact with her grandchildren after that.

But the prosecutor's decision to try the case rather than allow her to plead guilty to manslaughter turned out to be a wonderful development for my client, and most dramatically for me. Had she been convicted of manslaughter, my client would not have collected the life insurance her husband had—a substantial sum. Since she was found not guilty, Arkansas law had ruled that it was an "accident" to him, and the insurance company paid the entire amount of his policy to her! I took one-half, although I believe she would have given it all to me, and gave her the other half! Justice triumphed!

22

Although I had put Ham out of the house I had not filed for divorce. We were arguing mainly about the house, which my father had helped finance, and I was insisting that Ham pay my father back the down payment he had made. I could not understand why Ham was not willing to do so; he had signed the promissory note, along with me, but he was refusing to do so and simply said, "If you want a divorce, you're going to pay your dad."

I was extremely busy at the prosecuting attorney's office and taking care of the children, and I was reluctant to file a contested divorce. I really was living as I had always lived, and certainly was not interested in becoming involved with another man. However, Tommy Russell, the attorney who had been Ham's friend and had played a part in our lives, had taken a job as administrative assistant to Governor Faubus and had more or less turned his practice over to Ruby Hurley, a young attorney who became one of my closest friends. Ruby had suffered from polio as a child and was severely crippled, one foot being a great deal shorter than the other, and twisted. She had a beautiful face and was extremely smart, and kept Tommy's business going while he dabbled in everything, including establishing graveyards and financial ventures that Ham always financed, and that for the most part were lost causes.

I had talked to Ruby about the divorce, and she was aware of the situation, but nothing had been done. I had even found a wonderful split level house in Cammack Village in Little Rock and traded the house I had never liked on the highway in North Little Rock for it. I knew the North Little Rock house would go commercial and be worth lots of money, but I didn't have the time to wait. Gretel was reaching her teenage years, and the house in Little Rock had a wonderful den downstairs, which was really the first floor, with a fireplace and enough room for a pool table and a bar—for soft drinks only, of course.

* * *

Before I had moved into the Cammack Village house, I went to a psychiatrist, still hurt by the manner in which I had been treated throughout my marriage to Ham. After listening to my recitation, the doctor asked me, more or less surprised: "Has it never occurred to you that your husband is homosexual?" And then he gave me a book to read, which really shed a good deal of light on the situation.

My knowledge and perception of homosexuality was, like most everyone else's at that time, based entirely upon what The Good Book said about it. It was an "abomination" and should suffer the same fate as Sodom and Gomorrah. Individuals in those days who were homosexual were closeted, and certainly didn't congregate and march in the streets. I personally mourn the loss of the wonderful word "gay," which meant "happily excited, merry, bright, lively." I remember the song "Our Hearts Were Young and Gay," and my brother and his wife named their daughter "Gaye Carolyn."

And a governor scheduling prime time on television to announce that he is leaving his wife for his male partner, I confess that I am having a bit of difficulty in recognizing and accepting this state of affairs. I certainly do not care if an individual determines that he or she prefers an individual of the same sex, and I certainly feel that they should marry each other, rather than ruining other lives. I may be wrong, but I believe that homosexuality is determined at birth.

With the intelligence that accompanies hindsight, I now remember that my husband always had a very close male friend and companion, and that those individuals, and his relationship with them even in that day and age, invoked rumors and jokes. His friend Edwin Dunaway was as open with his sexuality as was possible in those days. He taught only one year at the University of Arkansas School of Law, and rumors of his sexual preference were widely circulated.

According to Wikipedia, the free online encyclopedia, the Rockefeller administration enthusiastically embarked on a series of reforms, but faced a hostile legislature and endured a concerted "whispering" campaign regarding Rockefeller's personal life. The "whispering" campaign was that Rockefeller was "gay." I heard it, and I remember Jeanette Rockefeller saying defensively, "Would I marry a gay?" I know that I met many, many "different" kinds of guests at Mr. Rockefeller's beautiful residence on the mountain, most of them from California, who rightly or wrongfully displayed the kind of behavior associated with homosexuality. One such guest loudly touted, in his high-pitched voice, that his pet monkey would eat only chicken if he had a choice!

Another friend of ours, Charlie Laster, was an attorney who paid frequent visits to our house, I assumed because we had like experiences as attorneys. I was greatly surprised when Charlie embezzled a large sum of money and was confined to jail (which at that time was in an enormous old building on the river). I was visiting a client there, and I heard Charlie calling me. I had barely said hello to him when Charlie said, "Virginia, I'm gay and it hurts—it really hurts." I was so surprised, but apparently his visits to our house were not to see me! I had originally meant to discuss with him that Judge Bill Kirby had contacted a group of attorneys in an effort to raise money for Charlie, so he might repay his client and avoid incarceration. I think I told Charlie about it in an effort to cheer him up, but we were not successful in getting very much money. I believe Charlie was sentenced to jail for a substantial length of time.

Ham must have been a very mixed-up individual, for occasionally when we were at the Officer's Club, the only place at that time where liquor was available with dinner, Ham would tell me that he loved me, almost angrily, and would compliment my ability to waltz.

I am sure he married me as a cover up and to have children, although he paid no attention to them and was actually abusive in unpredictable, strange ways. One day I had cooked carrots and was urging Ev to eat them, telling him they were "good for his eyes." He was not convinced and loudly proclaimed that he didn't want any. Before I could do anything at all, Ham took the entire bowl of carrots, dumped them in Everett's plate, and ordered him to eat every one, pushing spoonfuls of the vegetable into the child's mouth. Of course he threw up and has not eaten a carrot since.

* * *

Every year a group from the courthouse spent a day at the races in Hot Springs, usually on opening day. One year, I agreed to drive everyone to Hot Springs, but told them I would need to come back early because Gretel and her dance group were going to entertain at the State Hospital, and I was going to be there. My friend Van Legg was going to pick her up, get her costume together, and take her to the hospital where I would meet her and the rest of the dancers, one of whom was Van's daughter. To our surprise, Ham appeared at the races. This was during the time he was working for the government and making frequent trips to Hot Springs. I told Ham that our group was leaving early so I could see Gretel dance, and I assumed he would join us. "I don't get to come often to the races," he said when I asked if he was leaving, too. "I don't need to see a bow-legged kid jump around. No, I'm not leaving."

Ruby Hurley's mother was with us on that trip, and I remember that she, and everyone else, was furious. "I'll tell you one thing," Ruby's mother declared. "If he was *my* husband, he'd be there!" And I remember replying, hurt as I was, "Oh, no! If he doesn't want to see his little girl perform, I certainly don't want him to come!"

* * *

One Sunday afternoon Gretel asked if she and one of her best friends, Bonnie Hogan, who lived a block away, could bake a cake. "Of course you can!" I said, getting out the cake pans and a recipe or two, and Gretel raced down the street to get Bonnie.

She came back alone and very excited. "Are you sitting down, Mama?" she asked, and then "Bonnie is getting married!"

Bonnie had not finished high school; Bonnie was very young. "Oh! Is she pregnant?" I asked, and Gretel was furious. "NO SHE'S NOT PREGNANT!" And with that she slammed the door to her room.

Well, of course Bonnie was pregnant! There was a hasty announcement and a hasty marriage. And I remember thinking "I wonder how that happened!" Bonnie's mother was a stay-at-home mom, her husband had a good job, and she had never had to leave her children and go to work. The whole family was active in church, and although they had a good income, the children had not had everything they wanted and had not been allowed to do as they pleased. I admit that I am somewhat sensitive, because had that happened to Gretel, it would have been because I was a career person and too busy to care properly for my daughter.

* * *

Gretel was a beautiful teenager, taking dancing lessons, tap and ballet, and having all the problems that pretty girls have. I had a rule that she could not date older boys home from college, only high school boys her age. Across the street from us lived a boy, "Big Al," who was in her class, and of course when she asked if she could go to a dance with him, I always said yes. One night he picked her up for a dance, and Everett and I went to a movie. When we came home, we realized we had lost our key.

Not to worry, I told Ev. We'd run over to the dance in the school gym and get the key from Gret-Gret. We drove to the gym, and it was completely dark. There was no dance there, and there hadn't been one that evening.

Ev and I went home, Ev broke a window, and we went in. I put Ev to bed, and I took up watch at the front door until Gretel arrived, quite late at night, very surprised to find me at the front door. She had been drinking, of course, liquor, not soda pop.

"Gretel," I said, "you did not go to a dance at your school. Where did you go?"

"Mama," she said defiantly, "Nobody else's mother does this, and you can't, either!"

I think I kept my cool, but I remember saying, "I am not responsible for anybody but you, and I can certainly try! Go to bed! You are grounded. I'll talk to you in the morning!" I also called "Big Al's" mother to report that he had pretended to have a date with Gretel, and I think he got grounded, too!

Not too long after that, Gretel's dance instructor called to invite me and several other mothers to visit their studio to see a new dance routine he and his assistant were going to introduce. There were several patrons there, and we watched as the instructor and his assistant went through the routine. I watched not-approvingly. It was suggestive, almost vulgar, and when I was asked how I liked it, I told them. Gretel was terribly embarrassed and furious with me, refusing to talk to me on the way home.

When we got home, the telephone was ringing, and, as it happened, I picked it up in the kitchen at the same time she got it in the hall, near her bedroom. It was the dance instructor, and he had called to tell me that both he and his assistant had realized that the routine was too mature for this age group and they were not going to feature it. He thanked me for pointing it out to them. I said nothing, but it was wonderful to see Gretel's reluctant admiration. Her mother was not a complete idiot. She might even be able to walk erect and chew gum at the same time!

***

I purchased a new car and decided to take Gretel and Everett to Washington, D.C. When we took trips together, I always took a lot of things to eat, partly to save time and money. We had an ice chest with soft drinks and sandwiches, and we could travel quite a distance without stopping to eat.

We went first to Williamsburg, having heard from the Rockefellers how beautiful it was, arriving there at dusk. It was very strange there. There were no street lights and no cars, only horse and buggies. Little did we know that we had arrived during one of their celebrations when Williamsburg returned to the early years. Of course we were able to join in and thoroughly enjoyed it, but it was a strange introduction to Williamsburg for the children and me. We stayed in one of the beautiful hotels and had our meals in the lavish dining room. When we left, we all had a much clearer picture of the Revolutionary era.

When we received a telephone call from Duke Atkinson, he had some unexpected news, news that meant very little to me at that time, but became quite significant later. Duke was a member of the State Police, and little did I know at the time, but he would become my third husband.

"Ginger," he said, "I'm spending your money! The State Police have taken over the penitentiary! I just walked out in the field and killed a cow! These people have not had any meat for months."

I did not pay a lot of attention to what he was saying at the time, because we were enroute to Washington, D.C., and were excited about seeing everything there. Once there, we saw Washington street by street. We climbed the Washington Monument, saw the Jefferson Monument and the Lincoln Memorial, and spent hours in the Smithsonian. My feet were so swollen I could hardly walk, so I finally took off my shoes and kept going. We went to Mount Vernon, saw the Space Museum, with Lindbergh's airplane, and of course, the National Cemetery.

It was a very memorable visit, and the children couldn't have enjoyed it more than I did.

When we got home, Duke met me with an incredible story. I could not believe that the State Police had taken over the penitentiary. Duke told me that he and the other officers had been "digging" prisoners out of the woods on a daily basis, because everyone had been trying to escape. The investigation had revealed an incredible amount of fraud: the prisoners had had no meat for weeks, but an audit of supplies indicated that large amounts of prime beef had been purchased. In short, a top-secret report had been made, which I took to Rockefeller, rather than turning it over to Governor Faubus. It was very shocking to Mr. Rockefeller, who decried the "lack of righteous indignation" about the situation and created a new Department of Corrections. He named a new warden, academic Tom Murton, the first professional penologist Arkansas had ever had in that role. Murton was fired, however, largely because his aggressive attempts to expose decades of corruption subjected Arkansas to nationwide contempt.

My contact with the brutal conditions within the prison system was based on my association with Duke, who had been in charge of the prison before the official warden took over. At one time, I had possession of the disgraceful "Tucker telephone," an electrical device that was attached in some manner to the prisoner's genitals, sending out painful electrical shocks; the infamous whip; all of the cutlery and cooking equipment and other memorabilia. It was shocking to me, for while I was a deputy prosecuting attorney, I had been taken to the prison with one of our officers, and it was a wonderful experience. I was shown the entire organization: the bakery, which produced loaves of delicious bread; the rabbit hutches, where I was given two baby rabbits for my children; the laundry, run by the inmates; and a fascinating performance by the blood hounds and their trainers, not to mention a magnificent dinner prepared and served by the inmates, treating us like royalty.

* * *

My relationship with Duke Atkinson had, in fact, deepened, and for the first time in my life, I was having a wonderful time. Duke tried very hard to entertain me. One of the best times I ever had was when he took me scuba diving at Lake Ouachita, in Hot Springs. I had never been scuba diving, but Duke had all the necessary equipment. He hooked it all up, and I—one who really doesn't like being wet—followed him blindly into the lake, and loved walking around under water with my eyes open. Of course he kissed me, made love, and we carved our names together before we returned to dry land. Duke lost his St. Christopher medal, which really upset him, and he dived and dived trying to find it before he gave up and we went back to Little Rock.

I remember asking him if he really thought the medal had protected him, and his reply was, "I had some rough times and came out O.K.," which I thought meant "Yes"—he did believe. Anyway, I bought him another one, but a much more expensive one, with precious stones.

"Yes," I was "hooked," and at that time both children liked him, too, especially Everett. Every evening when I got home, I would find Duke there, shooting pool with Everett in our wonderful play room, or taking his pistol apart to teach Everett gun safety. I found myself looking forward to seeing Duke and being very disappointed if he didn't show up.

23

Each of the successive prosecuting attorneys after Frank Holt had retained me, and I continued as a prosecuting attorney throughout the various terms of the succeeding prosecutors. It was a great help to me, as I had no overhead. My office was on the second floor of the courthouse, and I could walk around the corner to court. I parked on the lot of the jail, reaching it by going through a connecting tunnel, and although I received only $300 a month, I could practice on the side, and I was beginning to represent a number of clients in various types of litigation. Of course it was only divorce actions, traffic violations, and collections, with personal injury cases only once in a while. However, for several years I was retained by Oklahoma Tire and Supply, receiving a thousand dollars a month, which I certainly earned filing dozens of replevin actions. I was able to start a savings account for my children's education, religiously putting a certain amount aside monthly.

I supported Rodney Parham for prosecuting attorney when he ran, working very hard on his campaign and of course voting for him. He lost to Richard Adkinson.

To my surprise, I received a call from Everett Ham right after the November election.

"What are you going to do after the first of the year!" he asked.

"I don't know," I answered, truthfully. I truly had not faced the situation. I guess I really thought that Richard Adkinson would keep me, a token woman and a very good prosecutor.

And then I heard Everett Ham saying, "I would hate to be in a position to help you and not do it!"

At that time, Ham was still ostensibly close to Mr. Rockefeller, who had just been elected governor. I learned later that Mr. Rockefeller was not going to take Ham with him to the governor's office, and that Ham had, in fact, been fired. Mr. Rockefeller's personal secretary was a friend and client of mine, and she kept me informed about the situation. In fact, she told me incidents of Ham's attempt to meet with Mr. Rockefeller, waiting for hours, falling asleep while waiting to see him, only to learn that Rockefeller had left through a different exit to avoid him.

He'd hate to be in a position to "help" me and not do it. I was furious. "I am an attorney," I said, "I'm a fine attorney, and I assume the Rockefeller administration will need attorneys. And if they approach me, and their offer is something I would like, then I might accept the position, but if you think I am standing on the corner with a bunch of pencils, you didn't learn very much about me when you were married to me!" And I hung up.

I was whistling past the graveyard. I had no idea what I was going to do, and it was November. My tour officially ended in December. I had no offers and very little money, with no prospects of anything.

* * *

During the days I was trying cases as deputy prosecuting attorney, it was common for individuals who worked in the courthouse to walk over to the courtroom when I began my closing arguments, as most of them enjoyed hearing me. I was known to be very dramatic and convincing. On one such day, I finished up and walked out to talk to my friends who had been listening.

"I sure hope that jury comes on back soon and doesn't stay out all night," I said to a woman who worked in the office that administered the GED tests. "Duke's sister is coming from Fordyce, and we're all going out to eat."

"Duke Atkinson?" my friend said. "Virginia, you know he's married, don't you?"

"He's divorced," I told her. "His ex-wife lives in Carolina."

"He lives in the same trailer court my sister does, and she carpools with his wife," my friend told me.

I was crushed. There could be no doubt. I got permission from the court to leave and went immediately home where I called my friend Faye Hill. By this time I was crying. "Faye!" I sobbed, "Duke's married; he's married! He's not divorced; he's married!"

"Well, I'll bet he will tell you. I think he's crazy about you, and I think he will call you!" she said confidently.

"He'd better not!" I raged. "If he calls me, I'm going to ask him why he doesn't bring his wife over for dinner!"

The children wondered why Duke wasn't at our house and not calling, and I told them that he probably was out of town. I did not want to tell them that he had a wife and maybe some children while he was "keeping company" with their mother!

My friend was right: Duke called. "Ginger," he began, and I started crying.

"I can't see you anymore," I told him. "I could just hear what people would say when I said, 'I didn't know he was married.' A deputy prosecuting attorney? And you didn't know? I can hear what people would say!"

"I know," Duke said. "Why do you think I didn't tell you?" And then he went on to tell me that his wife's previous husband had been his best friend during the war, and in fact he was the one who told her her husband had been killed. She had two children, and they had more or less gotten together after her husband died, and the marriage took place. To hear him tell the story, his marriage to Emily had more or less just happened. He told me he loved both kids, but that he and Emily had never really had a marriage. He said he had never been in love until me. He had "looked all over the world" for someone like me.

It seems Duke had made an appointment to have his teeth cleaned the day after he had met some friends of mine. He confessed to the dental hygienist, who knew me, that he was married and asked her if she thought I would continue seeing him if I knew he was married. Her answer was "she would not!" So he had not told me, because he wanted to keep seeing me.

Very shortly after that, Duke filed for divorce. I for sure couldn't see him then, and saw him only once: he entered the theatre after the lights were off when he knew I was taking the children to see *Hello Dolly*. He left before it was over and the lights were turned on.

* * *

Ham's threat that he might have an opportunity to "help" me and not do it was the second effort he made to cause me trouble. After I had begun dating Duke Atkinson, Duke called me and asked me how well I knew "THE MAN"—referring to Governor Rockefeller.

"Pretty well," I answered. "Why do you ask?"

Duke told me his immediate superior had called him in and told him that it had come down from "the top" that Duke should stop seeing Virginia Ham.

"That's ridiculous," I told him. "Mr. Rockefeller would never say anything like that. That sounds like Everett Ham! But I can find out."

I immediately called Mr. Rockefeller. "Could my friend Duke Atkinson and I come to see you?" I asked.

And he replied: "Of course," remembering Duke from his work with the prison. "I have a meeting with the National Association of Colored People this evening. But after that I'll be in my office. Come on up."

So Duke and I went to his office on the 17th floor of the Tower Building. I had been there many times, but it was Duke's first visit, and he was extremely impressed with the beautiful hangings and the wonderful bathroom with its telephone—the first one I had ever seen in a bathroom.

Duke told Mr. Rockefeller that he was dating me and that he planned to marry me as soon as his divorce was final. He went on to say that he had been ordered to stop seeing me, with the implication that it was from the governor's office.

Mr. Rockefeller chuckled and said, "Well, divorce is not unknown in our family!" Then Rockefeller said what I knew he would say, that he had never said anything of the sort and would never interfere with anyone's personal affairs. I knew that, and was glad that Duke had recognized that Rockefeller would never say anything like that. Again, I wondered why Ham kept trying to stir up trouble for me, and anyone he thought I might be interested in. Mr. Rockefeller was drinking rather heavily, and continued doing so while he and Duke carried on a great conversation about many subjects. Rockefeller was still very impressed with Duke's performance at Tucker with the convicts. Before too long, Duke realized that it was very late and that Mr. Rockefeller had had far too much to drink.

"Do you want us to take you to the airport?" he asked, and Mr. Rockefeller said yes. I shall never forget that night. Duke practically carried the governor downstairs and propped him up against the building. Then he turned to me: "Ginger, can you hold him up while I go get the car?" I said that I could, and spread my feet as far apart as I could, putting my head against Mr. Rockefeller. Duke released him and raced for the car. I managed to keep Mr. Rockefeller standing until Duke was able to carry him to the car. We then took him to the airport. Mr. Rockefeller's staff was greatly relieved. They had been calling in an effort to locate him, and Duke heard them talking to the "Mountain," giving information about Rockefeller in a code that Duke thought meant that the governor was very intoxicated.

Once his plane had taken off, Duke took me home, over and over rehearsing how vulnerable the governor had been. The dramatic Duke had been very alarmed about the situation. "Ginger, he was helpless. If we had wanted to abduct him, we could have had him in Mexico before anyone knew it!"

Throughout the time I had known Mr. Rockefeller, he had periodically gone from being "on the wagon," drinking nothing, to drinking excessively.

However, we had certainly learned that Mr. Rockefeller had not had any input on whether or not Duke should or could not continue seeing me.

24

I could never in a million years have anticipated the career opportunity that materialized for me almost at the same time my appointment with the prosecuting attorney's office ended.

One day when I was working away, an attorney by the name of Omar Greene walked into my office. I had met him and knew bits and pieces about his career, most of which was gossip. He had gone to Washington quite some time before as administrative assistant to Senator John McClelland, whom he regarded very highly. Omar had gone through a bad divorce, losing the only woman he ever loved, or so he told me, and two children, a boy and a girl. He admitted that he had had a drinking problem, and he left Washington and the practice of law and joined a traveling circus. He had, however, returned to Little Rock and entered into a law practice with Bill Butler and Casey Byrd, although at that time Bill was still a deputy prosecuting attorney, with an office two doors down from mine.

Omar introduced himself to me and said, "You're a woman. I really need to talk to you." And then he told me an incredible story. His divorced wife had just died, and he said, "I want my children."

"Well," I said, "if their mother is dead, why can't you have your children?"

"Her family would never let me have the kids," he said.

"Omar!" I said. "You are a lawyer! Her family has nothing to say about it. The children belong to you, particularly if their mother is dead. Go get your children."

"You don't understand," Omar retorted. "Her family is very wealthy and politically prominent. They would never let me have the children. The funeral is tomorrow."

"Go get your children. You are their father, and you are entitled to have them against everybody else. The grandmother has no rights. Go get your kids."

The next day, he walked into my office with a little boy and a little girl in tow. He had taken them from the funeral, telling nobody.

"Omar, call their grandmother. She may be hysterical, not knowing where the children are or what's going on."

"She will take them away from me," he said.

"Call their grandmother now!" I commanded.

He did, and again came into my office to report. "I was so wrong," he said. "My wife's folks are wonderful. They didn't know I wanted the children."

Omar put the boy in Subiaco Academy and the little girl in Mount St. Mary's, and little did I know that not only Omar but the children, too, would play a great part in my life.

It all began when it became apparent that I might not have a job after Rodney Parham lost his bid to be prosecuting attorney. Omar called me shortly after I had received the taunting call from Ham.

"What are you doing?" he asked.

"Working," I replied. "Why?"

"Go out the west door of the courthouse and walk west two blocks," he said. "I want to show you something."

I did. I walked down the steps on the west side of the courthouse and walked west on West Second Street to a building on West Second Street, just before State Street, where I found Omar standing outside a one-story building that was being renovated.

"Come on in," he said, and I followed him into the building. It had been a doctor's office, and it was being turned into a law office. Commodes were being removed from examining rooms, red carpet was being put down, and elaborate lighting fixtures were being installed.

"Thorp Thomas and I are going to buy this building," Omar announced.

"And part of the monthly payments go toward the purchase price. Do you have any money?"

"A little bit," I said, remembering the money I had put away for the children's college.

I thought everyone in the world had more money than I, but when Omar heard the amount I had, he immediately included me in the purchase of the building. Counting the two offices that had been the doctors' offices, one on each side of the building, with a closet and a row of beautiful shelves, there were eight offices. I now knew what I was going to do "after the first of the year." I was going to open my law office at 721 West Second Street!

* * *

As soon as Duke's divorce was final, he asked me to marry him, and of course I said "Yes," to the delight of my friends, and at that time, the children. Duke had taken the children and me to Fordyce to meet his parents, both of whom I liked instantly. Duke's father had been the sheriff of Dallas County for many years and was very popular. Duke's grandfather had been the only doctor in Fordyce in the early years, and if he was not the only one, he certainly was regarded as the best and the best known. His home was a fenced in mansion, still standing in Fordyce, and Duke used to joke that all the little boys in Fordyce were named for him. Duke's father and mother had married when they were both in high school, and his father went to work to care for his wife and the children. Duke and his sister, had approved. The doctor's second son went to college, becoming a high-ranking officer in the military, and the daughters attended private female schools. Duke's mother, although she was a lovely woman, had very little contact with her husband's family, by her own choice, and although he never talked about it, I think Duke felt that his side of the family had been discriminated against.

Duke wanted to show me off to everyone in Fordyce, and we even visited the Methodist Church, although I don't think Duke's parents were very active in church. His duties as sheriff took up a great deal of his time, Sundays and holidays, and his mother was not very gregarious. It developed that she was an alcoholic, although it was never mentioned. I found out about it only at the time of her death, when it was discovered that her maid had brought her liquor on a regular basis. She died from cirrhosis of the liver.

Duke's sister invited us to be married in her church in Oklahoma, where she lived with her doctor husband, and the children were entranced at the manner in which we arrived. Duke had allowed a prisoner who had been paroled and lived in Oklahoma to drive to his sister's home. We didn't know what crime our driver had been imprisoned for, but it turned out to be murder, which fascinated the children. He was an excellent driver, and thanked us profusely when he reached his destination and left us. I, for one, was relieved.

It was a lovely wedding. The church was decorated for Christmas, and everyone was gracious and happy. I had bought a beautiful outfit for myself, and outfits for the children, and of course an exquisite nightgown with matching robe and house shoes.

It all ended too soon. Duke had to be back the following day. I remember Gretel saying, "This is the happiest day of my life"— and that was certainly my sentiment. I was "Ginger" Atkinson. God was in his Heaven, and all was right with the world.

Which office at 721 West Second Street was I going to occupy? There was a tall hand-made sign someone had set up where each lawyer's name was to be placed. I argued that we should place the names alphabetically. (As "Atkinson" I would be first!) That went over like a lead balloon. We finally agreed upon drawing straws, and with my usual luck, I think my name went up last. I drew one of the back offices. No matter, I had a law office!

Duke helped me move from the courthouse to the new address. It was quite a job. I threw away what seemed to be tons of papers, and purchased a desk and chair of my own, as I had used office equipment that belonged to the State. When I walked into my new office, I found a bouquet of red roses and two signs saying "Ginger Atkinson," one attached to the wall near the door of my office and the other sitting on the front of the desk I had just purchased. Duke had put the finishing touches on my new office.

I had never been given a copy of the contract Omar and Thorp had on the purchase of 721 West Second, only Omar's word that part of the monthly payment went on the mortgage and that there was a balloon note due at some point in time. To tell the truth, I was in love for the first time in my life. I was practicing law, and my children kept me very busy, particularly Gretel who was a handful from the day she was born.

25

Gretel was only 12 when she experienced puberty. I remember that while we still lived in the North Little Rock house, Gretel's teacher called me and said that she thought Gretel was about to have her period, that she had all the symptoms. Remembering the manner in which I learned about menstruation, I bought a wonderful book and made plans to handle everything better for Gretel, although I hoped that her teacher was wrong and that it would not be occurring so soon. Of course everything went wrong. My parents were visiting, which they did often, driving from Russellville to Little Rock without notice, particularly on Sundays after church, because Mother knew I was working very hard on the other days. I had stayed home to prepare dinner, but I had sent the children with friends to Sunday school.

Mother and I had just finished making cornbread and getting ready to set the table for dinner when my friend dropped the children off, and an excited Gretel dashed in. "Mama," she shouted, "I need to talk to you." I knew what had happened, and quickly told Mother to go ahead and put the food on the table; Gretel and I were going for a drive.

I drove Gretel to a park, turned off the motor and put my arms around her. Then I told her as best I could, that nothing bad had happened to her; that she was experiencing a normal occurrence that all females experienced; that it was a wonderful process which would make it possible for her someday to have children of her own. She listened in complete silence. I then went to a drugstore that was open and purchased sanitary napkins before we went back to eat lunch. The following day, I picked her up after her dance lesson and noted dark circles under her eyes and signs of discomfort. I was right; she was experiencing her first cramps.

"Mama," she said. "Didn't you tell me all this is so I can someday have a baby?"

"Yes, Darling," I said. And then my practical Gretel said something for which I had no answer.

"Well!" she said. "Don't you think it's pretty stupid for it to happen before I get married?" We had reached home and Everett had run out to see his sister, sparing me from having to answer that astute observation.

* * *

While I was still a deputy prosecuting attorney, practicing on the side, and taking care of two children, my father's brother, Uncle Virge, and his wife, Aunt Nellie, had a situation that my parents, particularly my father, felt was wrong, and "Sister," being a lawyer, could and would take care of it. Uncle Virge and his wife lived in Belleville, a small town in Yell County that was a ghost town, with most of the buildings boarded up, until the chicken industry hit all the small towns in Arkansas. Everyone put up a chicken house and began to raise chickens for Tyson, and other companies, to such an extent that finally the whole town was overrun with chicken houses. The city council held a meeting and passed an ordinance that no more chicken houses could be built in Belleville.

Uncle Virge and Aunt Nellie lived next door to a huge chicken house, and the stench and flies were almost unbearable. Uncle Virge had been "gassed" in World War I and was drawing a small amount of compensation, and the feathers that blew out of the chicken house increased his discomfort. Imagine their shock when the town marshal, who owned the chicken house next door, began constructing an even larger chicken house on his property adjacent to the existing one. Aunt Nellie couldn't understand how the marshal could start one, when the city council had ruled that no more could be built. Yet there he was, strutting around with his badge and gun, while another chicken house was going up.

My father, Aunt Nellie, and Uncle Virge called me daily. There was no escape. "We'll pay you, honey," Aunt Nellie said, in her constant calls. "We don't expect you to work for nothing. But that ain't right, just to ignore the city council. And he's the law!" Aunt Nellie simply could not understand how the town marshal would ignore a valid ordinance.

Of course I knew how difficult the case was going to be. Court would be held in Danville, the county seat, a complaint had to be filed, service had, a bond posted. And I really had no free time available. There was no escape. Of course I waded in.

The judge was Paul X. Williams, one of the handsomest men I have ever seen, and certainly one of the smartest and fairest. He allowed Uncle Virge to post a property bond, knowing that nobody had very much cash—although after I agreed to file the case, Aunt Nellie took me to her bedroom and produced a jug filled with hundred dollar bills.

The trial date duly arrived, and the courtroom was crowded. Surprisingly enough, there were quite a number of people who sided with the marshal, and I saw my outlaw Aunt Icie among them. My father had bought a recording machine and was planning to immortalize the proceedings. I saw him unwinding the equipment and had him wait until I could ask the judge if such a procedure were allowed. The trial had not begun, and I approached the bench. "Your Honor," I said, under my breath. "My father has a new recording machine, and you would do me a great favor if you would tell him that recorders are not allowed."

Judge Williams broke into a wide grin. "He wants to record it? Why, sure. Mr. Harkey, come right up, sir." And before I knew it, I was wired up like *Meet the Press*!

Uncle Virge was the first witness and, being on the city council, produced proof that the council had voted unanimously to limit the number of chicken houses in Belleville to the existing number, and to allow no more. The proof showed that the town was overrun with debris and chicken refuse. The marshal began his second chicken house after that decision, and it was now completed and operating. Uncle Virge talked about his problems as a result of having been "gassed" in World War I, and how the feathers, which blew in his direction from the second chicken house, added to his breathing problem.

It was my father's performance as a witness that brought the house down. I called him as a witness because he was a realtor, and he certainly was qualified to testify that the proximity of two large chicken houses would definitely depreciate the value of my uncle's property. In addition, he and his wife, my mother, were frequent visitors at his brother's house, and he could describe the unpleasant atmosphere of sitting outside on a pleasant day and being subjected to offensive odors and an excess number of flies and fluttering feathers. As he testified, my father got more and more excited, pulling his trousers above his knees and raising his voice. "Judge," he said, "just last week—Sunday—we were here, sitting outside, getting ready to eat some wonderful cantaloupes Virge and Nellie bought back from visiting Vernelle, and when we sliced them up and started to eat them, the wind blew over from the chicken house, and you couldn't tell if you were eatin' cantaloupe or chicken sh…!"—and caught himself, did not complete his sentence, but sat, open mouthed, looking at the judge.

The spectators burst into laughter, as did Judge Williams, but he managed somehow to find his gavel and recess the trial. It was lunchtime anyway.

Mother had prepared a copious picnic lunch; she trusted no one except herself to provide food. She spread it all out on a snow-white tablecloth in a shady part of the courthouse lawn and invited anyone who was hungry to eat, offering a chicken leg to the passing judge. Although he declined, and continued on toward the nearby restaurant, he thanked her profusely and was still smiling from the testimony.

Judge Williams' ruling was as wise as any of Solomon's. The chicken house was complete, so it was too late to stop its construction. However, the judge required the town marshal to install blowers which operated in such a manner as to direct the feathers and the odors in the opposite direction from Uncle Virge's house. He also required the chicken house to be cleaned daily, with the litter and refuse to be removed. In short, he made the operation of the chicken house so burdensome and expensive that it went out of business and did not operate very long at all. I am sure the marshal regretted building another chicken house in violation of the city council's ruling!

* * *

All of the offices at 721 West Second were full of lawyers, and my favorite was Roy Finch. He had been a deputy attorney general under Bruce Bennett, and really had written all the opinions and done all the work while Bruce walked around and shook hands. Roy was one of the smartest and nicest men I have ever known, but he had a drinking problem, and it was well known. Everyone knew to call him early in the day, because later on it was too late, as he could no longer talk coherently. He died of cirrhosis of the liver, but while he was practicing, I really enjoyed him, as did everyone else. He had been in on the ground floor with Omar and Thorpe, and had had a part in the deal of purchasing the building, along with Harold Hall and Eugene Fitzhugh—and then me. I do remember that we purchased Harold Hall's part of the building because he was very far behind in his rental payments. Another lawyer, Gene Fitzhugh, started out with the group, but he first got in trouble for carrying a weapon on an airplane, and later he was involved in some manner with Whitewater and the Clintons.

I still represented Oklahoma Tire & Supply Company, and I was beginning to get calls from people I had helped while I worked in the prosecuting attorney's office. While I was at the prosecuting attorney's office and receiving a paycheck and paying no overhead, I had been able to help people with little or no money or income, and I could give them a long time to pay me. Unfortunately, many thought I could still do that! But little by little my clientele began to grow. I was practicing law!

26

Duke was wonderful to me—meeting me every day for lunch and doing simple things like not sitting down to eat until the meal was prepared and I was ready to sit down, too! Sometimes we lit candles and had a glass of wine, and he bragged about every dish I cooked. So far as I knew at that time, the kids still liked him.

When I moved from North Little Rock to the wonderful house in Cammack Village, there was a small Baptist church very near there, and of course the first Sunday morning found the children and me there. I had attended church on Sunday mornings all my life, and as I used to tell Ham, I was not going to reject religion for my children. If they wanted to do so when they grew up, they had that right, but I determined that I was not going to do it for them.

Gretel asked if she could sit with her friends, and of course I said yes, remembering that my mother required me to sit with her in the "amen corner"—I guess to make sure I was paying attention to what the preacher said. I don't know. Anyway when Everett and I got out of church, Gretel was always at the car, waiting for us. We drove home together, where the roast I had put in the oven, with potatoes, carrots, and onions, was ready to eat.

One Sunday, we came out of church, and Gretel was not at the car. We waited awhile, and then went to her classroom to see if she had left or was still waiting there, but she was nowhere to be found. I was trying not to panic. She had come to church with us; surely she was around there somewhere. We went back to the car,, and I saw her racing across the street to get to the car. That's when we learned that Gretel had not been coming to the baptist church. She had been going to Westover Hills Presbyterian Church, a small presbyterian church a few blocks away. The preacher was Dick Hardie, and he had a son about Gretel's age who went to the same school. The boys and girls at Westover Hills sat together during their class, and there was a pool table in the recreation room!

Duke's family was methodist, but he had not been active. So I decided that all of us would join Westover Hills, which we did. Dick Hardie and his wife, Kaki, who was a very gifted teacher at the University of Arkansas at Little Rock, were very prominent in the religious community, and "Preacher Dick," as we all called him, took a stance at the time of the integration conflict and marched to Selma! Many of the church members left the church at that time, and the rest of us simply said, "Good Bye!"

* * *

We went fairly often to "Fordyce on the Cotton Belt" to visit Duke's father, the sheriff for many years, and his mother. They had horses, and all of us rode them and ate wonderful meals prepared by Duke's mother's black maid.

I was in Seventh Heaven. My practice was growing, and I enjoyed every minute of my time with my husband. There were, however, a number of warning signs every so often, rare and short lived, but very strange. For instance, Duke was head of the drug division of the state police, and in that capacity wore no uniforms, but dressed in plain clothes. One holiday when large numbers of people would be traveling, the order came down that all troopers would wear uniforms. That day I came home and upon opening the door to our bedroom found Duke dressed in his uniform, complete with a "Smokey Bear" hat. It was the first time I had ever seen him in uniform, and I remember saying, "Oh, you look darling!" reaching out to embrace him.

With a look that was difficult to describe, an angry Duke pushed me away, and, with an epithet, almost shouted, "Don't you make fun of me!"

"I wasn't making fun," I said, bewildered, but he was gone. When he came home, he was exhausted from the strenuous day and went to bed, holding me close, and the incident passed.

A more dangerous and frightening occasion arose once when we were visiting his parents in Fordyce. We had a good time, but Duke had developed a headache. He was sitting at the breakfast bar holding his head when his mother came up behind him and very tenderly began to massage his neck and head. Duke, irritated as usual, stood up, turned to me, and said, "Let's go, Ginger!" And started out the front door. I quickly summoned the children, said goodbye to his mother, and followed him to the car. We had barely gotten in, me in the front with him and Gretel and Ev in the back, when he took off at a frightening speed, driving at an unbelievable rate on the narrow highway, muttering angrily under his breath, oblivious to our presence. "She can keep her damned hands off me!" he muttered. "She wasn't there when I needed her! She can leave me alone!"

I said "Duke! Duke!" trying to calm him down, and glancing at my frightened children in the back seat, as he continued to drive at top speed around all the curves, almost without consciousness.

"Are you talking about your MOTHER?" I asked, "Your Mother loves you, Duke! She was trying to make you feel better!"

Almost instantaneously, Duke seemed to, for a better word, wake up. He slowed down to a safe speed and drove in a completely different manner the rest of the way home, helping everyone out of the car, together with the accompanying gear we had taken with us. He was completely normal and said nothing about the weird action, and I certainly didn't. He was again the passionate, loving husband, and I put the strange behavior out of my mind.

27

The first hint I had that all might not be well with my being associated with Omar Greene and Thorpe Thomas was what Judge Kirby said to me when he learned that I had gone from the prosecutor's office to 721 West Second, allied myself with Omar and Thorp. "What are you doing down there with Ali Baba and the 40 thieves?"

And then, I had a jury trial in Judge Warren Wood's court, and before it started, we were all before the court, going over procedure. I happened to glance over at opposing counsel's notes and saw that one of his questions to the jury was going to be if they had ever represented or had any contact with Omar Greene and Thorpe Thomas. Quickly, I told the court that I objected to that question; that it was immaterial; and that by asking, opposing counsel was seeking to prejudice the jury; that I had no connection with either one; that I was only sharing expenses. The court asked his clerk to bring him a telephone book, looked up my name, found that it was listed by itself and that I was no part of any firm, and granted my objection.

My biggest surprise, however, came when the Martindale-Hubble representative interviewed me and asked me what my connection was to the other attorneys in the building. I answered that we were only sharing the rent and had no other connections, which was true, and his reply was surprising, to say the least. "That's good," he said, "for if you were partners, you could not have the rating you have." That reply made me somewhat uneasy, but I had no choice. The dye was cast; I had left the prosecutor's office and invested my money in Omar and Thorpe's project, and that's the way it was. Every month, Omar's secretary made out my bill, and I simply wrote a check, assuming that bills were being paid and equity in the building was accumulating. I did think that there was quite an amount spent for certain expenses, like cokes, for I don't drink cokes—never have. My father called them "belly-wash," and they were prohibited. But I occasionally served cokes to my clients, so I didn't object to paying my part of the bill.

One day when I came in, I was surprised to find a moving van at the side door. My good friend Roy Finch was moving out of the building.

"What's going on?" I asked, and Roy said, "Shut the door, and I will tell you."

I closed his door, and then he said, "I'm moving in with Claude Carpenter, in the 1515 Building near the capitol. Thorpe and Omar asked me to help them in a big personal injury case. I did, and they settled it without my knowledge and kept the money. Now if they had needed it, and borrowed it, promising to pay me back, that would have been O.K., but they didn't, and to me that's reaching in the till."

I really hated to see him go. As I said, he was my favorite of the entire group. I thought it very strange that nobody had said a word about any discrepancy or wrong doing. Thorpe, Omar, Roy, and I were the remaining lawyers with interests in the building, and I immediately asked Roy if he would sell me his interest and the copy machine the four of us had purchased. He agreed, of course, and I paid him, for that was an extremely valuable piece of equipment.

Omar and Thorpe called a meeting after Roy moved out and filed a motion to remove Roy from sharing in the purchase of the building.

"Look," I said, "you guys wrote the contract, but I didn't think it required that all of us actually stay in the building. Why couldn't we rent the whole thing for a whole lot of money? So long as we paid the doctor, what difference would it make?"

"He isn't paying any utilities," they said.

"Well, he isn't using any either!" I said.

"Well," they said, "it was agreed that if any of us moved out, we gave up our right to purchase the building." But they admitted that they did not have any proof of that, so Roy had an interest as far as I was concerned. We had enough money from renting all the offices to pay the utilities, and if we ran short, I told them I thought Roy would contribute his share. That ended the meeting, but I contacted Roy and purchased his interest, giving me two shares and Omar and Thorpe having two. There was never any problem renting offices at 721 West Second Street. It is in walking distance to every courtroom in the county except juvenile court out on Roosevelt Road.

(Top) Me at my office desk. (Lower left) Gretel, Duke, me, and Everett in January 1967 while Ev is home from military school. (Lower right) Henry "Duke" Harrison Atkinson, III, and me.

(Top) Gretel, Everett, and me at my brother's funeral at Easter in 1983. (Lower left) Me on Duke's "trails" bike. (Lower right) Duke and me with my parents on a motorcycle road trip to Danville with Everett.

(Top) Me with Gretel and Everett. (Below) Everett and me.

(Top) A portrait of me by Olan Mills. (Below) Dale Bumpers and me.

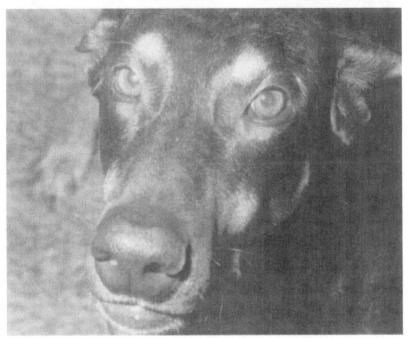

(Top left) Me at our house on West Markham in Little Rock with Little Bit, Satan, and Honey. "Who let the dogs out?" *(Top right)* Our Great Dane named "Little Bit" because he was a little bit too big. *(Below)* Satan.

(Top) Me and Gretchen, one of our dogs, in the living room at Querencia. (Lower left) Me in the kitchen at Querencia, "the last time I cooked." (Lower right) Querencia under construction in 1977.

(Top) Gretel and me at her wedding to Allen Branton. (Below) Gretel and Allen in a limousine after their wedding.

(Top) Gretel and Chandler, "breakfast and baby." (Below) Me with Chandler Branton.

(Top) Chandler Branton.

(Below) Chandler's funeral card with a drawing her brother Matthew did on the cover. Inside the card was this poem:

When you've said all of the
bad things and all of the good things
you haven't been saying,
you will find that what you've really
been withholding is, "I love you."

You don't have to go looking for love
when it is where you come from.

Chandler Elizabeth Hannibal
Adams Branton
November 27, 1987
February 17, 1990

(Top) Gretel and me on a trip to Antarctica with Everett. (Below) Me hard at work in my office.

28

I didn't escape menopause, but fortunately Jeanette Rockefeller gave me her physician's number at the Med Center, and after my examination, he recommended a hysterectomy. "If you were a housewife and you could lie down, we probably would not operate. But as a practicing attorney, you can't risk having blood gushing down you legs during closing argument!" How right he was, and the operation was scheduled. Imagine my surprise to learn that the doctor had died! I remember his successor talking to me, telling me that he had studied my case and was prepared to proceed, but of course it was up to me. I said "Yes, let's go!"

The procedure was routine, I assume, because I had no problems. Duke sat at my side and waited on me hand and foot. The day I went home, Gretel's friend Bonnie brought little Christina to see me. We could never imagine everything that subsequently transpired! Duke and I agreed that allowing Gretel to visit the young couple would show her how hard trying to make their own way and caring for a child really is. Little did we know that they might experiment with drugs. I think Gretel's participation was nominal, but Bonnie became addicted and spent some time in the State Hospital, losing custody of Christina. Gretel loved the little girl and helped Gary Clinton, Christina's father, take care of her from time to time.

* * *

And then I came home from work one day, and the owner of the neighborhood variety store called me with a surprising complaint. He said he had caught Ev stealing something, and when he was stopped, he gave the man a fictitious name. I couldn't believe it, and Everett had told me that he was not involved; that the villain was Walt Mason. The storeowner was a member of Westover Hills Presbyterian Church, and Everett's Sunday school teacher. I certainly didn't think he would report something like that to me unless he had good reason to. Needless to say, I was surprised and disturbed. Everett giving a fictitious name amazed me. Of course both of my children grew up in a law office, and attending all kinds of trials, including criminal proceedings. And neither of them was dumb! I grounded Ev until I could figure out what course to follow.

Duke knew my friend Jean McDermont from our prosecuting attorney days, and he was familiar with the fact that her son had graduated from military school. Looking back, I believe that Duke really didn't want either of my children around, but he had me mesmerized in those days, and the idea of sending Ev to military school, getting him away from Walt Mason and his like, didn't seem like a bad idea. I talked to Jean, of course, and she thought it would be wonderful for him, and even gave me the address of the Columbia Military Academy in Columbia, Tennessee.

That's what I did, when Ev was a fifth grader. To my surprise, Everett loved every minute he spent there, made wonderful grades, and still knows and sings the football fighting songs. If I had it to do over, I would let him complete his education there, but I missed him so much that I brought him home after the first year.

I remember a trip he made home during spring break when Ham refused to pay half of the cost of flying him home, and I elected to let him take a bus. There was some problem, and I met every bus until almost midnight, imagining everything in the world, but he was fine. We had a litter of puppies, and I put his bed down in the playroom in front of the fireplace, with all the puppies, and that's where we slept until Ham called early the next morning, asking when he could see Ev.

"Now," I said, and he replied he couldn't because he was going to the football game in Fayetteville, and he would see Ev when he got back. I told him that would be fine, but Ev had a deadline when he had to be back in Tennessee, and the school was very adamant about students getting back at a certain time. Moreover, he had a return bus ticket. It turned out that Ham, who would not pay one half of the fare for Ev to fly home, wound up visiting with him after he returned from Fayetteville, and then paying the entire fare to fly him back to Tennessee.

29

The days and nights flew by. My practice was flourishing, and I had hired a full-time secretary, Miss Betty. Her husband had been a client of Omar Greene in a very bad accident case in which he, her husband, had lost a leg. I can't remember her last name, but she was certainly a hard worker. All of the offices were rented, or so I thought, and once a month I received a bill for my share of the rent and expenses, and unquestionably wrote a check. I have mentioned that there were some ethical questions about my co-workers, but I personally witnessed only one episode that gave me pause, if nothing else. I came in one morning to find the secretaries, all but mine, trying on garments from a stack of women's clothes that was piled in one of the back rooms. Everyone was laughing and excited about the garments, which apparently were available to them for little money, if any. It seems that Omar represented a ladies' dress shop that had just been burglarized, and I think Omar was dealing with the insurance carrier on behalf of his client. Either that, or he had a client charged with burglary involving a ladies' dress shop. I remember that I closed my door, avoided the garments, and asked absolutely no questions.

On Good Friday 1966, almost at closing time, my fellow attorneys Omar Greene and Thorpe Thomas dropped a bombshell. My secretary had already gone home when I returned from Saline County where I had had a major victory. I had set aside a will, and I was jubilant. I was going through the mail, for I had been gone and I have always opened my own mail, when there was a knock on my door, and Omar and Thorpe walked in.

"Ginger," Omar said, "The $10,000 balloon note on this building is due Monday, and we have decided not to buy it. In fact, we have bought the building across the street. What are you going to do?"

I could not believe my ears. "What am I going to do?" I repeated. "Well, I guess I'll sit here and practice law! I guess I can rent your offices like we rent the other offices."

And then came the real bombshell: "No," Omar continued, "they have been working with us all along, and they are moving with us."

There was nothing further to say, and it would have been useless to protest or complain. My husband was furious when I got home and told him, and the kids were upset, but the following Monday things really fell apart. We had started compiling a library, and I had paid for my one-fourth of it. So when they started taking all of the books out, I intervened. "You may take your part, but every fourth book belongs to me!" And I marched in and started taking down every fourth book. Omar reached in his pocket. "Just how much do you think your part of the books are worth?" he asked.

I did a quick calculation. "I think I have $2,000 in them," I said. He handed me the money in $100 bills and continued moving the books out. Even worse, they took rubber bands, every paper clip, even the telephone, which they had put in Thorpe's name because it was cheaper than a business number. But what was the worst, emotionally and financially, when people called me at their number, they simply said, "She is no longer with us," rather than taking a number for me.

* * *

At the same time that bombshell hit me, an even worse event transpired, none of which I understood at the time. As it happened, Gretel didn't go to college after graduating from Hall High, as we had planned, and much, much later I learned that the man I thought was a wonderful step-father to my children and an adoring husband to me was truly a Dr. Jekyll and Mr. Hyde. The stories I am hearing even now, after all these years, are hard to believe. The children told me nothing at the time, and I have asked repeatedly, why not? There answer is that Duke had told them if they told me anything, he would kill them, and they believed him.

Gretel was 18 on May 18, 1969, and a few days later she charged two sleeping bags to me at Montgomery Ward's and ran away with Ray Robinson, someone I did not know and had never met. Everett gave false information to Duke concerning with whom she had left and in what direction she had gone, false information for which he received physical punishment—all completely unknown to me. It seems impossible now that I was so oblivious to what was going on, but I truly was. Duke's role with me was that of an adoring husband, making mad passionate love every night with breakfast in bed every morning. I was a sole practitioner, with more clients than I had ever dreamed of having, working around the clock, traveling throughout the entire state, even as far away as Harrison.

I was devastated when Gretel left. Not only did I miss her and worry about her, but she had planned to work in my office during the summer, and maybe part-time if her schedule allowed it, for she had planned to go to UALR for her first college experience.

* * *

After Omar and Thorpe had moved out, taking all the other tenants with them and transferring the utilities that had been in Thorpe's name, I remember sitting in the dark alone in my office and saying out loud, "What else can happen to me?" And suddenly there was a swarm of small-flying insects, and I burst into laughter. I had to ask! Of course they were termites, although I had to report my termite carrier to the authorities before he would repair the damage.

Of course I got a different telephone number and had it installed as quickly as I could. Then I had flyers printed saying "Same Address, Different Telephone," giving the number, and mailing the flyers out to all of my clients and friends. I think I also published it in the *Daily Record*.

When the rent on the building came due (I ignored the balloon note), I wrote a check for one-half of the amount, mailed it to Omar and Thorpe, asked them to put their half in the envelope and mail it to the doctors. It came back to me, with a letter saying, "We are not going to pay any additional rent; however, we will retain our interest in the building like Roy Finch did."

They must have contacted every real estate dealer in the city, because people began to knock on the door, which my secretary and I kept locked, wanting to look at the building. I would meet them and say, "I am buying one-half of this building, and my half is not for sale. You may purchase one-half," which put a stop to any further invasion.

"Well, I'll talk to Mr. Thomas!" the irate real estate salesmen would state, and my answer was just as clear.

"Fine. Talk to anyone you like. Talk to Jesus," I have been known to say. "The fact remains: my half is not for sale."

It was my husband, Duke, who took over the situation at that time. I simply watched. I really never knew exactly what transpired, but Duke was well known to carry not only a loaded gun but also knives in his boots, and he apparently expressed his concern about the situation. As I said, I never really knew exactly what took place, but Omar and Thorpe came up with a very reasonable figure for their interest in the building, which I was able to pay.

Dr. Chears' and Wengar's real estate dealer was Russ Meeks, whose son was an attorney friend of mine, and when Russ came to discuss the situation, I simply told him the story and that there was no way I could pay the balloon note. In fact, I had never signed the contract that Omar and Thorpe had made with the doctors, and I suppose they had simply defaulted. At any rate, Mr. Meeks arranged a meeting with Dr. Chears for Duke and me, and we reached an agreement on a purchase price and more agreeable payment schedule. I paid the payment on 721 West Second before I paid my tithe to the church! I am sure the doctors had written building off, for it was quite old at that time, but nevertheless they saved my practice, and I shall be eternally grateful. Every year at tax time, I would contact the doctors' accountant and ask how much I had paid, to be sure I deducted the correct amount. Imagine my surprise when he replied to one of my inquiries as follows: "You paid it off six months ago. Where do you want your refund mailed?" I was so busy taking care of other people's problems and business that my own went begging.

30

I missed Gretel and worried about her until we were able to find out where she was, using the facilities of Governor Rockefeller, the State Police, and Everett, who finally went to visit her in California. She was being a real "hippie"; I believe she was at Haight-Ashbury for awhile. She had married Ray Robinson, whom she later divorced, and thank God, there were no children. Although I am sure she experimented with drugs, apparently she was not addicted to anything but cigarettes, which is bad enough.

    I shall never forget one day when she was still in school. I went home at lunch to see about her, for she had not felt like going to school that morning. When I went into the house, she was not in her room, and I found her sitting outside on the patio with a long cord on her telephone, busily engaged in a conversation with someone and smoking a cigarette. I was heartbroken. I had never smoked and assumed that Gretel was too smart to get "hooked" on nicotine, not that it was recognized as being so bad. I made a rule: she could not smoke in my presence. I even argued with my friends who took the position that they would rather their children smoke in their presence than to slip around and do it. I felt then and do now that if I can keep her from smoking one cigarette, I will feel better about it. I remember how glamorous smoking was portrayed in the movies when Gretel was a teenager, and I am eternally glad that the cigarette companies have had to pay something for what they, apparently, knowingly did.

* * *

I had Gretel's first year's tuition in the bank, and Duke and I used it for a trip to Japan. Duke had been stationed there during the war, and he often talked about it and how he would like to take me there and show me, among other things, the famous high-speed railroads. We took a trip first to Thailand, then to Japan and Hong Kong. Almost all of the trips I have made out of the United States were arranged or sponsored by law firms or bar associations, as was this trip. The sponsor said that a portion of the expense could be taken off my income tax, but my accountant would not take it off because he had once worked for the Internal Revenue Service. However, the things we saw and did were things I would have wanted to see anyway—like the judicial system and a train in Hong Kong, which I saw on my second visit there. There was a bunch of lawyers and their wives in attendance, including Judge Warren Wood.

I had seen Yul Brynner in *The King & I* on Broadway, and to see the ornate buildings of Thailand and how the people lived on the water, buying from the boats that regularly dispatched groceries and other necessities, was an exciting experience. Until we left for Japan, it was a perpetual honeymoon, and Duke gave me a gorgeous pair of jade earrings.

Our hotel in Japan was built high on a hill, with flowers of every description blooming on the grounds surrounding it. The melodious sound of birds chirping emerged from the bedside radio, and a welcoming assortment of fruit and candy was on the bedside table. We rode the famous high-speed railroad to a nearby seaside city where we dined on exotic Japanese fare before the trip back on the swift train. We visited the Royal Palace and its grounds before returning to the hotel for our last night in Japan. We were scheduled to fly to Hong Kong the next day.

Early the next morning, our tour director assembled all of us together for a breakfast of doughnuts and coffee before we went to the airport to be flown to Hong Kong. I was looking forward to seeing Hong Kong, which still belonged to Great Britain at that time, subject to being returned to China on July 1, 1997. After we finished our breakfast and heard a report on where we were going next, we all went to the elevators. When our elevator opened, we discovered it was already full, and Judge Warren Wood's wife, who was directly in front of me, jumped backwards as the elevator door closed, and one of her spike heals landed on the top of my right foot. She apologized, and although my foot was a bit red, it did not even tear my silk hose. "I think I'm fine," I told her, and we took the next elevator and continued on our way.

The harbor at Hong King looked exactly the way I had pictured it from all the movies I had seen. It was beautiful and I was excited, but when I examined my foot, it was swollen double, and I could not stand on it. Hong Kong! And I couldn't walk. What a disappointment.

A wheel chair that must have come over on the Mayflower was obtained, and Duke lifted me into it after we landed. A doctor was waiting in the hotel. He determined that my foot was not broken, but it was severely bruised. I was ordered not to walk or stand on it, and he prescribed some pain medication. By this time, I was sobbing more from disappointment than pain. Hong Kong! And I couldn't walk. I never expected to return to Hong Kong, but as it has happened, I have several times. But I certainly didn't know I would ever see Hong Kong again at that time.

"Don't cry, Sweetheart," Duke comforted me. "You're not going to miss anything!" And I didn't. Duke rolled, carried, and lifted me the length and breadth of Hong Kong—up and down hills and off scenic boats and buses. Both of us were exhausted, but we had missed very little, if anything. My foot finally healed, although I limped around for quite some time even after returning home. The judge's insurance company paid for most of my medical expenses.

* * *

Our friend Winthrop Rockefeller was still governor, having been re-elected in 1968. Ham no longer worked for him, and one day I was served with a summons. Ham had filed for a reduction in child support. The lawyer who represented him and had me served was David Bogard, and I was furious. Many times when I was deputy prosecuting attorney, I had gone to court in North Little Rock for David's father who was practicing law at that time. I called him and raised cain, and the elder Bogard apologized. "He's just young," he said. I am sure he contacted his son, for David called me and apologized. I remember telling him that I did not intend to answer the complaint, nor did I intend to appear in court. I added that he should find out what Ham wanted to send to take care of his children, to write it up, and let me know, and if he didn't want to contribute anything toward their care, I certainly would take care of them! In retrospect, I really don't know why I was so agitated by the occurrence. I guess I thought Ham should have called me, although I realize that that probably never would have occurred. The amount of money I received was greatly reduced, and Gretel had attained her majority. In addition, Ham paid sporadically, owing various sums at different times. I believe Everett III collected a substantial amount of money that he was owed one time, but that's another story.

31

From time to time, I have interspersed this narrative with stories about clients and incidents that occurred during my many years of practicing law, and I just remembered another one. A tearful black woman came to my office one day with a legal problem. In her hand were some crumpled up bills of various denominations, which she handed to me after she sat down.

"Ms. Atkinson," she said, still almost crying. "My ex-husband has paid no child support, and its prom time at school. I can't afford to buy my daughter a ball gown. Do I have enough money there for you to take him to court?"

I was amazed that she had brought money to me rather than trying to pay for the garment someplace; she was intelligent enough to know it would be better to try to get all the money owed to her than to go bargain hunting, and although the wadded up bills were barely enough to cover the filing fee, I assured her that we certainly could make him face the judge for his failure to follow the court's orders and maybe make him pay the attorney fees, too.

On the way home, I realized that we had to file the action, serve the defendant, who resided in another county, and give him time to answer. The prom was not that far off. I thought of all the beautiful formals I had seen at Elle's and found myself driving in that direction.

"Miss Rita," I said to the proprietor, "I want you to help me make somebody very happy," and I told her the story. "Could you sell me a formal maybe at cost, or near it so this girl can go to the prom? I promise her father is going to pay up!"

Rita took over. I gave her the address, and that was all it took. It was after the affair was over that I met the happy young woman, who gave me her picture and thanked Miss Rita and me over and over, as did her mother.

The real drama, however, came when the culprit, the child-support dodger, was confronted in court by his daughter. She did not raise her voice at her father. She simply gave him her picture wearing the stunning evening garment and said, "I could not have gone to the prom without these ladies, Daddy. Mama couldn't do it by herself."

The court did not have to incarcerate him. He paid all the arrearage and promised not to get behind again. I think he was truly sorry and chagrined that rank strangers had been more helpful to his daughter than he.

* * *

Mr. Rockefeller expected to face Orval Faubus in the 1970 campaign, but Dale Bumpers of Charleston, Franklin County, won over a host of candidates, and along with his lovely wife and children, became my close and cherished friends.

Mr. Rockefeller had inoperable cancer of the pancreas in September of 1974 and died in Palm Springs, California, when he was only 60 years old. I barely recognized him the last time I saw him, but his Winthrop Rockefeller Foundation and the Winthrop Rockefeller Charitable Trust lives on, as does the wonderful Museum of Automobiles on Petit Jean Mountain. He purchased the collection of James Melton (and added to that), and I, along with my children, attended its opening, a very thrilling thing for us. His dramatic last act as governor was the commutation of the sentences of every prisoner on Arkansas's death row, and he urged other governors to do likewise, having been a long time opponent of the death penalty.

* * *

A very successful businessman in North Little Rock, Martin Burnett, walked into my office, with its wonderful location a block or so from all the courts, and asked if Dale Bumpers could use it as his campaign headquarters. I remember telling him I couldn't afford to donate it, and he said, "Oh, we aren't asking that; he'll pay," and it was settled. The rent was not very much, but it was a welcome addition to my income, and every room in the building except my small section was filled with earnest, excited young workers for Dale Bumpers.

Once you met Dale Bumpers, you were immediately for him. His appearance and demeanor revealed his statesmanship, and he spoke often of his father, who thought that public service was an honorable profession. He easily defeated Faubus and then unseated Rockefeller in the general election. I shall never forget the night he won. My building could not contain the crowd, and although the air conditioner was pumping as hard as it could, the temperature in my building was sweltering, a condition that the *Arkansas Gazette* did not overlook. "In his headquarters, no larger than a bus station john," it reported, "his fans and followers celebrated in the steamy, crowded quarters," or something to that effect! "A bus station john!" My wonderful Harkey Building!"

* * *

But, I am getting ahead of myself. The most devastating experience I ever encountered happened shortly after Dale Bumpers and his campaign workers came into the Harley Building.

My parents had sold their property in Russellville, including their lots in the graveyard, and returned to their early home, Danville, Arkansas, where they purchased a lovely smaller home near the First Baptist Church and within walking distance of the post office. My father had built an enormous shed directly behind the house, with an enviable collection of tools, spare parts of electrical equipment, and other bric-a-brac neatly stored and carefully labeled. If either of them had legal questions of any kind, they called "Sister," which was perfectly natural and expected. I, of course, really did not mind, but Duke always complained, ostensibly because I had to make the trip alone, as he was almost always on active duty.

On one such trip to my parents, I took my friend Faye Hill with me in an effort to keep Duke from worrying about me. I made tuna salad for him to eat while I was away and called him when we arrived safely, for we had driven through a blinding rainstorm.

Faye and I enjoyed the feast my mother had prepared, then I took care of the problem, which had to do with the preparation of a quitclaim deed for a relative, and we returned to Little Rock before dark. Faye had left her car at my house, and had departed for her home, when I went inside the house and down the hall to our bedroom, where I found Duke just replacing the receiver on the telephone located there. The bedroom telephone was Duke's alone, to be used for his job, and in retrospect I remember his having a strange look on his face that evening.

"Ginger," he said, "Those goddamn hippies are going to tell you that I am cheating on you."

I kissed him "hello" and said, "Well, what could I do about that if you were?" thinking he will be proud of me for being tolerant and confident.

Well! Just the reverse happened. His face darkened, and in an accusative voice he almost bellowed, "Well, *some* wives would be jealous!"

I was astonished, but I quietly said, "Well, I'd be jealous," and left the room to check on Everett, who was spending the day with a friend.

I had a case the next day, which I tried in small claims court before Judge Holt and which I really wanted to win, for it involved a friend of mine. She had bought a beautiful coat with a fur collar, and when she had it cleaned, the cleaners had damaged it. The cleaners vigorously defended their work, but we won and recovered a judgment for the cost of the coat. I was elated and called my office to see if anyone was waiting to see me. If not, I had planned to go home early, which I did often to prepare gourmet meals. It was not to be; my secretary said a young woman was waiting, and she was being docketed for not being on her job.

I rushed to my office, through the political crowd that was there, to my niche, and the client was sent in. I remember that I put on my glasses, for I had been away all afternoon, and picked up my mail, which my secretary had put, unopened on my desk. I have never done only one thing at a time, and this was no exception. Slicing open my mail and stacking it to the side to be studied at a later time, I addressed the client, a buxom young woman wearing slacks and a T-shirt.

"You have a problem, dear?" Her name was Marilyn.

"Yes, ma'am," she said tearfully. "Ms. Atkinson, a few weeks ago I met a wonderful man, and we fell in love. I know it was wrong, because he's married, but we were *so* in love, and now I'm preg... pregnant, and he's supposed to help get an abortion ... and he won't answer my phone calls, and I don't want to hurt him ..." and she dissolved in tears.

I was furious. "And why not?" I questioned, "He's hurt *you!*"

And with that she collapsed: "Oh, Ms. Atkinson," she sobbed. "It's Duke!"

So that's what Duke had been talking about when I got back on Sunday. This was one of the hippies who was going to tell lies about him. "Oh, really?" I said, sarcastically. "What are you trying to do? Blackmail me? I have no money. I make payments on that Lincoln just like everyone else."

With that she reached into her purse and produced medical evidence. There was no doubt; she was pregnant. And then she said, "Do you remember when you had the dinner party and Duke had to leave?" And of course I remembered. The dinner party was for a client of mine, a wealthy entrepreneur and his wife, in an effort to interest them in forming a company or a business handling motorcycles, with Duke as the manager, something he desperately wanted to do. "Well," she continued, "I had locked myself out of my apartment, and he came to let me back in; he has a key. I thought he'd be mad, but he was sweet. He said that could happen to anybody."

Knowing that she had hit pay dirt, she continued. "Somewhere in his jewelry box, you will find a St. Christopher's medal," she went on. "I gave it to him."

I had never gone through Duke's jewelry box or the personal belongings on his dresser, but I remembered the replacement St. Christopher's medal I had given him after our scuba diving experience. Sure enough, I found another one, with "All my love, always" on the back.

I could no longer question the situation, and I marveled at Duke's effort to discount it. My office was full of Bumper enthusiasts. I couldn't scream, couldn't faint, couldn't cry; I couldn't even swear. I stood up. "Ma'am," I said, clearly, "This isn't my problem. It's yours and his. When he comes home, I will have him call you," and I ushered her out of the room.

And then I went home to await Duke's arrival. It didn't happen that night; he didn't come home until after I went to the office the following morning. But Miss Marilyn called me quite late that night—on Duke's private telephone, of course, in my bedroom! "Oh, Ms. Atkinson," she sobbed. "It's storming where he is, and that state police car he drives has no fog lights."

"He's a big boy," I told her. "Go to sleep." And I hung up the phone.

I went to the office the following morning, which, as I remember, was a Friday. It was almost noon before the lady at the front desk called to tell me my husband was on the line.

He was his usual self. "Hi, honey. I'm off to a high school to demonstrate to the teachers how marijuana smells. What's going on?"

"Not much," I replied. "It's Friday. Why don't you pick me up and take me with you?"

"O.K., pretty girl. I'll be right there," and he was. I had gone through his jewelry and found the St. Christopher's medal with the message "All my love, always" on the back, and I put it around my neck, under my blouse. Once we were on the highway, I said, "Duke, who besides me knew you were going to Jonesboro?"

"All those damned hippies knew," he replied.

Then I asked, "Did Marilyn know?" And I pulled the medal out. "I understand you have a key to her apartment?" He pulled over to the side of the highway and killed the engine. Silently, he took from his key ring a single key. He had once given me half of a special double key ring with the words "The Lord watch over you while we are absent from the other" on both halves. He had one, and I had the other. When I saw him take the key off his half of the key ring that day in the car, I lost it. I was crying inconsolably, and hitting him in the head and face with my purse as hard as I could, calling him everything but a child of God. I truly was irrational. I opened the car door and started walking down the highway, oblivious to the traffic or which direction I was walking.

Duke turned the car around and slowly followed me, saying "Ginger, get in the car. I will take you home." I ignored him, except to scream, "Whore monger! Whore monger! Whore monger!"

Duke stopped the car, got out of it, followed me, knocked me down, then picked me up and put me in the car, sobbing, "I'm sorry, Ginger. I'll take you home." And he did. When I got home, I went inside the house, gathered up as many of his clothes as I could handle, took the beautiful nightgown and robe I had worn the night we were married, and threw all of the things I had gathered up into the boat we had bought and spent so many wonderful hours in. Then I told him to go and never come back!

My eye was turning black, and before he left, Duke got a piece of steak from the refrigerator for me to hold on my eye. He was contrite, saying over and over, "I'm sorry. I'm sorry I hit you. I had to stop you." Everett came in while all this was going on; it must have been time for school to let out. I remember telling him that I was O.K. and for him to go to his room. Duke went downstairs to retrieve some of his possessions, and on the walk upstairs, he stopped, breathing heavily and holding his heart. I remember saying, "There's nothing wrong with you! You get the hell out of here!" But there might have been. Duke died of a heart attack not many years later, but not before he made many, many more mistakes.

The next day, I typed up a divorce complaint and took it to my good friend Roy Finch at the 1515 Building. I told him the whole story, something he could hardly believe. He and all my friends had witnessed Duke's apparent devotion to me from the beginning—his constant attention and concern. I told Roy the whole sorry story, and I told him that I wanted him to talk to Duke. I said that if Duke wanted that young woman and a baby, then I wanted Roy to file the divorce. If he didn't, and she had in fact more or less snared him, then I didn't want Roy to file it. Duke had two grown daughters, and I could hardly see him with a new baby.

And then started the harassment, totally unexpected and constant. Every day when I opened my mail, there was an unsigned letter, with incredible items attached. Shades of Monica Lewinsky! She sent me a handkerchief they had used to clean themselves up with after their first intercourse. She sent me postcards of every hotel in the state in which they had spent the night, with the room circled. I raved and ranted on the telephone to Duke. "Get your whore off me!" I would yell.

He would reply, "I can't, Ginger. The more I ask her to leave you alone, the more she's going to do it!" I really don't know how I survived that episode in my life, but I was extremely busy, which helped. And of course my wonderful friends Dale and Betty Bumpers and their loyal supporters were campaigning constantly, oblivious of my situation.

And then one day, I got a call from Roy Finch with the following message. "Ginger, Duke says it's all a bad dream, and he loves you." I am sure Duke had procured an abortion for the young woman and had broken off the affair.

"I don't know, Roy," I said. "I don't think I could ever trust him again. But, thank you."

Roy said, "I'll hold it," and hung up.

* * *

Dale Bumpers won the election over the horde of candidates, including Orval Faubus, who were running in the run-off, as well as over Winthrop Rockefeller in the general election. There was an unbelievable number of people at his victory celebration, and they stayed and celebrated, drinking cokes and probably everything else, and making Betty Bumpers' effort to keep the spilled cokes off the carpet impossible. Everett was with me after the crowd left, and as we were trying to clean up the place, we were interrupted by the Little Rock Police, who ordered us to vacate the building. There was a bomb threat!

The bomb squad searched everything as we watched in disbelief from across the street and some distance away. I have no idea what time it was when the police let us back in, but Ev and I were still trying to get the office presentable when there was another knock at the door. Duke was standing outside.

"Ginger!" he exclaimed when I opened the door. "You don't need to be down here this late!"

"Ev and I had to clean up the place," I said. "You should have seen the mob!"

Wordlessly, Duke picked up a bundle of debris and took it to the trash container outside, then returned for another load. When we had completed the task, Duke said, "Let's go get some coffee or something to eat." Of course it was too late to go anywhere but home, and that's where we went, Duke following Ev and me in his car.

When we got home I made a pot of coffee. Ev didn't want anything to eat and went straight to bed, leaving Duke and me alone. Duke made an overture, as if he were going to embrace me, but I pulled away, and he made no further attempts. "Good night, Ginger," he said, then left. I spent a sleepless night.

32

The beautiful little house in Cammack Village had so many memories that I simply could not cope with it, and Ev and I on the following Sunday answered an advertisement about a house on Markham that had a swimming pool. It was a sprawling ranch house, and the swimming pool was Olympic size, but the entire house was pink. An elderly woman and her husband lived there and had decided they wanted a smaller house. There was a large room, complete with pool table, that led out to the swimming pool, and Ev was ecstatic.

"Do you think my son and I can maintain the pool?" I asked, and the lady replied, "Oh, my, yes! Every spring I just get down there and fill it up! Of course you can."

We bought it, but it was winter time. When spring came, I decided to call the pool service—to find out how to handle it, for one thing. Imagine my surprise when the man immediately said he knew the pool well, that it would not hold water and never had!

I filed a lawsuit and was successful, although I was disgusted that I had taken the woman's word and had made no attempt to find out the true status of the property. With the proceeds from my lawsuit, I hired a workman I had known from attending court in Malvern, and it was completely made over. The only thing I was told about the pool that was true was its size!

* * *

Duke knew we had moved, but he did not know my address, and I didn't want him to know it. I was still so hurt and disappointed that I truly did not know if I could ever forget. In the meantime, we learned that Duke was in trouble. It seems that he had procured an abortion in a city where abortions were against the law, and on the day he had gone there, the police had, in some manner, placed cameras in the clinic and had pictures of his being there. The head of the State Police was a member of Preacher Dick's church, where Duke and I had been members, and because of that, Duke was allowed to resign from the State Police and no further action was taken.

I did not know that all of this was taking place, but I remember I received a telephone call one day from Preacher Dick, and when I answered the telephone, he asked if I was busy.

"Not too busy to talk to you, Preacher Dick," I answered.

He said, "Do you think you could come over now?" referring to his office at the church.

"Of course," I said, and immediately drove there. When I opened the door to his study, he was not alone. A red-eyed Duke was sitting there.

"Duke wants me to try to save his marriage," Preacher Dick said. "He's sorry for everything and wants to renew his vows, and there's a precedent for that in this church. I can't tell you that it won't happen again, Miss Ginger, but people do change, or I'm in the wrong business."

And of course that's what transpired in the chapel of Westover Hills Presbyterian Church, complete with guests, music, and flowers. Duke bought Everett a new suit, took him aside, and told him about temptations. He told Ev when he was older, he would understand how these things could happen, and he added he was sorry and that he would spend the rest of his life making up to Ev and me. Our friends at the air base had a big party, and my marriage was back in force. Duke did not have a job or a car, so his father, the sheriff, let him borrow his Hog—

a beautiful big motorcycle. Later on, his father let him have another motorcycle, one which was not quite as large as the sheriff's. Trouble started almost immediately. Duke would accuse Everett of riding his "bike." Ev would deny that he had been on it, so Duke started marking the tires and checking to be sure Eve had not been on the vehicle. Finally I intervened. "Duke, that's an attraction nuisance. We cannot have it around and not expect a teenager to get on it."

Duke agreed. "Ginger," he said, "why don't we sell this one, and I'll get us a bigger one—one that you and I can ride on together." And against my better judgment, I went along.

Duke had begun his career as a motorcycle policeman, and he knew all the safety rules. Every Sunday, he would get on his bike, and Ev would get on his. We went out in the country, and Duke taught him safety rules, grounding him if he disobeyed any one of them. I think it is safe to say that Everett became an expert motorcyclist, taking no risks. I gradually overcame my fear and thoroughly enjoyed my perch behind Duke, riding through the summer evenings with my son and his girlfriend. Sometimes we rode up to Petit Jean Mountain, where we ate watermelon and took pictures; sometimes we went to the drive-in movies. One summer we even went to Mexico, taking the bikes and one of Everett's friends.

Duke had taken a job with the sheriff's department, but he missed being on the State Police and really was not very happy with his job.

* * *

One day I answered my telephone, and it was Gretel! I asked her where she was, and she replied that she was at her father's. Ham and his friend Tommy Russell, who was divorced from his wife, Maxine Brown, had either rented or purchased a lovely home in Wildwood, North Little Rock. "When can I see you?" I asked her.

"How about lunch?" she said.

"Today? That's great!" It was almost lunchtime. "Where do you want to eat?" I asked, and then added, "How about the Train Station?"

The old train station in Little Rock had been purchased and refurbished, and the restaurant there was the latest word in Little Rock. Gretel agreed to meet me there, but of course I was delayed, and when I got there, she had been there for some time and had ordered a cocktail, or two. When the menu came, she ordered filet mignon, which was fine. It was great seeing her again and having her home. As I said, Gretel had had a cocktail or two before I got there, and after she had hugged me, she said, "Mama, you don't want to know where I've been or what I've done, but through it all I could hear your voice telling me what was right and what was wrong."

I was somewhat taken aback, but I said, "Sweetheart, that wasn't me; that was God."

Taking another swig from her cocktail and blowing smoke from her cigarette, she said, "Might've been, but he used your voice!"

She had come back to Little Rock with Ray Robinson, who ended up in the Veteran's Hospital in North Little Rock. Gretel planned to divorce him, which for some unexplainable reason infuriated her father, and she was no longer welcome to stay with him.

That's when she learned that Bonnie Clinton was a heroin addict and had run off with somebody, leaving Christina with Gary. Gary was living with his parents. When he learned that Gretel had no place to live, he suggested that they get a place together. He would pay the rent in exchange for her taking care of Christina.

When Bonnie found out that Gretel was taking care of Christina, she immediately filed for custody. I had no inkling about these developments. I only knew that Gretel was taking care of Christina for Gary.

One morning, I went to the courthouse to file a case, and when I entered the clerk's office, the place was in turmoil.

"What's going on?" I asked and was told that there was a custody suit set for trial that morning and that the defendant and his girlfriend had taken the child and left town.

I didn't have to ask the name of the defendant, and for sure I knew who the girlfriend was!

Gary, Gretel, and Christina had left Little Rock.

Once again, I pulled strings and located Gretel. She, Christina, and Gary had been to Mexico, New Orleans, and Pensacola, Florida.

I put all my jewelry in a lock box at the bank, located where they were staying, and knocked on the door. A surprised Gretel opened the door and almost swooned. "It's my mother," she shouted to Gary, and I entered the room.

Christina was a darling little girl, about three years old, and I suggested that we all go out to eat, which they were happy to do. After we had located a suitable restaurant and everyone had ordered, I told them that I had been at court the morning they failed to appear and left town, and I told them that the situation was not good. I pointed out to Gary that he couldn't stay hidden and gone forever, that his parents still lived in North Little Rock, and that he had a job there. I also told them that they could never get custody of Christina, no matter how unfit the child's mother was, as long as they were "shacking up" together. I told him that someday in the future it might be looked upon as O.K., but that at the present time it was not. I suggested that they come home and get married, and I would see if I couldn't get custody of Christina, since both of them told me that the mother was not free of her drug addiction and that she had been married two or three times. After I took them back to the place where they were staying, I left. There was really nothing more I could do.

Some time later, after I had reached home, Gretel called me. "Mama," she said, "I don't know why we didn't know that was what we had to do." And they came home. I called Bonnie's attorney and told him what I had done and what the situation was. Believe it or not, I was able to get the charges against Gretel and Gary dismissed, and to get liberal visitation with Christina—almost joint custody.

Gretel was pregnant, and we had a wedding that was very different from the wedding I had envisioned for her. I gave her money to buy a dress, and she had a long dress made from dark, printed material, and she wore boots on her feet, of all things. Of course, she was still beautiful and so was the ceremony, which was held outside on Petit Jean Mountain, with music, poetry, and lots of apple cider. It was truly beautiful.

* * *

I had a wonderful baby shower for Gretel, inviting everybody she and I knew. My gift to her was particularly beautiful, or at least I thought it was. It was an antique baby carriage in excellent shape. I found it at a church "rummage sale," and I am not sure just how old it was, but I remember that I put ribbons on it and placed most of the gifts Gretel was to receive from the other guests in it before it was rolled into the big living room of the house on Markham.

Liberty Mikell Clinton was born March 16, 1972, my first grandchild. Gretel was an excellent mother, breast feeding the child with no embarrassment when the child wanted feeding. She had an apartment in Hillcrest and called me one day saying she needed milk and bread. I had a good friend who worked at the Veteran's Hospital on Roosevelt Road, and I thought I'd pick her up at lunchtime, and we would take the milk and bread to Gretel and show my friend the baby. After I picked my friend up at the hospital, I hurried to the grocery store, dashed in, got a loaf of bread and a gallon of milk, and made my way to the checkout stand. There was another shopper, a black woman pushing two overloaded carts and advancing toward the checkout stand, and I knew it would take much longer to check her out than to check me out.

Waving my two items in the airs, I said to her, "Ma'am, I wonder if you would let me go ahead of you?"

To my great surprise, the woman scowled, and in her nastiest voice said to me, "Why should I?"

It flew all over me. "Because," I said, "I have two items and you have two hundred! And I have a friend with me who has only 30 minutes for lunch, and I am taking these two items to my daughter who just had a baby and needs them, and IT WOULD BE A FINE CHRISTIAN THING TO DO, BUT YOU THINK IT IS BECAUSE I'M WHITE AND YOU'RE BLACK!" And with that, I turned my back to her.

Suddenly, there was a voice from another checkout station: "Will the lady who has only 30 minutes for lunch come over here?"

I marched over to the newly opened checkout stand, where the cooperative checker swiftly totaled my two items. As I paid my bill, I suddenly heard everyone in each of the checkout stands, except of course the angry black lady, turn to the person standing next to him or her and say: "You don't have very much; would you like to go ahead?" It was a fruit-basket turn-over for the next few minutes. I couldn't believe it. I thanked the checker and dashed out the door. I had no time to spare if I was going to show my friend my grandchild and get her back to her job on time.

I related the incident to Duke when I got home, and he just shook his head. "Ginger, Ginger," he said. "You're asking for trouble. One of these days somebody is going to stick a knife in you."

"I don't think so," I countered. "You should have seen how everybody suddenly offered to let others go ahead. I think most people are just thoughtless. The woman with the overloaded baskets was deliberately being rude, and I couldn't resist pointing that out to her when I had a legitimate reason to go ahead of her."

I did not have my first grandchild very long. In the summer of 1972, Gretel and Gary moved to Colorado—with both little girls—and it was three years before they returned to Arkansas.

33

My parents were terribly unhappy living in Danville. It had changed from how they remembered it, and Daddy had an unfortunate relationship with the hospital there. I could never determine if his complaint was valid or not, but I do know that he would not go there for treatment, so I was making trips to Danville to pick him up and bring him to Little Rock for various examinations and treatment.

The Presbyterian Church has an outstanding facility in Little Rock known as Presbyterian Village. It was designed by a man for his mother when she became unable to live alone, and it offers three levels of care. There are apartments where couples live with their own belongings, and there are covered walkways they can use to go to the cafeteria if they do not want to cook. There are single rooms with private bathrooms for single individuals and an infirmary for occupants who require medical attention. My brother came to look at the facility, and he was greatly impressed. "I wonder if Dottie and I could make arrangements to come here when we need to," he said.

It is truly a wonderful facility. If a resident falls, a notice to that effect goes off in the infirmary. I didn't just want to pick my parents up and move them in, but I did make arrangements for them to come and look at what was available.

Mother was very impressed with Presbyterian Village, primarily because there was a place for her African violets. She also met a woman she had known since childhood who, together with her husband, had taken an apartment there. She was instantly at home and ready to move in. My father was not enthusiastic. Mother never met a stranger and really enjoyed meeting people and talking to them. Not my father, but he didn't veto the idea. He didn't embrace it, either. He just toured the entire Village, making no comments.

The folks visited with John and me, and it was decided that they would sell the house in Danville and move into Presbyterian Village. The Danville house was a very desirable piece of property, largely because of the enormous workshop, and it sold almost immediately when the folks listed it for sale. I notified John that their property had been sold, and both he and I thought they would be moving to Presbyterian Village as soon as they disposed of some of the personal property they would not need in smaller quarters.

I was working away in my office a few weeks later and received a call from a realtor. "Ms. Atkinson," he said, "do you know a Mr. and Mrs. Harkey?" Had I heard him correctly? Mr. and Mrs. Harkey? Do I know Mr. and Mrs. Harkey?

"Well," I said, "not very well." I said, truthfully. "They are my parents!"

"Well," the salesman continued, "they are in my office, and they have several pieces of property they want to look at."

"Don't sell those people any property!" I said. I might just as well have told water to run up hill. Of course the realtor showed them the properties they had cut from the newspaper, and the one they chose was on Mississippi, not too far from "Sister" on Markham and within walking distance of a baptist church. The lady who owned it had gone into a nursing home, and she wasn't as old as my parents! There was nothing to be done. They purchased the property, located at 7717 Ohio Street, and went back to Danville to get their belongings and move to Little Rock.

On a very cold, rainy day, with no prior notice, I received a telephone call, again at my office, and it was Mother and Dad. "We're here, Sister," my mother said.

"You're here?" I echoed, "Is the moving van here?"

"They wanted too much money," Mother said. "We moved ourselves."

And they had—with all of the possessions they had elected to keep piled on their car and a trailer attached. I rearranged my schedule and joined them at their new home, only to find that none of the previous owner's furniture had been moved out. It was very fine furniture, and I was desperately trying to stack it out of the rain in the adjoining carport, covering it as best I could to keep it dry.

The house had been vacant for some time, and it badly needed cleaning. I first purchased mops, brooms, and cleaning supplies, then picked up the woman who cleaned my office and took her and everything to Ohio Street, stopping first to buy some hamburgers and a gallon of milk, for it was long past noon by this time. Needless to say, whatever I had scheduled at my office for that day had to be rescheduled.

John just shook his head when I called him and reported the latest development. Presbyterian Village had to be forgotten.

34

Two and a half weeks later, there was a real catastrophe, an event that changed our lives forever.

It was Halloween 1973—one of those gorgeous fall days with brilliant sunshine lighting up the bright red and gold leaves. I left my office about the time everyone else in downtown did and found myself in a stream of traffic, going west toward my Markham Street home. As I approached St. Vincent's Infirmary, I found a police car stopping the cars in my lane to make way for a screaming, redlight-flashing ambulance to turn into the hospital's emergency room entrance, and in an incredibly short time I learned that the patient in that ambulance was my son—Everett.

When I reached home and entered the kitchen, whose windows face the busy street, I hurried to answer an insistent telephone.

It was Susan Dixon, the wife of my attorney friend Phillip Dixon and the mother of Everett's best friend, Phillip, Jr. Her message left me strangely numb. "Ginger," she said, "there's been an accident. Everett is in St. Vincent's."

I don't remember thanking her. I think I dropped the telephone. I know I ran to the car and reached St. Vincent's Infirmary, only a few blocks away, in record time.

Everett was in a hospital bed, lying on his back, eyes wide open and completely rational. He felt no pain. That was because he could feel nothing. He was paralyzed from the neck down. It was obvious that his back was broken.

Duke arrived from his job across the street at Montgomery Ward's, and Doctor Wardlaw, Everett's orthodontist, was there, cutting out the braces he had installed on Everett's teeth. Preacher Dick and other parishioners from my church appeared. I was totally numb.

At that time, Ham was still employed by the federal government, working out of town, and I thought that he should be notified. I got him on the telephone and began, "Ham, there has been an accident. Everett is in St. Vincent's Infirmary!"

"You and that goddamn motorcycle!" he shouted, and I collapsed. Preacher Dick, who was standing at my side and heard what was said, put his arms around me, and unlike a man of cloth, said angrily, "Tell him to go to hell! You don't need that!" And he hung up the telephone. I have always been grateful to Preacher Dick.

* * *

The ensuing days, weeks, and months are a busy blur of pain, despair, hope, prayer, fear, regret, and a million other emotions. The lady who hit Ev was brought by her husband to my home the night of the accident, a total basket case. "I didn't mean to hurt him," she moaned over and over, and I found myself trying to comfort her!

"Of course you didn't," I agreed. The four of us, she and her husband and Duke and me, had coffee and shared our misery.

A bevy of doctors at St. Vincent's examined Everett. Some thought they should operate immediately; others thought they should wait until the swelling went down. They asked me what I chose to do, and I have never felt more incompetent and helpless. I had no idea, but I had been told by some of my fellow lawyers who had handled serious injury lawsuits that Dr. Tom Fletcher was the best surgeon in the state. He advocated waiting for the swelling to go down, and that's what we did.

Meanwhile, Everett was on a circle bed, in an effort to prevent bedsores and other complications.

* * *

Of course I had to check on my parents daily, as they had no transportation. My father could not hear nor see and had been stopped several times by the police when driving. One of them who knew me from my prosecuting attorney days said, "Miss Ginger, we thought we had a drunk. He was all over the road."

My brother called him and told him that he thought that he should not continue to drive. Daddy thanked him, hung up the phone, and continued to drive. How we finally got him to give up the car was to tell him that we would save it for Ev to drive—that Everett would need a car—and that was good enough for Daddy. His grandson was the light of his life.

When I would go by the folks' house, they were eager to hear how Everett was. I remember once telling them that Ev had had a collection of fluid in his chest that had to be drained off, and immediately Daddy began to cry. "You're gonna lose him, Sister. He's hurt too bad. He ain't gonna make it!" I quickly and silently left. After that I avoided giving them any information about Ev's condition.

The operation was scheduled. The doctor told me, "Bring everyone home who is interested in him."

"Why?" I asked, and he minced no words.

"Surely you know he may not make it," he said. I heard the words, but somehow they didn't soak in.

I sat with Ev a long time that night before the operation. We watched a movie, *Patton*, together and also watched the fish in an aquarium that a friend of mine had given him. An aquarium is an amazing gift for somebody who cannot move around.

When I left Ev's room, I ran into the Catholic priest who was making his nightly rounds. Impulsively, I spoke to him. "Father," I said, "my son is scheduled for surgery early in the morning. I wonder if you could say a few words for him?"

"Yes, of course," he replied and followed me into Everett's room. Everett was wide eyed. He had not expected to see me, let alone a priest.

"I understand you are having surgery in the morning," he said to Ev. "Let's say a prayer, shall we?" Ev bowed his head, as did I, and the priest's short, but sincere supplication comforted me. I left the room again, along with the priest, and many years later Everett told me that during that prayer he felt hot from head to toe, and was never afraid again from that time on.

I know that he was calm the following morning when I went to St. Vincent's very early on a beautiful fall day. "Mama," he said, "I don't think anything is going to happen, but if I don't make it …"

"Hush!" I interrupted. "I'm not going to listen to this!"

But he overruled me. "Mama! I have heard you tell your clients over and over, 'Get your house in order!' If I don't make it, I want Butch to get my camera, Phil to get my …," and one by one he named each of his friends and the treasured possessions he wanted each to have.

"Okay," I said, but that didn't satisfy him.

"Repeat it, Mom," he demanded, and I did, winding up just as the attendants arrived to transport him to the operating room. As they rolled him out, Everett raised both hands and extended his thumbs up as he disappeared down the hall.

A group of my friends from church came to sit with me. I had refused a doctor's offer "to take the edge off." I wanted all my facilities; I didn't want to miss anything.

Ham stuck his head in the room, asked how long it was going to take, then left the building, and did not return. Wild horses could not have moved me from the waiting room. I had sent money to Gretel in Colorado for her to come home to be with Everett, but her husband suffered an injury moving a mobile home, and they had to use the money to get treatment for him. Also, I apparently did not send enough—something I did often, not realizing how expensive things had become and how limited her assets were.

* * *

The operation lasted 13 hours. It was the longest operation that St. Vincent had ever had at that time. Two doctors, Dr. Steele and Dr. Fletcher, and an anesthesiologist, Dr Pollard, didn't have a dry thread on their bodies when they came out of surgery to report to me.

Dr. Fletcher explained that he had placed a "Harrington" pin in Everett's back. I asked him if that would stay in his back forever, and his reply was "It can," an answer I didn't like. It also might not. And of course, it didn't. It was removed many years later after Everett had gone to Washington, D.C., to work for President Bill Clinton.

Everett had been taken to Intensive Care, and Dr. Fletcher told me that I could go in, but he warned me that Everett probably would not know me. "And I'm sorry, Ms. Atkinson, but he will never walk. There's not enough left of his back to support his weight."

With that I walked alone into Intensive Care.

When I saw Everett, it took all my will power not to scream. His face was so swollen and spotted from lying face down for 13 hours that I barely recognized him. But as I leaned over him, he opened his eyes and said, "Mama, Butch doesn't get my camera yet!" And I burst into laughter, interspersed with tears. Thank you, God; Thank You, Thank You, Thank You! Is all I could say to myself. Everett was alive, but he was injured so severely that recovery was going to be a long, long haul.

* * *

When he was dismissed from Intensive Care, Everett was assigned to a room on the top floor of St. Vincent's, and his friends were allowed to visit until quite late. Everett was on a circle bed, which was regularly turned, first on back with face up, then face down. I came in one afternoon to visit, and Everett was face down, with the mattress still on his back, and the young black nurse was apologizing. "I couldn't undo it," she apologized, and Everett said not to worry about it because it wouldn't be long and he'd be O.K. "He's so sweet," she said.

Another evening I went to visit, and when I opened the door, there were wet towels all over the room, and Everett and the nurse were laughing as she picked them up. "I came in with a wet towel and woke him up," she said, "and he threw it at me! Well, I figured if throwing one made him feel better, maybe throwing a lot would make him feel really good!" So she had gone back and got a handful of wet rags, given them to him, and ducked as he chunked them at her. I marveled at the patience and understanding of that young woman. She could have handled that situation much differently and yelled at him for throwing a towel at her when she was doing her assigned duty, even though it required waking him up. I appreciate her and all the others who patiently did what they could to help Everett pass the seemingly endless hours, not to mention alleviating the pain as much as possible.

Early on, Everett discovered that daytime television had little to offer, and he complained about it to me. I understood, but that room at St. Vincent's was his only destination, and would be for many months.

"Ev," I said, "Look around this area and see if you can find something to do, because we can't change the location right now."

The next day or two when I came in, I found him learning to play chess. One of his therapists was a fine chess player and participated in competition events. It was a godsend. Everett never tired of playing chess and became an excellent player, which didn't surprise me, considering his intelligence and the many hours he had to play.

I continued taking breakfasts to him from the International House of Pancakes restaurant across from St. Vincent's, then going to the hospital at noon and back in the evenings, unless he had company. The hospital allowed as many guests as he, or they, wanted. I remember Everett's being disappointed in some of his friends, because they would use visiting him as a gimmick to stay out at night. They would tell their parents they were going to visit Everett in the hospital, then go wherever they wanted, instead.

It was getting close to Christmas, and since he had been unable to work, Everett had no money to spend, either for himself, his family, or his friends. Ham was behind several months on child support. I took the amount he was behind to Everett and told him that if his father paid the arrearage, I would put it in an account that he could write checks on to buy gifts for people he wanted to give gifts to. I thought Ham would be more likely to pay it to Everett than to me. Sometime after that, I went to visit Everett and found him face down. I greeted him, and he gestured toward his dresser. There I saw a check for the entire arrearage.

"Good!" I said. "He paid it!"

Everett nodded, and then said, "But he tried to give me stock in a new enterprise that he and Tommy Russell are entering into. I told him I didn't think I needed stock at this time, and he wrote that check. He also said he didn't think he owed that much, but I showed him your figures."

I brought a copy of the newspaper that had several pages of gifts available at the various stores to help Ev choose items if he needed to. The gift he chose for his father was a very inexpensive shaving item, which tickled me. After he made decisions about various friends, both boys and girls, I bought them, had them wrapped, and took them to him to be given to his friends when they visited.

I also got a beautiful small, living Christmas tree and carried it to his room, thinking he would enjoy the smell and the trimmings. Suddenly over the loudspeaker I heard, "Would the lady who brought the Christmas tree in please remove it from the building?" So much for that. I should have known it would be a fire hazard. Of course I took it home and brought an artificial tree for Ev's room.

* * *

I also did something else. Ev had pictures of "240 Z's" tacked up all over his room at home, and they meant nothing to me. I had no idea about the vehicle—only that I had seen pictures of it tacked up on the walls of his room. I took one of the pictures and went to the dealership. I don't remember if I used some of the money Everett had received from an earlier accident he suffered when a young man hit the car Gretel was using to take Everett to school or if I borrowed the money, but I purchased a 240 Z, and on Christmas Day, we parked it on the hospital lot. The parking deck had not been built at that time, and cars were parked on the yard. I remember that Duke moved the vehicle two or three times, for it had to be visible from Everett's bed. He could not walk to the window to view it.

We had a good visit at Christmas. Ev gave me my gift first, and it truly was beautiful. He knew the shop downtown that I frequented: Ms. Jack Fines, and he had called the lady who often waited on me, asking her to select a gift for me, and she outdid herself. It was a slack suit with a leather jacket. I still have it hanging in my closet, as anyone who knows me would expect!

When all of the gifts had been distributed, I handed Everett the key to the new 240 Z and pointed out the window where it was clearly visible, having been moved several times to be sure he could see it from his bed.

"We're going to drive it," I said. "You and I."

It was close to two years before Everett could drive his 240 Z. After he was released from the hospital, he would sit in it, and often he would summon me from the kitchen, and I could see him sitting in the car. I remember his calling me: "Mama," he would call. "Come take my shoes off. Maybe with my shoes off I could lift my feet," and I would oblige, untying his number 12's the way I did his little blue shoes so long ago. But taking off his shoes did not do the trick, and I remember him stumbling past me on his crutches, sobbing in pain and frustration.

Duke and I took photos of his learning to walk, because I thought we would have to file a lawsuit to recover damages for Everett. Of course, we knew no amount of money would be adequate, but he certainly deserved some kind of compensation, and his expenses were enormous. I had insurance for him, and so did Duke, at least he did while he was a member of the State Police. I was proud of Everett's efforts to walk. I had never witnessed the process before. Everett would stand on a moving platform, with a rope around his waist, and a very strong man would pull him forward, slowly one foot in front of the other.

* * *

During Everett's long stay in the hospital, I had a dear friend—actually a former client—who was a devout Christian Scientist. She called me daily, checking on Everett and, of course, me. She was a remarkable woman in many ways, living alone miles out of the city, taking in numerous dogs who had been abandoned. She knew more scripture than I had ever known, and I truly enjoyed hearing from her, for she was never upset or perturbed. God was in His heaven, and all was, or would be, right with the world. And when she spoke in her soft, comforting manner, I believed it.

She would say, based apparently on her vast knowledge of Christian Science and her faith, "God sees Everett as being perfect! He's going to be all right." And little by little, Everett was improving. I cannot tell you how much she helped me, and how I looked forward to her calls.

35

While Everett was in the hospital, I got a call from my mother and father one evening wanting me to come over to discuss some "business." I went after I got home from work and visiting Ev to see what was going on. My father handed me a written letter that he had sent to my brother in answer to a letter from John.

When my parents bought the house on Ohio Street, there was a mortgage on it that they had assumed, and it was necessary for Daddy to write a check every month. Daddy had never made payments, and I remember that I had fixed 12 envelopes for him to write the amount of the mortgage and mail it each month. It seems that Dad had complained to John about the process and was going to pay off the mortgage, and John had asked if he, John, could assume and pay the mortgage, as it carried a very low interest, in contrast to the loans that John was having to pay for his two daughters' college education. It seems that Daddy and Mother decided that I should assume and pay the mortgage, as I needed the money worse than John, particularly since Everett's injury. "Mother and I want you to have it," Daddy said.

I really didn't know what to say. I was afraid my brother would think that I had intervened, but Daddy was quick to assure me. "No," he said, "John knows that this is mine and Mama's idea," he said. We want you to have the money and let you assume the debt. You may need it for Everett."

I thanked them and told them I would let them know after I talked to Duke.

Duke's response surprised me, although in retrospect, I should have known. "Why don't I assume it, Ginger?" he said. "That's a very low interest rate. I could pay that without any problem. And we could pay off both our cars."

Thank Heaven for a law degree. "Well, Duke," I said, "that would be fine, but don't you think you'd better have some insurance? That debt is over $10,000, and if something happened to you—you lost your job or got sick or something—you'd need to have insurance so the folks wouldn't end up losing their home."

Duke agreed to get insurance, largely because I think he knew I wasn't going to do it otherwise. He called and made an appointment with a doctor, the insurance company having required an examination, but before he had met with the doctor, I inadvertently discovered that he was at the theatre with a young woman with whom he worked at Montgomery Ward's. I had gone to the warehouse to see him after he had told me that he had to go there to check out a batch of stolen tires. When I got to the warehouse, it was dark as pitch. I thought I had missed him and he would be on the way home. Imagine my surprise when I had stopped at a red light and just happened to look across the street and saw Duke and a young woman coming out of the theatre and walking toward a nearby restaurant.

I was in shock. I said nothing about it at the time, but I continued to check, and I found his car at her home the following night.

Then Ev told me that all of his friends had seen them together at the drag races in Benton, but had been reluctant to tell me. All that time, I thought he was working late.

It got worse. The next morning I received a call from a small mobile home company, telling me that I needed to sign something. Bewildered, I asked their address and drove rapidly there. It was unbelievable what had transpired. Duke and his paramour had purchased a mobile home, using my name, for heaven's sake, she pretending to be me. The salesman was apologetic, for my proof was clearly correct. "We will pull it today, Ms. Atkinson," he said. And they did.

The amazing thing was Duke's reaction. He called me, crying. "Ginger," he moaned, "what are you doing to me?"

What was I doing to HIM? It was almost ludicrous. He and the young woman—I can't even remember her name—left Little Rock and went to his sister's home in Oklahoma. I think he sold all his guns for enough money to get them there. He had a fabulous collection of guns, most of which he acquired when he made arrests and did not turn them in or restore them to their owners. When I first married him, I found a wonderful old cabinet in which his father had stored hay, and I spent a fortune having it refinished and lined with red silk and turned into a gun cabinet. When I think of all the years it was in our home with young people coming and going, and all the guns loaded to the nth degree, I shudder.

* * *

Meanwhile, Everett, who had been schooled in the hospital his junior year, walked on crutches to graduate with his class at Hall High. Ironically, the only other student graduating on crutches was the son of the woman who hit Everett.

The lawyer who represented her brought me a copy of her insurance policy and displayed it to me. It was for $100,000. "That's all she has, Ginger," he said. "And of course we will pay that to you for him."

I began to cry. "When we pay the doctor bills, there won't be anything for Everett," I sobbed.

"What bills?" he asked. "I'm not on notice of any bills."

I couldn't believe my ears. He was going to allow the settlement right then and there, and I accepted. As I said before, both Duke and I had insurance, and the doctors received some compensation, but I am sure it was only a pittance of the bill we owed, of that I am sure.

We went to the courthouse with the proposed settlement, and Judge Jernigan asked about the "boy's father."

"I have custody your honor," I told him.

"Well, I still think he should be notified," said Judge Jernigan.

We left the judge's chambers to discuss this development, and the other attorney said, "Miss Ginger, Judge Warren Wood is downstairs. Let's talk to him." And that's what we did.

Judge Wood examined the documents, and then said to Everett: "Son, if you sign this document, you will have accepted this settlement, and you can never receive anything else. Do you understand that?"

"Sir," my son said, balancing himself on his crutches. "My mother thinks this is the thing to do. Please show me where to sign."

He signed, and we left the courtroom.

Structural settlements were not common at that time—or if they were I didn't know about them. I was obsessed with trying to be sure Everett would have some compensation, and I had talked with every leading attorney in the city. I finally met with Sid McMath, who recommended that I set up a trust for Everett, and that's what I did. Everett could not get his money until he was 21 years old, but he was entitled to a certain amount on a regular basis. If he wanted something, he had to make the decision that he wanted it badly enough to use "his money," the money he received. He was very careful with his money, and years later said to me, "Mama, you don't know how smart you were."

I replied "Yes, I think I do." At that age, and with no experience, he thought $100,000 was all the money in the world! It would last forever!

I was so grateful and proud of the way Everett worked to be able to walk again. He went from crutches to a cane, and often said to me, "Mama, just to be able to swing my feet off the side of the bed and stand up! You can't imagine how great that is. Everybody should have a little bit of back trouble—not as bad as mine, but enough that they would know how to appreciate their backs!"

36

On June 26, 1974, my faithful father died. On his birthday that year—June 20—I had given him an electric toothbrush, which he was never able to use.

He and Mother had redone the backyard of the Ohio Street house, taking out the many beautiful flowers and creating a vegetable garden. They knew exactly when to plant everything—the dark of the moon, and so on. How I wish I had learned all their methods, for witchcraft or scientific performance, it worked. They had potatoes, roasting ears, okra, green beans—you name it, and there was not one weed to be found.

One morning in June—only six days after his birthday, Mother called me and said he had a stomach ache and "I think he needs to see a doctor. Can you pick us up?"

I was at the office, and my car was in the shop. I called a friend and asked if she could take me to get my father, and she said, "Of course," so we took the folks to the Baptist Hospital emergency room. It wasn't long before they got him a room and my car was ready, so my friend took me to pick it up. I thanked her and went back to the hospital to get Mother, for she had been up for hours.

The doctors were examining Daddy, and I told Mother that I thought she should let me take her home to rest awhile, and if anything went wrong I would come and get her. She was reluctant, but got in the car, and I took her to her house. When we opened the door, the phone was ringing. It was the hospital; Daddy had taken a turn for the worse. Of course we got there as fast as we could.

Daddy was on a heart monitor that was beeping away, and a nurse said to me, "Talk to him. We don't know if he is conscious or not."

I leaned over and said, "Pawpaw—you can't leave right now; we have to grabble the potatoes." And without opening his eyes, he said, "Not until the vines die, Sister." And the monitor stopped.

He was rational to the end. Ninety-one years old!

* * *

We decided to have his funeral in the wonderful "Shed," as he called it, that he had built at the Scott family graveyard at the foot of Blue Mountain Dam, for he had never joined any of the baptist churches that Mother had joined everywhere she went. Little Rock was no exception. Mother joined the First Baptist Church, and the children and I continued to be Presbyterians. Although Mother was disappointed, she never complained or talked about it. When she and Daddy moved to Little Rock, I told her that I did not want to go back to the baptist church. I even took her to Westover Hills, thinking she might like to go to the church the children and I attended, but she was never comfortable anywhere but at a baptist church. I took her to hear one of Preacher Dick's sermons, thinking that she might understand that there was not a lot of difference between the two churches, but that Sunday, he happened to mention "the universal catholic faith," and on the way home, she said, "He's for them old Catholics!" and I never mentioned her going with us again. On special days, I went to her church, and I'm sure she was disappointed that we did not go back with her, but that was one thing that I remained adamant about: we did not go back to the baptist church.

Of course John and his family and many of Mother and Daddy's friends attended Daddy's funeral, and Everett walked with the pallbearers with his hand on the casket, but he could not physically help carry it, something that broke his heart. He remembers everything that his grandparents said or did during the many hours they cared for him when I was so busy being a sole practitioner.

Mother's long-ago desire to "outlive your father" materialized, but only for a relatively short time. I was determined that she should be happy and do many things that she had not been able to do. The first thing we did was cut her hair and get a permanent. She had worn her hair in a bun during her entire marriage, and she loved her new hairstyle. But the thing she enjoyed most was wearing slacks. My father had never allowed her to wear "pants." I remember trying to convince him that wearing pants when I was pedaling my bicycle was much more modest, but Daddy remained adamant. Mother loved her new attire, particularly in the wintertime, and had a wonderful time shopping for her new wardrobe.

I think she was relatively happy during the last three years of her life. Her neighbors were wonderful, particularly the Rosells, and she enjoyed living directly across from the Anthony School, where she could watch the children constantly through her picture window. Her garden was also her pride and joy, and she supplied all her neighbors' vegetables. She never failed to call me and tell me that she had "supper ready," when many times I had just had a late lunch, as I had been in court most of the day. I never failed to go by and eat with her or take food home, although many times I passed it on to other friends.

* * *

My accountant brother John managed our parents' money and, after our father's death, Mother's finances, and did a wonderful job of it. He arranged their investments and the income from them in a manner that gave them a steady income each month. It was John who managed to persuade my father to accept his social security, something he never felt right about. "I didn't earn it," he used to say, "and my taking it will make it hard on John and his generation; it will use up money they earned." At John's continued urging, he finally signed up for it, but he always referred to it as his "rocking chair money," and he was never sure that he was entitled to it.

Mother wanted a fence around her vegetable garden and must have contacted John to give her the money to get one, for one day my brother called me and said, "Virginia, Mama doesn't need a fence round that garden."

I talked to Mother and surveyed the backyard where the fence was to be installed. Then I called John. "John," I said, "Mother wants a fence. Send her the money." Of course he did, and the fence was installed. I know of nothing that gave Mother more satisfaction. She opened and closed that fence gate a dozen times a day, happily sliding it open and shut, as she went about gathering the produce that she mostly gave away to me and her neighbors. She loved the house on Ohio Street, and from her experience with the real estate business, she knew she had made a good purchase. She used to survey her property with great pride and boast about how much it could be sold for. She never would have believed it brought as much as it did.

* * *

One Sunday, after church, Mother complained that her "chest hurt," and I made an appointment with her doctor, who specialized in geriatric medicine, and made arrangements for Everett to take her to the appointment. I was working away in my office that afternoon when Everett called me. "Mama," he said, "can you pick up Mam-Maw? They want to keep her overnight and do some tests, and I have a date."

"Overnight?" I said, wondering what had transpired, but of course I said I would go get the things she needed for overnight in the hospital and then go to the hospital so he could go on his date.

When I got there, Mother was restless and wanted to go home. I told her we'd talk about it in the morning, that the doctor wanted her for awhile. When he came in, he took me to the examining area and showed me her x-rays. "Here's her chest the last time we x-rayed it, and here it is now," he said, holding up the x-rays, and I could not believe it. One side of her lungs was gone! "We are going to test it, of course, but it doesn't look good."

It wasn't. It was cancerous, and the doctor recommended that we take no action. I called my brother, and he flew in, although we told Mother that he was on a trip to Memphis, where he went often, and had just run by to see her. Both John and I disagreed with the doctor on everything. First, he thought she should be told that she had cancer. John and I both said "NO" instantly and together. I knew my mother. She would have been scared to death and would have given up completely. Also I wanted her to have whatever treatment was available, and so did John.

"Don't tell her she has cancer," I told the doctor, and my brother agreed. "I think she deserves to know," he argued, and I disagreed. "Why?" I asked. "She's already a Christian. She's been baptized. She doesn't have to repent or anything. Her estate is in order—don't you tell her anything. It would scare her to death and hinder her possible recovery." And finally I said, "We are paying your bill and we do NOT want her to know."

So far as I know she did not find out about her having cancer. She was given massive doses of medication and finally was told that she could leave the hospital, but that she could not live alone. Before she was discharged, John and I made the rounds of nursing homes, and it might have been because we went just at dinner time, but I saw many elderly people tied to their chairs, helplessly waiting to be fed. We left, and I said, "Johnny, I'm not putting our mother in one of those places."

"Well, Honey," he said, "you can't run a nursing home and a law office."

"I'll have to try," I said, then told him good-bye before he had to go back to work.

I went to a temporary hearing the next morning on behalf of a client who had sued for divorce and was asking use and possession of the marital home. It was a short marriage, the second for both, and the husband had already found a place to live, thinking the court would grant her request. As it happened, Judge Bullion, who was, in my opinion, a very difficult judge, suddenly, after hearing the proof, said, "I'm not putting this sick man out of his home! Denied," and we left the courtroom. My client was devastated. She had leased her home when she married this man and had nowhere to go. Her daughter had a very small house, a husband, and four children; they had no room for her.

I was giving my client a ride back to her car, and it suddenly occurred to me that she could live with my mother at the house on Ohio Street. Why not? "You probably will think I've lost my mind," I said to her, "But my brother and I have just learned that our mother can't live alone, and she has a wonderful house on Ohio that has three bedrooms and a bath and a half. If you will move in and take care of her, I will pay you $50 a month and give you free room and aboard." She jumped at the prospect. She had been a chef at a country club, and the last days of my mother's life were wonderful. My client made magnificent meals, particularly at Thanksgiving, and had her children and mine, at least Everett, to it, and Mother continued her gardening, part of the time on her walker.

* * *

In those days the graveyards all had Decoration Day, and we never failed to travel to the Scott family graveyard for that event, which included picnic lunches and gospel singing. Mother looked forward to that event every year. I am convinced that had she known that she had inoperable cancer, she would have given up and made no effort to do anything.

When my father died and Mother was left alone, I took Honey, the cocker spaniel that I had bought for the children, and left her with my mother, just for company. It was love at first sight, for both. My mother had always wanted a dog, but my father would not agree for her to have one. Mother enjoyed the little dog so much, and her last instruction to me dealt with Honey. "I want her took care of," she said, and I assured her that she would be.

Mother was hospitalized for a short time, and I went every day as soon as I could leave my office. It was one of the most difficult times I have ever experienced, and I was never able to get in touch with my brother when I really wanted someone else to hear what was going on. My mother's eyes were closed, and she gave no signs of recognizing I was at her bedside. But she was not quiet. She called her deceased brother's name over and over, making me wonder if she were seeing him. He had died with Bright's disease before I was born, but I remember my mother grieving for him, so apparently they were very close as children. I wanted to discuss it with John, but I could never catch him at home when Mother was calling her brother.

Every once in awhile, Mother would suddenly open her eyes and smile at the sight of me, but her recognition was fleeting and she said nothing. On June 28, 1977, while I was sitting at her beside, she slipped quietly away. The transformation was startling. In death she was beautiful.

My wonderful client and friend, her caretaker, rode in the family car for Mother's interment in the Scott family graveyard at the foot of Blue Mountain Dam, next to her husband of so many, many years. And of course there is a beautiful headstone that my mother purchased for them after she had informed "John Henry" that if she outlived him, which she did, she did NOT intend to use the homemade markers he had designed for them both.

Everett took Honey home with him, to the house on Markham Street, where she was loved and petted. But she missed my mother and went hunting for her one day. While trying to get to 7717 Ohio, she was hit by a car. She didn't know Mother was no longer there.

* * *

Mother was correct in her conclusion that she and Daddy had made a good deal when they bought the Ohio Street property. Mother used to brag about the house and say to me, "I'll bet you could get $50,000 for it!" A staggering amount of money for Mother. Well, as it happened, I got a great deal more than that, and I really didn't want to sell it, because I was getting a substantial amount of rent for it. But the Anthony School was expanding and buying up all the property on the street. Mine would have been the only one standing, so I sold it, as everyone else on that street did, and my parents' last home was torn down.

37

From time to time I have recited experiences I have had as an attorney for well in excess of 40 years, but my story would not be complete if I omitted the unbelievable case that all of us who were working for the prosecuting attorney at the time experienced. We saw and prosecuted a living, breathing necrophile. In case you don't know what a necrophile, or a necrophiliac, is, that is an individual who is sexually attracted to corpses.

Believe it or not, it has apparently always existed, for Herodotus writes in *Histories* that, to discourage intercourse with a corpse, ancient Egyptians left deceased beautiful women to decay for "three or four days" before giving them to the embalmers. This practice originated from the need to discourage the men performing the funerary customs from having sexual interest in their charges.

While I was serving as deputy prosecuting attorney, there was a series of grave robberies in a cemetery in Jacksonville. All of the graves were those of beautiful young women. The culprit was parking his car up to a new grave, putting a rope around the tombstone, pulling the casket out, and stealing the corpse.

I don't know how the mystery of what was going on was solved, but I do know that the individual who was engaged in this bizarre activity was a member of the United States Air Force stationed at the Little Rock Air Force Base, a married man with two children. All of this occurred while his wife was gone to visit her parents in another state, and when he was arrested and they were informed, they refused to believe it, maintaining that he was a good husband and father!

He was also a necrophile. The proof was unmistakable. The police raided his residence, found a corpse being warmed up in his bathtub, obviously to enable him to have sexual intercourse with the dead woman. His mouth was eaten away from formaldehyde. When he was brought to the prosecuting attorney's office, he admitted everything, but only after he had requested that I, the only female present, leave the room.

I was happy to do so!

Researches in 1958 and 1989 commented that, although rarely described, necrophilia fantasies may occur more often than is generally supposed. The authors reported that, of their sample of necrophiliacs, 68% were motivated by a desire for an unresisting and unrejecting partner, 21% by a want for reunion with a lost partner, 15% by sexual attraction to dead people, 15% by a desire for comfort to overcome feelings of isolation, and 11% by a desire to remedy low self-esteem by expressing power over a corpse.

Minor modern researches conducted in England have shown that some necrophiles tend to choose a dead mate after failing to create romantic attachments with the living.

As of May 2006, there is no federal legislation specifically barring sex with a corpse, but many states, including Arkansas, have laws against it. In Arkansas, it is a Class D Felony.

I have heard nothing more about the "wonderful husband and father" that I witnessed brought into the office that day, except that he admitted everything to the "boys" after I left the room. I hope the reports of Klaf and Brown in 1958 are not correct, namely that necrophilic fantasies may occur more often than supposed. Surely there are only an isolated number of people who are that sick. In my 40 years of practice, I saw only one, which was quite enough for me!

* * *

Gretel and Gary moved back to Arkansas in 1975 and lived in the "Goose House." That's what we called a little house at 14 Del Rose in Little Rock that I had taken in as a fee, comparing it to Mother and Dad's first home in Harkey's Valley—called The Goose House because geese nested in it before they fixed it up and moved in. Gretel's house was really a nice little place, with a wonderful backyard, and Gretel redecorated it in a very unusual and attractive manner. I remember that she had a big Thanksgiving dinner that year for a group of friends and her and her husband's parents. I remember that there were people seated in every room of the little house, and I chose to sit in the back bedroom, quite far away from Gretel's father who she had also invited.

Gary got a job as the manager of a pizza place, and Gretel worked as a waitress, making sure that the customers were properly serviced and happily pocketing the tips. I remember her asking a patron who was about to leave if everything had been all right. She was asking the question because he had overlooked leaving a gratuity. Once she questioned him, he quickly left some change on the table.

In the meantime, I had looked at a wonderful, unfinished house on Southridge Road in Walton Heights overlooking the beautiful Arkansas River. The upper story was finished, but the downstairs was not, and it was listed at a bargain. It was furnished with a heavy Mexican dining room, a wonderful kitchen that opened up on a huge deck with a magnificent view, and a beautiful bedroom with adjoining tub and shower. I was hearing regularly from Duke and felt as though he was asking to come back, and if so, he could finish the house. I purchased it and moved from the Markham Street house, and Gretel and Gary moved in.

Gary had promised to help me hang pictures at the Southridge house, so when I got home, I called to see if he was coming that evening. I got more or less excited call from Everett. "Mama," he said, "Gretel was bathing the girls and all of a sudden, she left them in the tub, got in her car, and left. What shall I do?"

"Everett," I said, "Take the children out of the bathtub."

He did. There was no use looking for Gretel. We had no idea where to start.

Late that night, there was a knock at my door. I knew who it was, but nevertheless I checked by looking from my second story window to be sure. Gretel was at the door.

I opened it, let her in, and asked if she were hungry. She said "Yes," and I fixed her a bowl of soup and put her to bed.

Then I called Gary, who was at Everett's. I told him that I was worried about Gretel. The day before I had gone by the Markham Street house on my way to the office, and I found Gretel sitting on the bed with a mountain of clean clothes which she was silently and methodically folding.

"Gret-Gret, Honey, you can't do all of this." I told her.

And almost unconsciously, she replied, "I have to." And kept folding.

"Gary," I told him. "We have to get some help for Gretel. If you don't, I'm going to see if I can."

That evening, Gary called me. "Mimi, can we come see you?" And of course I said yes.

They came. I had made coffee and some snacks. After they had been there for a little while Gary said, "Mimi, Gretel's ready to go rest for awhile."

"Oh, Mama, could I," she asked. "I waited till I got home, Mama."

"Of course you can, Darling," I told her. The next day I bought her a new outfit to wear, and we went to the hospital.

I have forgotten how long she stayed, but she was simply exhausted, according to her doctor. After she was released, they moved to Fort Smith, Arkansas.

* * *

Gretel took some classes and worked part-time, but she hated Fort Smith, and I don't think she was particularly happy with Gary.

One day, she called me on the telephone and said, "Mama! I'm sending you $100!" they had borrowed some money, but not much, and nobody had asked for it to be repaid.

"Well, thank you, Sweetheart," I said, "but what's the occasion?"

"Gary sent his mother $100!" she stormed.

"Well, do you all owe them some money?" I asked.

"Ye, ma'am," she replied, "but his mother doesn't even work! And I said we needed to send you some money, that we owed you too, and he said you didn't need it!"

"Well, thank you, Gretel," I told her, being proud of her principles. And when the $100 arrived, I opened a checking account in a Fort Smith bank in her name. Every payment that they made to me went into that account.

When she had decided to leave, she called me. "Mama," she said, "I'm going to leave, and I am afraid my tires won't make it. I don't have any money."

"You have a little bit," I told her and sent her the Fort Smith bank account. It wasn't a lot of money, but I think it was enough to get her home. I put her and Liberty in the spare bedroom at Markham Street, and she, Liberty, Everett, and I had a wonderful time. The living room was full of everybody's furniture. I was afraid to get rid of it, afraid somebody would need it. So we just stacked it up, and each of us had our private bedroom, getting together when invited to do so.

I remember a wonderful football game, which Arkansas was supposed to lose. It seems that Lou Holtz, the coach, had ruled the best players were not eligible to play because of his "Do Right" rule, and Everett was furious.

We won! It was hysterical, the way Everett would shout out of his bedroom, then Gretel, then me—all cheering, or booing, or screaming! I think it was against Oklahoma ... but we won!

* * *

I had decided to sell the Southridge house and build what I had always wanted to build: a house overlooking the Arkansas River. Meantime, we were looking for property for Gretel to live in, as we both knew we didn't want to continue living together indefinitely. A friend of mine, Sue Ann Stephens, who sold real estate showed me a wonderful duplex on Kavanaugh in the Heights, and Gretel and I bought it. She and Liberty lived in one side, and we rented the other side, which helped. In fact, I seem to remember that I took it over because I needed the tax deduction, and Gretel, who had gone back to nursing school, did not. I put an extra bath in on Gretel's side, and a dishwasher. Gretel hated the location of the second bath, which admittedly was not the best since it was right off the living room. But that was the only spot that was available for another bath, and I knew they needed two bathrooms.

It was a wonderful location. Liberty could walk to school, and Gretel got a job as a hostess at That Little Restaurant. It was there that Allen Branton, with whom she had attended high school, met her again when he and a group of his friends had gone there for dinner. One of his friends said later, "I saw Allen lose it!"

Not long after that first encounter, Gretel called to see if I could take care of Liberty, which I certainly could and loved doing. "Allen has invited me to Chicago to see Diana Ross," whom he represented as a lighting designer.

38

I wish I could say that when Duke took his young paramour to his sister's home in Oklahoma we had heard the last of him, but we hadn't. He called me at least once a week crying and telling me what a terrible mistake he had made, that he still loved me and asking me if he could come home. Of course I should have told him not only NO but *Hell* No, but I didn't. I let him come home, and he appeared, long hair and all, ostensibly thrilled to be home, and certainly giving me the honeymoon treatment. The maid who had worked for us before all the problems started was working the first morning after he came home, and she was excited to see him back. "Oh, Mr. Duke," she gushed, "It's so good to have you back!"

"It's so good to be back!" he replied.

That day, he had his hair cut short again and picked me up for lunch. It certainly looked like everything was the same.

Meanwhile, Everett was planning to take a trip around the world on a Windjammer, something he had always wanted to do. I thought it would be therapeutic for him, as well as educational. I knew that Everett was going to have to live with his broken back, and I was turning loose of him, something that was going to be difficult for me to do. We used some of the money from his settlement, and he had arranged to earn some money as a navigator on board ship, but he was getting rid of things he didn't need and trying to accumulate money for the trip.

One night, he came into our bedroom where Duke and I were watching television and showed me an insurance policy that his father had given him. "Mama," he said, "Dad said he wasn't going to pay the premiums on this policy anymore now that I'm 18. It isn't worth very much, but I think I'll cash it in. What do you think?" I didn't look at the policy—a grave mistake—but remember saying, "Well Ev, I guess you can do what you want to with it; it's yours," and I thought no more about it.

Some time after that, very close to the time he was scheduled to leave, Everett went to his dad's to show him his passport pictures and tell him good-bye. Late that night, I was awakened by a ringing telephone. It was Everett, and there was no mistaking it: he was drunk.

"Everett," I said, "you have been drinking!"

"Yes, ma'am," he said slurring his speech. "Mama," he said crying, "He kept my money, Mama. He kept my money!"

"Ev," I said, "where are you?"

"I'm at your office" was his reply.

"Well, you stay there," I told him. "I'll pick you up."

When I found him, he was devastated. He was hurt and angry, and remained in that condition for many years with respect to his father. And of course, I could do nothing. I found it hard to believe that Ham had kept such a relatively small amount of money from his son who was so severely injured, but I said nothing. There was nothing to say. It was many years before Everett had any contact whatever with his father.

* * *

In the meantime, Duke was seeking employment, going first to the sheriff's office in an effort to regain the only job he really knew and enjoyed, law enforcement. He was still very solicitous toward me, picking me up for lunch every day at noon, and being very good to Everett.

Everything changed very abruptly one day after he had been unsuccessful in obtaining employment. Duke was taking me back to work after we'd had lunch together, and he turned to me and said, "Ginger, I may have to borrow that $10,000 so I can get something started," referring to the money my parents had given me when I assumed the mortgage on their home.

I don't know why I lied, but I did. "I don't have it any longer, Duke," I told him, and his attitude toward me from that day on changed. I hated to think that he had returned solely for the purpose of getting that money, but subsequent developments made it obvious.

Not long after that, I was at work and completely worn out after a crazy day. I had stretched out to rest a short time before I left the office to go home and begin dinner preparations when I was awakened by a phone call from a furious Duke, swearing and calling Everett names.

Suddenly, my secretary stuck her head in my office door and told me Everett was on the other line. I put Duke on hold and when I picked up the other line, Everett began to tell of his catching Duke in Boyle Park and had fooled Duke into thinking he had taken a picture of him with his girlfriend. I interrupted Everett, telling him that Duke was on the other line confessing and that Ev should go to see Preacher Dick.

I shall never forget that evening after I got home and told Duke he had to leave. Duke claimed he couldn't find his clothes, and when I went to help him get them together, he began to swear and scream, yelling at me, "Have you looked in Sweet Thing's drawers?"

"Do you mean Everett?" I asked, and then made him follow me to Everett's room where I opened each drawer, one at a time, showing Duke that nothing of his was in Everett's possession. Duke stood next to me as I opened each drawer, and he was unsteady on his feet and acting very peculiar.

Meanwhile, Gretel appeared, and she lost no time in going through the wash, locating Duke's clothes, and putting them in a sack for him. While the officer stood by, Duke started to leave, then came back in and asked if he could have the little television set, and I handed it to him. At that point, I would have given him anything he asked for! I wanted him to leave!

I did not know at that time that he had actually shot live bullets at Everett and the friend who was with him, or that Everett had driven recklessly through 5:00 traffic to escape.

I do know that Henry Harrison Atkinson, known as "Duke" Atkinson, was a sick man, and I guess, all things considered, we all were lucky not to have had even more serious difficulties than we had.

After he left, I found my attic full of marijuana, evidence that Duke had failed to turn in when he made arrests, selling it or using it—or both. I found that an investigation had been opened on him, but not pursued.

Sometime later, a friend of mine and I were scheduled to leave on a trip to Portugal, and I just happened to pick up the newspaper as I started to pick her up and saw an obituary. It was March 30, 1986: Henry Harrison Atkinson, III, was dead, in Hollandale, Mississippi.

39

Gretel was taking her nurse's training and loving it. It was amazing to me to see a young woman who had slept until noon and never wanted to get up suddenly waking up while it was still dark and dashing off to St. Vincent's Infirmary where she was learning to be a nurse. I fixed breakfast for Liberty and got her off to school before I went to my office. She and Liberty were with me at the Markham Street house for awhile, but after we got the duplex in Hillcrest, she and Liberty lived there.

One day, Allen Branton, who had been a regular visitor at Gret's after the trip to Chicago to see Diana Ross, called me and said that he wanted to take us to lunch—Gretel and me. I told him that was great and met them at one of the city's nicest restaurants, arranging my schedule in order to spend time with them.

"Mimi," Allen began, after we had ordered and were being served. "Gretel and I want to get married." Gretel was nodding.

"That's wonderful!" I remember saying. And then he dropped the bombshell.

"Gretel wants a big wedding, and I'm going to give her one, but I don't have time right now. I have a house near the Art Center, but I don't think it's the right place for Liberty. She would have to change schools. What I would like to do is move in with Gretel until I have time to make plans for the wedding."

I remember going over and over in my mind what he was saying. I had to be sure. "You mean," I said, "you want to move in my apartment with my daughter and my granddaughter *before* you get married?"

"We'd pay the rent, Mimi," he said.

I remember being completely taken aback. "Do you think that would make any difference?"

It was time to go back to work, and I could tell that Gretel was furious, but I couldn't help it. I don't think I could possibly have endorsed that situation.

I think Gretel is still angry about my attitude, but I could not, in good conscious have allowed that.

Allen simply rented another house, not too far from the duplex and still in the same school district, and Gret's side of the duplex became available to rent.

I picked up Liberty every Sunday morning for Sunday school, but I did not go in the house. I pulled up in front and waited for her to come out and get in the car. Liberty loved the new house, particularly her bedroom, which she told me had matching bedspread and curtains.

"Mimi, I want you to see my bedroom! It's so pretty!"

Liberty," I said firmly, "I am not going to visit in that house, so just forget about it."

"Well, Mama says different people have different ideas," Liberty started, and I interrupted her.

"That's right, Sweetheart," I said, "and Mama is wrong about this right now, and that's all right. We love Mama, but she's wrong." And I didn't talk about it anymore. Allen certainly gave Gretel a beautiful wedding at Marlsgate Plantation, the last that occurred there before David Garner purchased it and re-did it. Her dress was stunning, with an enormous train and shoes to match. Allen demonstrated his considerable talent for lighting by placing lights strategically high on the surrounding trees, and the ceremony transpired without a hitch. Preacher Dick, who officiated, called it a performance, not a ceremony. Liberty, who was eight years old, was her maid of honor, and when Gretel tossed her bouquet from Marlsgate's spectacular staircase, Liberty ran to me, embracing me as high up a she could reach, and declared, "Now, Mimi, you can come see my room!" It was evident that the child had recognized the conflict.

* * *

The day before the wedding, when we had the rehearsal dinner, I was standing at one of the fireplaces with Preacher Dick, trying to get warm, for the lovely old house was drafty, when suddenly I had a terrific pain in my left hand, which was behind me, near the fire. An enormous wasp flew off, and it was obvious I had been stung.

"Take your rings off," Preacher Dick said, and I did, not a moment too soon. In fact, the swelling was so pronounced and painful that I was taken to St. Vincent's Infirmary, missing the rehearsal dinner entirely. I was placed in bed in a darkened room, and an examination revealed that my blood pressure was greatly elevated.

The doctor thought that my high blood pressure was the result of my severe wasp sting, and while that might have alerted us to a problem, I am convinced that it was genetic! Both of my parents took blood pressure medicine from my earliest recollection, and I have been on it since Gretel's wedding.

I attended the wedding the next day in my lovely white formal with a bandaged hand, which I put behind me when pictures were taken. Allen had sent a limousine to bring me from my Walton Heights home, and the young black man who was driving had no idea where Marlsgate was! I leaned over from the back seat and gave him directions.

* * *

I enjoyed the time I had with Liberty and missed her when Gretel and Allen moved to Jackson Hole, Wyoming. She loved Sunday school at Westover Hills, although there was never a large number of children there at that time, and sometimes Liberty was the only one.

I picked her up one rainy, cold Saturday, and she was dressed with no petticoat or jacket.

"Sweetheart," I asked her, "don't you have something warmer to wear?"

She shook her head. "No, ma'am."

We were nearing Dillard's Department Store, and I pulled in and opened our umbrella. They were remodeling Dillard's, and at that time it was necessary to go down quite a long distance before reaching the store. It was pouring down rain, and on the way down to Dillard's, we passed a children's store, and on impulse I took the child's hand and turned in, out of the rain. We were in luck. They were having a sale, and the first thing we noticed was a long-sleeved burgundy velvet dress that was just her size. We also found stockings and sandals, and forgot about Dillard's.

The next day, Liberty was almost ready to go, dressed in her new finery. I was brushing her hair, which has always been beautiful, long, and naturally curly. "Weren't we lucky to see this outfit?" I asked. "I'll bet God looked down, and said, 'You don't need to go all the way to Dillard's. There's a dress right there in that shop that will be just right for that little girl …'"

I was brushing away and piously talking about God finding the perfect outfit for us. I did not realize that Liberty was shaking her head and trying to say something. Suddenly she stamped her foot and butted in. "NO, Mimi!" she said. "God wouldn't have said 'that little girl.' He knows my name!"

I was silent. Of course He did. I should have known that. She might even have been able to ask Him to remember her grandmother's name.

40

I have traveled extensively—literally all over the world. I have seen all seven continents, fulfilling a vow I made to myself. I remember visiting my paternal grandmother at her dog-trot house in Harkey's Valley and thinking "surely there's more to the world than this, and I'm going to see it!" And I did.

Most of the trips I took were designed by attorneys and judges, so in addition to visiting the sites and attractions that most tourists visit, we also took in prisons, trials, courts, and the like. Lawyers could even take tax deductions for some of the trips, but my accountant, as I've mentioned earlier, would not allow me to do that.

On February 3, 1981, I went to Africa—on a photographic safari. That adventure started with a near disaster. I was going alone, scheduled to meet the other members of the safari in New York City. Gretel took me to the airport, and we had gone to the cafeteria for coffee and doughnuts, Gretel assuring me that we had plenty of time and the flight would give us notice when it was time to get on board.

Well, if they gave us notice we both missed it, because Gretel suddenly looked up and shouted, "Mama! Isn't that your plane?" And it was backing out! I ran to our station, waving desperately. The attendant came out and took my hand. "Come on," he said. "There's another airplane just about to take off that will make contact with that one," and he began to run, pulling me with him.

"Do I have time to go to the bathroom?" I asked.

"No, ma'am you do not!" he replied, continuing to race toward the next station where passengers were being loaded for take-off. My escort held my ticket in his hand and waved at the passengers being herded in. The attendant handed over my ticket, and I hurried on board, almost the last person to do so! My trip to the bathroom had to wait until I was finally en-route to New York, but on a different airplane from the one I was scheduled to take.

I met my group and breathed a sign of relief. We were routed first to London. I called Gret to tell her that I had been united with my group, because I knew she was afraid I had missed them, but all was well. Our tour director gave us a "care package" in London consisting, among other things, of soap, toilet tissue, and, of all things, a lightbulb. I thought it was a joke until I reached Dar es Salaam, Tanzania, and discovered that the hotel to which we had been taken had no air conditioning, very little food, and no lightbulbs in the wonderful tall lamps!

* * *

We finally found ourselves "on safari" in a small armored jeep-like vehicle, steel plated, with a top that could be opened for picture taking. We were in the famous wildlife sanctuary. There were lions everywhere, elephants, giraffe, Thompson gazelles, ostriches, flamingoes, cheetahs, and zebra.

From Tanzania, we went to the Seychelles for R&R, and what a wonderful experience that was. The Seychelles once were known only to pirates, and only recently had got an airport, being accessible only by ships for many years. The islands were first French and then British and now are self-governed. There was a viewing stand built for Queen Elizabeth and many dragon blood trees planted by the children of slaves when the English abolished slavery and brought the children to the missionaries. We learned the legend of the *coco de mer*, found nowhere except on Praslin Island. Male and female trees produce no fruit until they are 25 years old, and then a strange double nut resembling the pelvis of a woman. These are now museum pieces and quite expensive. When cut, the trees drip "blood"—bright red sap.

From the Seychelles, we went to Nairobi, Kenya, where we visited a tea plantation and a ranch where Masai warriors were dancing. The Masai straddle the Kenya-Tanzania border and at that time numbered about 120,000. Our travel director told us there was a great deal of conflict between those who wanted the Masai to come into the 20th century and those who wanted to preserve their culture, and I often wonder what the situation is now. It was a very hard life, particularly for women. Cattle are the coin of the Masai realm, and blood is an important supplement to the basically dairy diet. A rope is drawn tightly around the animal's neck, a specially blocked miniature arrow is shot from close up to pierce the vein, and the blood is caught in a gourd. Just enough blood is taken not to weaken the animal, then mixed with milk and consumed. The women built their huts of leafy branches, woven together and plastered with a waterproofing of cattle dung. There are three rooms—one for the young livestock at night, a combination living, sleeping, cooking, and eating area, and the wife's private room where she and her smallest children sleep.

Circumcision is an important ritual. It may be recognition of the boy's maturity as well as merely a ritual for marking arrival of puberty. But the saddest custom was that young women underwent a clitoridectomy before marriage arranged by their parents. I seem to remember that there is an effort to stop this practice, and I believe Hillary Clinton is involved in that attempt.

* * *

I loved my stay at The Ark, a game lookout built in the shape of Noah's Ark. A comfortable lounge overlooks the pool, and there are open verandas on all floors where we could sit to watch the animals come eat. There were elephants, rhinos, buffalo, leopards, giant forest hogs, and some rare bongos.

Of course, the highlight of the trip was our stay at the Mount Kenya Safari Club, once owned by actor William Holden. What a fabulous resort—advertised as "one of the last bastions of the vanishing art of gracious living." The lawns were manicured, and peacocks, cranes, flamingoes, Egyptian geese, and marabou storks strolled at will. My cottage had a huge fireplace and a tiled sunken tub.

41

In the halcyon days of my marriage to Duke, we planned our "ideal" home and talked of building it on acreage I purchased in the country on the edge of Saline County.

I had seen the beautiful "Faye Jones" houses when I lived in Fayetteville and had been totally enamored with the unusual rock floors that became his trademark. I also was a fan of Frank Lloyd Wright and wanted touches of his homes in mine. I had lived in Walton Heights and visited the homes located on the river side and had been amazed at how many people had failed to expose the magnificent view. I found myself alone—a divorcee whose children had grown up and left an "empty nest." It was time to build the "ideal" home. And I did.

Everett was just leaving for his trip around the world on a Windjammer when a lovely level lot on the river side of Rivercrest Drive became available. I bought it, drew my plan out on a lawyer's yellow pad, hired a builder, and watched him drive stakes into the ground. When Everett returned, the dream was a reality.

I hired every workman and purchased every piece of lumber and all the beautiful stones that adorn my one-of-a-kind house. Basically, it is one enormous room—living room, dining room, and kitchen—with bedrooms and baths on each side and an unencumbered view of the river from every room, including the master bath! There are two fireplaces, one in the living room and one in my bedroom, and closets to spare. The beautiful flagstone floors are bare in the kitchen, but carpeted in the living and dining rooms, and there is a magnificent cedar-shake roof.

There is a third bathroom off the kitchen, for convenience, and a spacious laundry room with a deep mop sink, a washer and dryer, and a built-in ironing board that folds away into the wall and is always there for a quick press-up on the way to work.

For many years, I maintained a hot tub, mainly because it was good for Everett's injured back, but I, too, really enjoyed it, as did many guests, particularly the attorneys who put on the *Gridiron* every two years! There is also a sauna in the second bathroom.

There is no garage. I had experienced garages that were totally full of junk, leaving no room for a car. So I planned a spacious covered parking area for my car, a circular driveway, and a large storage room with a window. The beams supporting the cathedral ceilings, which extend from the front of the *porte cochere* through the entrance and to the rear of the house, are another Faye Jones feature.

I never liked the pantries in the houses where I had lived. Most of them were located in cabinets, which required one to stand on his or her head to retrieve canned goods when preparing a meal. So I had carpenters build shelves on piano hinges that fold out, like pages in a book standing on end, in a large separate pantry, with doors and a light, making it incredibly easy to organize groceries and to get them when preparing a meal. I have seen pantries like mine in a few homes that have been built since I built mine, but at the time, mine was the only one I had ever seen. I had clipped the idea for it from a magazine many years before.

My beautiful home is named QUERENCIA, which is Spanish and means "affection for the place one calls home, and the sense of well-being that the place affords." Could it have had any other name?

* * *

One of the most unexpected things that ever happened to me occurred in early 2001 when Miss Ruby, Ruby Davenport, my friend and secretary of many years—took a call for me and said, "Ms. A, there's a man on the line from Los Angeles. He wants to talk to you."

"Los Angeles!" I exclaimed. "I can't practice law in Los Angeles! What does he want?" Of course, I picked up the phone.

"Ms. Atkinson," a nice male voice said. "My name is Matt Miller." Then he asked, "Do you watch *Power of Attorney?*" I recognized the name of a syndicated law show.

"Lord, no! Does a postman go for a walk on his day off?"

He thought that was the funniest thing he had ever heard, particularly since he was trying to tell me that one of my cases had been selected to be tried on the air! It seems that *Power of Attorney* featured small claims court and had chosen one of my cases to try on the air. I had sued a client who had failed to pay me for a great deal of work and owed me $5,000.

"We will fly you out here," Mr. Miller went on, "and there will be a lawyer to represent you, and a judge. We will try your case, and if you win, we will pay you $5,000." He went on to name some celebrity lawyers who had appeared on some of his cases. I really didn't see what I had to lose, and Liberty, my granddaughter, lived there. I called her, and she checked it out and called me back. "Mimi, its legitimate! I'll be there." And she was.

I was picked up and taken to the airport on a cold day, with snow on the ground that prohibited me walking down the driveway. I was totally shocked to arrive in Los Angeles to find a beautiful warm evening with the sun shining. The limousine was no faster than the myriad of cars going home from work, but I finally arrived at my hotel, which was near the *Power of Attorney* set.

It was a very interesting experience. There were several cases to be tried, and the various participants were directed one after another first to a young woman who groomed our hair and put make-up on us, then to the "courtroom," which was strikingly accurate. I had met the attorney who was to represent me. He was a real attorney from New York City, and the judge was a real judge, who had retired. I saw the client who owed me the money and who no longer lived in Little Rock, and met the attorney who had been provided for him.

Although the defendant put up a good fight, the judge ruled in my favor, and he was very complimentary in so doing, referring to my long and successful career. I received my $5,000, and I remember asking if the former client didn't have to pay it back to the company. I was told that he did not, which explains why he made an appearance. It also explains why *Power of Attorney* did not last very long!

* * *

The staff at *Power of Attorney* not only paid me $5,000; they allowed me to change my flight, which was supposed to leave the same day the trial ended, to the following day so I could visit my granddaughter. I met the man Liberty had been living with, enjoyed a wonderful meal, and got to see Liberty at work for HBO. On the way to the airport, I had to tell Liberty that I could not condone her lifestyle, and her answer was "I know Mimi, but my marriage didn't work, and this man has really helped me. I couldn't have the job I do and make the money I make without his help. And besides that, he makes me happy."

She didn't explain what that meant, but my years of taking Liberty to Sunday school were not in vain. When Liberty realized that if she was going to have children, she had to do so before too much longer. She told her companion that she did not intend to bring illegitimate children into the world, and unless he married her, she was moving on.

She now is Mrs. Tim Bock, and they are doting parents of Spencer Bock, who is three and reading on a sixth grade level, and Ryan Bock, who just celebrated her first birthday. They are the ones who married in Africa, and there has never been a better set of parents. God moves in a mysterious manner.

* * *

Both my children, my son Everett and my daughter Gretel, had the same problem that I had with respect to marriage. Our collective experience would tend to make one cynical, if not completely against the institution!

I have already mentioned that Gretel ran away, that she came back and went to school, that she is a registered nurse, that after two marriages she married Allen Branton and has had an outstanding relationship with only one heartbreaking experience—the loss of a beautiful little girl to leukemia. Everett, on the other hand, has had two failed marriages, and apparently, like me, has recognized that he is a dropout.

I have to admit that I was obsessed with Everett having some kind of a career, despite the seriousness of his injury. He has always loved photography, and he and his friend Danny Paluch went to New York City where they took a course in photography. Both Everett and Danny are superb photographers, but except for a short effort to establish a photography business at The Harkey Building, neither pursued that route. Everett did edit Dillard's magazine for a relatively short period of time, and that endeavor lead to his first marriage to Jeri Hainey, who also worked for Dillard's. She had been Miss Arkansas and was 10 years older than Everett.

Preacher Dick married them at Querencia, and everyone had a marvelous time. The bride's father paid for a wonderful band, all of whom ended up in the hot tub before the evening was over. Although Everett wanted them to live at the Markham Street house, Jeri wanted him to move into her house, and of course, he did. I don't remember how long they were married, but one day Everett called me and said, "Mama, can you pick me up?" Of course, I could and did, a devastated young man with only the clothes on his back and his dog on a leash. His wife allowed him to take nothing, not even the computer I had given him. It seems that they had added other parts to the computer, using money the bride's father had given them, so Jeri felt that the computer was no longer Everett's sole property.

I filed a divorce action immediately, giving my tenant, Roy Finch, free rent to represent Everett, and the fight was on. I thought Roy was joking when he enumerated what all Jeri was asking for. Her father had allowed her to have all the proceeds from a trucking company he had given her, and she was requesting that Everett pay part of the cost of the operation. Roy told me that the judge, who was Lee Munson, asked her if Everett would then have an interest in the trucking company, and upon her response that he would not, Judge Munson denied her request for payment. Everett also got his computer, but the entire experience was extremely traumatic for him.

* * *

At some point, Everett and I went to Australia, New Zealand, and Tahiti. It was not long after Everett got out of the hospital, for I remember that the long flight was very hard on his back, and he got very cross with me when I told the pretty young flight attendant that he needed to lie down somewhere.

Tahiti was a beautiful tropical paradise. We ate delicious food, swam in the wonderful water, rode the crowded little buses, and visited the Mataiea Village where the famous painter Paul Gauguin lived when he painted "By The Sea," "Ave Maria," and other depictions of Tahitian life.

I loved Australia with the little Koala bears munching on Eucalyptus. We went to Sidney, and not only did I do a tour, I attended a wonderful performance at the unique Opera House, sitting on the front row! No one thought I would be able to get in, let alone have such a wonderful seat, but it is a great deal easier when you want only one ticket! Everett said he didn't feel like going, but I suspect he had plans to go to places his mother would not be interested in seeing.

We did, however, go together to an enormous sheep ranch and saw a demonstration of how the sheepdogs miraculously herd the sheep, seemingly effortlessly, and Everett bought some beautiful sheepskin seat covers for his car.

It was New Zealand that was the highlight of the trip for me, mainly because I knew absolutely nothing about that country until we got there. Everett had no problem driving on the wrong side of the road, but it was very strange to me, and I was glad I didn't have to drive. And how different was the South Island from the North Island—not only the terrain, but the people as well! The South Island was exactly like England. The North Island was populated with dark-skinned Polynesian people, heating their homes with boiling water that came out of the ground. It was a very striking difference and one I would never have believed if I had not seen it.

I did not know at that time that I would have a son-in-law who would make regular trips to New Zealand to fish, and that my daughter and Matthew, their son, would accompany him there many times. It is also near the equator, and many people who go to the Antarctic leave from New Zealand. When the children and I went to Antarctica, we left from South America.

42

Back when my husband Duke had left me (I'm really not sure which time, but I think the break was not entirely made), I was invited to go to Las Vegas with a good friend who had won a free trip and wanted company. I knew Duke was working in some capacity in the gambling part of Las Vegas, and I accepted the invitation. My friend was unaware that Duke was there, or that I intended to look him up. While she was visiting some people she knew, I located Duke, but we had only a few minutes together, and nothing of value was said or accomplished.

My friend and I dressed in our finest that evening, for we had tickets to a show. I remember skinning off my slacks, bathing quickly, and leaving my dirty clothing on the floor of the bathroom, for we were pushed for time. It was a wonderful experience. We loved the show and returned to our hotel room a little past midnight. I believe my friend went in first, and I was unprepared for her scream. But I joined her when I realized everything was gone—the closets empty, with only the dirty slacks still on the floor. We had been robbed. Everything, including my irreplaceable leopard coat, was gone!

Of course, we notified the hotel, but they accepted no responsibility, and with regard to my coat said that if it were that valuable it should have been put in their safe. Both my friend and I had to wire home for money, for our airplane tickets were also missing. Duke called me, telling me that he had heard the news about the theft and immediately thought of my coat.

When I called my Christian Science friend, who had been so comforting to me while Everett was in the hospital, she was confident that Duke had had a hand in it, but "Never mind," she said. "There is no loss. You will see."

I paid no attention to her. No loss? Maybe she had no loss, but I certainly had a loss! My wonderful leopard coat—priceless and irreplaceable—gone. There was no use crying. I dived into my regular business routine! Practicing law in the daytime and visiting Everett's hospital room in the evenings.

One busy day, I had a call from my friend the furrier in North Little Rock. "If you're not busy, come over here. I want to show you something," he said. My curiosity was aroused, and I hurried to leave work before his closing time, rushing into his showroom just as the last customer left.

"I want to show you something," he said, moving swiftly to the back of his shop. When he returned, I was too astonished to say or do anything! He was holding my coat, complete with the black mink trim he had added to increase its length! The only difference was this coat was made from much younger fur. (There had been patches of fur in my coat that were in danger of falling out.) I was speechless.

"An older woman brought this in and wants to sell it. She has no idea what she has, and she only wants"—and he named a very reasonable amount. I bought it on the spot. My Christian Science friend was correct. There was no loss.

I wear my priceless leopard coat with a great deal of pride, and it is the only item my two children are going to argue over when I'm no longer around. My son thinks it could be made into a gorgeous masculine coat, and he is not going to take the seven remaining furs that I have, so maybe my daughter will agree that seven furs are sufficient.

* * *

My collection of furs is like almost everything else that has happened to me: it was not planned. My first beautiful full-length mink cost me relatively little money, and its purchase was not planned. The same furrier called me one day with a legal problem. It seems he had sold a beautiful full-length ranch mink to a woman who had incurred sufficient debt to be forced to file bankruptcy, and the bankruptcy court had declared that the furrier's self-written contract was not sufficient to protect the furrier and his debt. The coat was to be sold, along with all other items, to help pay off her creditors.

The sale was scheduled to take place at a law office, and my furrier friend wanted me to go with him to the sale. I picked him up and we were on our way to the sale when he said, "Miss Virginia, the coat is used, and I can't put it back in my stock, even if I were able to get it." He told me how much was the purchaser still owed. "If you will pay that amount," my friend went on, "I will clean it and re-line it and put your name in it."

Of course I agreed, but when the auction began, my friend was not the only bidder. Thank goodness he began very low, and I held my breath as a very persistent lady added to his bid—not once, but several times. When he raised the bidding to cover all the purchaser owed, it was more than the other bidder wanted to pay, and the coat was mine! It was a fraction of the cost of a full-length fur, and I am still wearing it many years later.

* * *

I splurged and bought a full-length black mink coat, paying it out in time to wear it to the first cold days of winter in 1990. As a matter of fact, the first place I wore it was to Salt Lake City, Utah, where my daughter's almost brand new baby girl, Chandler, was fighting leukemia. Planned, wanted, loved—that she would be so ill was never imagined. I remember Gretel calling me when she was on her way to Children's Hospital in Salt Lake City for the child to be examined, saying, "Mother, the doctor thinks my baby has leukemia!"

My reply was, "Oh, no, Gret-Gret! He's just being a very thorough doctor," and that's what I thought—and hoped!

But the tests were positive. It was 1990, and we had only had Chandler since November 27, 1987. Never was a home designed more elaborately for children than the one that Gretel and Allen built. There was an upstairs playroom big enough for their son Matthew's toy train to stay up all the time, whistling and rolling merrily across its ample route. Each child had his or her personal bathroom with miniature commode and bathtub, and they all had closets where they could reach to pick the garments they wore each day.

All of the very young doctors at Children's Hospital, some of them wearing ponytails, were confident that their beautiful young patient was going to recover. I had never been in an exclusively children's hospital before, and it was a never-to-be-forgotten experience. Chandler did not particularly like her hospital bed, but she tolerated it, standing up most of the time, and reaching out to pick the flowers that had been given her. When the nurses came in to give her medication, she would retreat as far back as possible to try to avoid the whole procedure.

In the hall directly across from each little patient's bed was a rocking chair, and I, and other grandmothers, took advantage of the chairs, particularly when our grandchild was sleeping or being bathed or fed. One day, one of the nearby grandmothers noticed my beautiful mink coat and approached my rocker in an effort to see it more closely.

"You have a beautiful coat," she said. "May I see it?"

I was flattered. "Of course," I replied. "Thank you." I was very proud of the new coat and certainly was not shy about showing it.

The lady, whose daughter had a sick little girl as we did, took my coat and sat down with it in her lap. She began very carefully pulling the fur apart, running her fingers across it and through each section of the heavy garment while I watched in complete bewilderment.

And then she said, "I raise minks. I sell them for coats. You have a very fine, female mink coat."

My sales person had been vindicated.

I still have the beautiful coat, but we lost little Chandler, an unbelievable tragedy. She would have been a grown-up young woman by now—wearing her own furs.

* * *

I worried needlessly about Everett not being able to take care of himself financially, forgetting that not only was he very smart, but he was determined to be as normal as possible and do and see everything he could, despite his staggering injury.

He enrolled in UALR and did quite well. He had previously taught himself to use the "new" electronic machine known as the computer, and he loved the course he was taking in Chinese. In fact, he went with a group of professors from the universities of Utah, Southern California, and UALR to China, Hong Kong, and the Philippines—a trip he enjoyed immensely. The tomb of China's first emperor, which had been lost to history until 1974, had just been found, and the life-sized terracotta soldiers, horses, and chariots arranged as if for battle were being evacuated. I don't think all of the vast army had been found even several years later when I went to China and saw the exhibit.

At one time, I had 10 rent houses, and Everett was an excellent manager and rent collector, although the money he earned was not a handsome amount. All the houses were under the auspices of the City Housing Department, and the rent was relatively low. He also was the janitor at my law office and experienced the bomb threat I mentioned earlier after Dale Bumpers was elected. He was instrumental in my project of putting a second story on 721 West Second Street, and what a project that turned out to be!

The wonderful little building that had fallen into my hands had a flat roof, and I remember that my father hated flat roofs and fought one for many years, trying to keep the roof from leaking. I had the same problem. It seems that there was a constant leak somewhere, and the workman who came regularly was dabbing it with tar in an effort to keep us dry.

Finally one day, I remember him saying that we simply had to re-roof the building, that he could no longer repair that flat roof.

From the time I acquired the building, I had toyed with the idea of altering it to make it more effective for my purposes. It obviously was not a lawyer's office. The front room was enormous, obviously a doctor's office where patients could gather with room for their families. The room surrounding the front room and all of the other rooms were quite small, much too small for the taking of depositions where there were two lawyers, a court reporter, and clients. Fortunately at that time, the beautiful Arkansas Bar Association building was available to lawyers who needed extra space, and I was quite close to that facility, being right across from the courthouse.

I questioned several builders who had told me that the walls of the front room were weight-bearing walls and could not be altered; otherwise, they would collapse. But imagine my surprise when one of the architects I had contacted told me that my building was designed for a second story! In fact it was Gretel's father-in-law, Eddie Branton, and one of Eddie's sons, Andy, and one of Eddie's relatives who helped Everett and his roommate, Gordon Young, put the second story on 721 West Second Street. Gordon was known as "Stumpy" because he was missing a foot. I never knew how he lost it, but he called himself a builder and had built two houses and wanted the job. So that's what transpired.

To put a second story on a building would elevate its size, making it twice as large, and that fact opened up a can of worms. There was a city ordinance that required additional parking for a building of that size, and I would have understood that if I had intended to rent the enlarged space to additional tenants. But that was not what I intended to do. I simply needed additional space to take depositions and have lunch upstairs.

Roy Finch and I paid a visit to the planning commission to plead our case and ask for a waiver on that requirement. We were successful, and I proceeded to borrow the money to complete the project, and that was not an easy thing to do. Everywhere I went, I was told they didn't lend that small amount of money! Ten thousand dollars was a "small amount" of money? Well, I guess it might have been to them, but it surely was not for me!

Of course, I gave my son and his roommate the job, and not a moment too soon, as the roof had continued to leak and the entire place was deteriorating as a result. I remember one of my clients who sold business real estate saying that she didn't think the building would pass inspection.

I arranged to move my practice to Willis Lewis's building just a couple of blocks away, and I thought everything was ready to roll. Roy and I went to the meeting of the City Board of Directors, presented our waiver given us by the Planning Commission, and the board overruled it! I stood there in utter disbelief. There was nothing to do but file a lawsuit.

Roy and I researched the problem and thought that chancery court would be faster, so we filed it there, getting the earliest date available. When we went to court, the regular judge, Lee Munson, was on vacation, but the attorney who was sitting had no problem with finding that the waiver was legal and ordered the remodeling to continue.

Before anything could be started, the City appealed, and we were back to square one, dipping out the leaking building and paying interest on borrowed money.

I had a contempt citation scheduled in Judged Judith Rogers' court the date of the hearing in the appellate court, but Roy Finch was available, and I had no problem with that.

When I was free after my hearing, I raced down the hall, only to find Roy sitting on a bench, alone, everybody else having left. He even had his head in his hands.

"What happened, Roy? What's going on?" I asked.

His incredible answer was, "He sent it to circuit court."

"You mean we have to fight it again?" I almost shouted—visions of the leaking room and the monthly interest payments rushing through my mind.

I cannot remember the name of the city attorney who called me, but he was a friend of mine who was desperately searching for a compromise.

"Ginger," he said, "why don't we do a bill of assurance setting forth that the second floor created by the proposed improvement will not be leased or otherwise occupied as a private office space, but may be used as a library, conference room, storage area, or other similar use to accommodate the tenants of the first floor? Would that work?" So he prepared one and mailed it to me.

I read it and blew a fuse. "I will NOT sign it!" I told Roy. "That is not fair; it's limiting my use of my building! I can't do anything with my building until January 1, 2008!" That was a lifetime in 2003.

"Sign it, Ginger, and let's get on with the remodeling. They will never check on anything," Roy said.

I grudgingly signed it, and Roy was correct. Nobody ever checked anything—from that day until this—and of course it is now far past 2008. To my knowledge, I lost nothing by the bill of assurance, and as a matter of fact, it is highly probable that it was not enforceable because it was signed at a time when I had deeded the building to Everett, but I have forgotten why we thought that was necessary. Roy and I planned to try to get the blamed thing reversed, but Roy became ill, and it never got filed. He called it reverse foreclosure and thought it was unenforceable, and he was a very smart lawyer. He died, and I still miss Roy. He had stopped drinking, but it was too late. His liver was gone. He was a true friend and the funniest man I ever knew.

The second story has been a wonderful addition, but we really need an elevator, and the time will probably come when one will be required, because not everybody can climb the steps, although we have handholds and carpeting.

43

Everett became an intern for Dale Bumpers, achieving that position entirely on his own. Dale did not know Ev was my son until I told him one day, which is not surprising since our names were totally different. Dale hired him and kept him on, which was a first for any intern. He was also instrumental in the hiring of a very competent young man, Vince Shoptaw, who has turned out to be a close friend and a practicing attorney.

Everett became very competent with veterans' affairs, and his ability did not go unnoticed. And about this time, our perpetual governor, Bill Clinton, ran for president. He had been defeated once as governor by Frank White, and I, frankly, did not think he had a chance against George H. W. Bush—not to mention Ross Perot, who was running as an independent. I shall never forget the night he won! I and what seemed like the rest of Arkansas were jammed together in front of the Old State House, and I believe that was the most exciting thing that has ever happened to me.

I also went to the inauguration—feeling that it probably would be the only time I would ever have the opportunity to attend a presidential inauguration. Bonnell Rice and I stayed with my friend Evangeline Legg, who lived very near the White House. We had wonderful seats for Barbara Streisand's performance. I could reach out and touch her. And of course, I still am very close to the Clintons—Bill, Hillary, and Chelsea.

Herschel Gober was a veteran, a member of the National Guard, and very politically inclined. I met him when Bonnell Rice and I had lunch at the Flaming Arrow, a private eating place and bar, and I remember when I was introduced to him, he said, "You're Everett Ham's mother, aren't you?" Of course I was eager to claim my son, and then he said, "If Bill Clinton is elected president and if he takes me to Washington, I'm taking your son with me, because he's the first person Dale Bumpers ever had who knew anything about veterans, or gave a damn about them!"

I remember his saying that, and it materialized! Bill Clinton was elected the 42nd President of the United States of America and took office January 20, 1993. He even served a second term and left a surplus, which is more than you can say for his successors—both parties.

I was invited to a big party attended by a large group of people Bill Clinton was taking with him to Washington, and Herschel Gober was among them. I did not attend. I did not feel I could possibly survive if Bill Clinton had decided take Herschel Gober and he was not taking Everett. But he did! I later knew why he took Everett; he could do nothing alone.

* * *

Everett's move to Washington, D.C., changed everything. First, he had to find a place to live, and of course, he could not leave his Doberman behind.

He decided to get an apartment in Maryland because there was no suitable place for his dog in Washington. He found an apartment located near a small stream, with plenty of room for Raven to run. He could take the shuttle and be in Washington and at his office in a very short time. Even so, I thought his routine was pretty taxing—having to drive from his apartment to the shuttle, travel to Washington, work his regular hours, drive back, walk Raven and take care of her, be sure his clothes were laundered and that there was food in his refrigerator, then start it all over again. It seemed to me that he would not be able to keep up that pace with his broken back, and I was right. Everett called to see if I could take Raven until he could get home. I used my frequent-flyer miles for a friend of Everett's to fly to Maryland, then we rented a car, and he brought a very confused Raven to me.

She knew me, of course, but she missed Everett, and she was afraid I was going to leave, too. I would take her to work, and she would lie at my feet, but if I got up, even to go to the bathroom, she struggled to get up and follow me, ignoring my reassurance that I was not leaving and would be right back. I did not realize that she was as old as she was, and she was heartbroken without Everett. I used to take her outside to do her business, and if a white car went by, she immediately stood still and watched it until it was completely out of sight. Ev had a white car, and she never failed to watch any white car until it was out of sight, then look mournfully and questioningly at me. If I had something I had to do, I paid Ruby, my secretary, and her family to watch Raven, and they loved her. Ruby had a magic touch when Raven had sores on her legs. I took her once to the emergency vet, who took one look at her and asked how old she was. When I told her, she said, "That breed doesn't live that long!"

"This one has," I replied. "And we want her to keep on living! Please take care of her."

I loved her dearly, but she had so many problems, I was afraid she could not live until Everett came home. And she didn't. I had taken her to the vet, our friends who had helped us with all our pets, Joan and Larry Nafe at Hillcrest, and I went every day at lunch to visit her. She was so sad when I left that I don't know if it was the right thing to do or not. I kept telling her I would be back—and that I loved her, but she was always inconsolable.

The doctor had prescribed some kind of medicine, which I wrapped up in peanut butter, and although she was not eager to swallow it, she would reluctantly do so. One night, however, she kept turning her head, first one way and then the next, demonstrating very clearly that she wanted nothing to do with it. It was quite late, and I remember telling her, "O.K., Sweetie—if you don't want to take it, that's all right." And I went to bed, as did she. The next morning she was not lying in her place at the foot of my bed. I called her and called her. There was no response.

I was alarmed and went from my bed toward the kitchen. I found her. She was dead.

I could do absolutely nothing. I had wanted her to live until Everett came home, but I guess I knew that wasn't going to happen. I called Vince Shoptaw, and he wrapped her in a blanket and took her to our vet, who had been expecting her not to recover. They took care of everything except notifying Everett. I knew that was my job, and I really hated to have to tell him, although realistically he knew Raven had lived as long as she was going to live.

* * *

At that time, Everett had his own problems. He was going to have to have surgery. Some of his friends donated leave time, but not as much as he was going to need. I think he was off work nine months, and Gretel came from Jackson Hole and stayed almost that long. I remember her saying that she had been unable to come when he was hurt, but she certainly could come now. Ev was in the Washington Medical Center in Arlington, Virginia, and had a wonderful doctor, whose name eludes me. I tried to get him again after Everett came home and had additional surgery, but he had retired and was not available. Of course, we were so fortunate to find Dr. Richard Peak, a very competent specialist on backs. In fact, he and Everett were little boys together in Cammack Village.

I picked up Gretel at the airport the day Everett had surgery in Washington, and I have never been so scared in my life. It was bitterly cold, and I had never seen that much traffic in my entire life. In addition, I was not really sure where the airport was, or how to get there. Somehow I found it, and Gret and I sat together at the hospital for what seemed like an eternity. The doctor came in afterwards and gave us a great deal of information about the operation—what he had done and what to expect. The Harrington pin was gone, and the doctor felt Everett was going to benefit from the procedure, and he did, although it was several months before he was able to go back to work.

During the time Everett was recuperating, a sensational news event took place. A woman, Lorena Bobbitt, cut off her husband's penis! Fortunately for him, she did not destroy it, and the doctors were able to reattach it, but for quite some time there was nothing else on television, and Gretel, Everett, and I kept the lines busy anyway without such unusual excitement. I remember both children calling me about the episode—Everett maintaining that the wife should have been hung, or at least prosecuted, and Gretel maintaining that she should have been given a medal! I remained neutral; I knew better than to take sides!

* * *

After he went back to work, Everett moved to Crystal City, in Arlington, Virginia, across the bridge from Washington, D.C. It was a wonderful place with a complete city underground. Everett had a parking place for his car, and he could go down on the elevator to a grocery store, a shoe shop, and expensive restaurants or hamburger joints. There was everything one could possibly need or want. It was unnecessary to go anywhere else.

Along about this time, Everett met a young woman from Russellville, Arkansas, where I had lived so many years earlier. She was a school teacher and was attending a Democratic function at the White House. When Everett heard her say she was teaching school in Russellville, he immediately joined in the conversation, telling her that his mother had been valedictorian in Russellville many years before, and from that time on we knew Mary Jo Ballard. She had a darling little girl, Maegan, and Everett asked if he could bring Mary Jo and Maegan for

Christmas that year. Of course, I was delighted and hurried to set out my Christmas china and prepare my best dinner. Maegan was a darling little girl, very well behaved and polite. When she had eaten all she wanted, she very quietly asked if she could be excused, and if course, I thought that her mother must be a particularly good mother. Apparently, the little girl's manners were taught her by her grandmothers, but how could we have known that then?

Mary Jo wanted to live in Washington, D.C., by hook or by crook, and it makes me sick to think that I went along with all of this, mistakenly thinking she would be a wonderful companion for Everett. She had a master's degree in elementary education and had been married at least once before, because she had Maegan. She took out after Everett, visiting him regularly, running errands for him, and cleaning up the apartment before she left. I remember Everett telling me that she did that regularly and not just when I was there to see it, and I remember her calling me on the telephone almost crying saying, "Mrs. Atkinson, if you'll get in touch with Dr. Roy and get Everett's medicine, I'll fly it up to him. I can't stand for him to hurt!" And I would tell her that he would be all right, that he would contact Dr. Roy if he needed to.

They married, and it wasn't until I talked to her former mother-in-law, Portia Short, that I understood why they didn't marry right away. She wasn't divorced! She had filed for divorce, but it had not been finalized when she was chasing Everett and spending a great deal of time going back and forth to Washington.

* * *

Everett rented a larger apartment at the beautiful apartment house, and Mary got a good job teaching school. Everett enjoyed every minute with Maegan and took her to all the available historical sites in and around Washington: Mt. Vernon, the Washington Monument, the White House.

Everything was apparently going well, and then the Republicans took over the House and Senate, and Herschel Gober came to Everett and told him that there was a lot of criticism because Herschel had so many appointments. He said if Ev would give up his appointment, it would be better, and that there would be no change whatsoever, that everything would be exactly the same. Trusting Herschel and being a "team player," Ev surrendered his appointment. When it came time to renew everything, Herschel told him that he, Everett, was not a veteran and therefore Herschel could do nothing for him. Everett was out of a job.

He was devastated and began searching for a replacement. I sent word to President Clinton, who got on the ball, and Everett went to work for Rodney Slater at the Department of Transportation. Everett loved it, but walking up and down the hills surrounding the Capitol had taken its toll on Everett. His doctors told him he was killing himself and needed to retire. We held our breath until he received his disability status, with insurance. He was coming home.

I redid the Markham Street house from top to bottom for Everett and his family. It had been rented the entire time Everett was in Washington, and it really needed to be refurbished. I recarpeted, repainted, bought a new refrigerator, new washer and dryer, and of course had the swimming pool and the yard reworked. Maegan loved the pool, and although Mary had to have a hysterectomy, everything seemed to be working out. Mary had a teaching job, and Maegan was enrolled in Pulaski Academy.

Mary was still trying to get Everett to take her on vacation. He repeatedly told her that they could not afford a vacation, that he was not earning money the way he had been in Washington. But then she told Everett she had a cousin who had a cabin on the River at Denton, Florida, and they could stay there free. Everett, not wanting to disappoint Maegan, agreed to go, thinking the only expense would be the gasoline, and he could handle that. I learned they were going by checking my answering machine.

"We're gone, Mimi. Back Saturday, Love."

On Friday, Ruby, my secretary, and I were working away when the phone rang, and it was Everett. "Mama, file for a divorce and pick me up at the airport tonight."

"Oh, Everett!" I said.

""Mama," he said. "File it!" And he was gone.

I immediately filed for divorce, taking it to the courthouse just before closing time. Fortunately, I had all the necessary information because I had gone to Russellville to change the visitation Mary's ex-husband had with Maegan since it was impossible to have the same visitation after Maegan and her mother moved to Washington, D.C. I had charged nothing for my representation.

I had plans after work, and I called a friend of Everett's and asked him to pick up Everett. He did, and at the same time told me not to contact Everett until the next morning. "He's pretty upset," he told me. And he was right. Ev was a basket case.

I got to Everett's about noon on Saturday morning, and that's when I learned that things had not been going well for quite some time. Mary had run up an incredible amount of debt on a joint credit card, even taking out a substantial amount of cash, and leaving the marriage at one time, only to be sent back by her parents, according to her. But the most serious thing she had done was to take Everett's hard narcotics and use them or sell them, leaving him in pain, because he cannot get them at will. His doctor had suggested that he keep his medicine in a safe, but Everett found that difficult because he never knew how much he was going to require from time to time.

He also found that she had lied completely about the money for the trip, taking the payment out of their checking account, so all of Everett's checks bounced. Not only that, but she had come into the marriage with a car that was on its last legs. Mary was spending a fortune just to keep it running. Everett, while he was working in Washington, helped her get another car. It was a used car, but in much better shape than her car. It was a Jaguar, and Mary loved it, and was furious when Everett would tease her that it really was just a Ford, since Ford owned Jaguar at that time. After the divorce was filed, Everett found the Jaguar sitting in his front yard at Markham Street, with two payments due, a flat tire, and all the pictures of me that I had given Mary lying on the front seat.

She refused to make any other payments on the vehicle, and since Everett had co-signed with her, he, of course, was responsible for the payment. She also had run up an incredible amount of money on credit cards, and when the court ordered he to pay her share of the debts, she took bankruptcy. When I filed Everett's complaint for divorce, we couldn't find Mary Ballard Ham. She did not appear at her job when school started, and when I subpoenaed the records, I found that she had resigned, giving as her reason that "her husband had filed for divorce." I was amazed. That would be the time she would most need a job! But not Miss Mary. She tried to get alimony, with Everett drawing disability. I can still hear her former mother-in-law telling me that I was going to be surprised at what was going to happen when the divorce was taken, and I certainly was. First of all, I learned that none of the Little Rock attorneys whom Mary contacted would handle the case, because of me! I thought I might have to testify, so Everett retained another attorney.

The worst thing Mary did was not allowing Everett to see Maegan, something I never would have thought she would do, because she knew Everett loved the little girl and had been a wonderful step-father. Fortunately, her former mother-in-law, Portia Short, brought Maegan to see Everett, and he has been able to maintain a relationship with her. She is a beautiful young woman who finished high school a year early and is presently in college.

44

Every time I hear somebody complaining about how expensive his or her medication is, I think of the medicine prescribed for Everett that gave him instant relief. Needless to say he loved it, because there was no waiting for it to take effect. I remember when he first went to Washington he would call me late at in the evening and ask me to talk to him until his medication took effect, and I would chatter away about everything I could think of until he got drowsy and his pain medication took effect. "Thanks, Mom. Good night," he used to say, and I, many times, cried myself to sleep.

Everett called me one day and told me that his insurance company was no longer going to pay for what he called his "lollipops," the medication that gave him instant relief. When he got his monthly supply, he used to give half of it to me for me to put away at my house for him, so he would not be tempted to take it when he was hurting so severely.

"Not going to pay for it?" I asked. "Why not?"

" I don't know," he replied. "We can appeal," he said. "But I can't afford it."

I was furious. "By George, I can! And appeal I will! Bring me the information."

When I went to the pharmacy, I almost fainted. Almost $1,560! For one prescription?

That's what it was, and it would last a month if Everett used it carefully and didn't have too much "break-through" pain.

I filed an appeal. It was denied. I filed a second appeal, buying the prescription in the interim. It was denied the second time, but in the information I received, I was told that the next appeal was to Washington, D.C.

I did not understand what the difference was, and I still don't, because my earlier appeals had been to Blue Cross and Blue Shield. Be that as it may, I was reading the information I had received and was trying to decide how and where to lodge my next appeal when I received a telephone call from Everett.

"Mom," he said, "are you sitting down?"

"I'm at work, Everett. What's going on?"

"I just got a call from Blue Cross and Blue Shield, and they are going to pay for my lollipops, and refund our money!"

Neither Everett nor I ever had any explanation of why the insurance company stopped paying for that particular prescription, and unfortunately, Everett did not receive the warning that patients should brush their teeth constantly after taking the medication because it was hard on one's teeth. By the time Everett learned he should have taken certain precautions, it was too late. He has lost several teeth, which have to be replaced. I believe it is too late for Everett to join the class-action lawsuit that has been filed, and that prescription is no longer available. It really is too bad, because it really relieved Everett's pain instantly, and had he known about the need for extra dental care, he could have done it. Everett has dealt with severe, constant pain since he was 17 years old, and he is in his mid-50s as I write this. He is the bravest individual I have ever known. How I wish some medical miracle could eliminate scar tissue and constant pain.

* * *

Everett once said to me, "Mama, what do people do if their mother is not an attorney?" And I have often wondered the same thing. And sometimes even when their mother is an attorney it's rough.

Several months before the doctors sent him home from Washington, Everett had been calling me with a question. "Mama, what kind of business did Dad have? There's a man named Harris who keeps calling me wanting to buy Dad's interest in the business. What kind of business did Dad have?" Gretel was calling from Jackson Hole asking the same question. My answer was the same to both. I had no idea, I told them. I seemed to remember a piece of property that was not worth very much, and maybe wasn't even paid for at the time we got a divorce, but I gave up my interest in it and had heard nothing about it since that time. Everett says that he remembers his dad going out to the property when he, Everett, was a little boy, and his dad was living in a houseboat on the river.

It seems that Ham had undergone some kind of surgery and had suffered from not having enough oxygen, which had left him more or less disabled. He had given up the houseboat he had lived in so long and had been placed in an apartment at first, and then in a nursing home. Everett had made peace with his father, visiting him regularly in the nursing home and furnishing him with diapers and whatever else he needed or wanted by using Ham's social security and the $1,000 a month that Wayne Harris was paying him, ostensibly for his part of the business that nobody knew anything about and which Mr. Harris wanted to buy.

After Everett came home, he had his father's power of attorney and made a trip to his father's business. It was a mini-storage business—American Mini Storage and Retail Sites at 4807 Rixie Road, Sherwood, Arkansas—and was being operated by Ham's old friend and drinking buddy, the same Wayne Harris.

Everett tried very hard to get in touch with Mr. Harris, even going so far as to hide his car and sit in the office when Mr. Harris arrived, but that didn't work, either. Mr. Harris took one look at Everett and said "I have a dental appointment," then left the building.

I had tickets for a wonderful South American trip. I really wanted to see only the lost city of the Incas, Machu Picchu, but the tour included all the countries in between, starting with Brazil, with its wonderful statute of Christ, Argentina, Uruguay, Chile, and finally, Peru. I was scheduled to leave in about two weeks when Everett walked into my office at quitting time with a letter from John Thurman, an attorney, dealing with the Mini-storage property and ending with the following language: "You will no longer be allowed on the property."

I could not believe my ears. Was this not his father's property, too? And did he not have a power of attorney? What was Wayne Harris and John Thurman talking about?

After both children had contacted me about their father's business, I called Cecil Bailey, the smartest accountant I have ever known, and turned him loose on tracking down "the business," and he did a wonderful job. Ham owned a one-half interest, and Wayne Harris had been paying himself substantial sums of money each month and giving Ham $1,000 a month. Harris also had failed to report and pay taxes, and Cecil Bailey had definite proof.

If I were going to leave for South America, I had to file a lawsuit at once—and I did. With Cecil's help, I filed an action for Gretel Branton and Everett Ham, III, asking for an *ex parte* emergency hearing and the appointment of a receiver. Cecil's affidavit was wonderful. I attached it to my complaint and rushed to the courthouse. We fell in Collins Kilgore's court. I took the file to the judge's office, just as he was finishing up a divorce with the litigants getting ready to leave. I was due in Robin Mays' court on a contempt citation, and I put my file on the judge's desk, "Judge, the plaintiffs are my children," and I turned to go to my contempt citation.

When I reached the door I heard Judge Kilgore, loudly, asking a question: "You want an *ex parte* hearing?"

And almost tearfully I replied, "Yes, sir, I do!"

I had to concentrate on my contempt hearing, leaving me no time to worry or contemplate what to do if the judge failed to grant the hearing, which I fully expected him to do. (Judges do not like *ex parte* hearings.) After my hearing, I walked out, only to encounter Bobbie Vinson, Judge Kilgore's clerk, who had come out in the hall hunting me.

"He granted your motion, Ginger," Bobbie said, handling the pleadings. I almost collapsed from relief. Cecil Bailey's affidavit set out exactly what was going on, and it was obvious that something needed to be done about it.

Our case was set for a hearing, with a receiver to be appointed.

I believe if I had represented Mr. Harris, I would not have sent a letter to my partner's legitimate representative telling him that he would not be allowed on the premises!

* * *

I went to South America, starting with Brazil and its beautiful beaches. Then the enormous moment of touring Christ the Redeemer and the cascading waters of the Iguaçú Falls. Next was Argentina, then Uruguay, Chile, and finally Peru and Machu Picchu, the lost city of the Incas. I walked every step of the way, and it is a truly beautiful sight, 8,000 feet above sea level. Historians say it was constructed around 1462, at the height of the Inca Empire, and abandoned less than 100 years later, probably because the inhabitants were wiped out by smallpox before the Spanish conquistadores arrived in the area. There is no record of the Spanish having known of the remote city. In 1911, an American historian named Hiram Bingham was led up to Machu Picchu by a local 11-year-old Quechua boy named Pablito Alvarez, and Bingham undertook archaeological studies and completed a survey of the area. It has since become an important tourist attraction.

Upon my return from South America, the case involving Wayne Harris blossomed into a perpetual lawsuit. Harris at first tried to say Ham was incompetent and could not have set up a trust, which we had, but on its face was a witness, Mr. Harris' wife, who had sworn that Ham was competent and had signed everything in her presence.

The next thing that happened was that the mortgage on the property was foreclosed by the bank, and that took a bit of manipulation.

Then Mr. Harris filed a completely new lawsuit in another court and served Everett. When we had gone to court the first time, in Judge Kilgore's court, he had told Everett, on the side during a recess, that Ev really needed a different attorney because I was too close to the case—too involved. I didn't agree, and was really hurt by that attitude, but I called a friend and asked who he thought was the most competent attorney to deal with that type of case, and upon learning the name of the attorney, I called him, with Everett on the line with us. I remember that he asked for a retainer of between $5,000 and $10,000, and I remember saying that I liked $5,000 better! He said that would be fine, and Everett took a check to him the next day along with the pleadings. It was in Chris Piazza's court, and our time was running. Although both Everett and I called regularly, we heard nothing, and on the next to the last day, in a pouring down rain, we were contacted by the senior member of the firm, who apologized to us and accompanied us to Judge Piazza's court to ask for a continuance, because our attorney was in Bridgeway under a suicide watch!

Phillip Dixon's son was Everett's best friend, so Ev called Phillip, whom he knew was a fine attorney, and although Phillip was retired, he met with Everett and introduced him to a fine attorney who met with Everett immediately, and Everett was relieved. He came to my office and was completely confident that he was going to win. "Mom," he said, "I'm sorry that attorney is sick, but I am really glad that got us a good attorney."

And he really did. The only problem was that Phillip Dixon called me on the Friday before the Monday of our court date to say that he was extremely sorry, but he had just learned his firm represented the bank that handled all of the Mini Storage's business. This created a conflict of interest, so the firm could not represent Everett.

The case was back in my lap. We left it there. I got the cases that had been filed in Chris Piazza's court combined with the case that was pending in Judge Kilgore's court and filed an answer, completely defeating whatever strategy the other side was contemplating.

We went to court. Gretel had come from Jackson Hole, and Everett had taken enough medicine to be able to appear. We had also agreed that each side's accountant could stay in the courtroom. I believe Gretel was one of the first people to testify, and I remember asking her if she remembered Mr. Harris being at her father's home many times when she was very young.

"Oh, yes," she said. "My father called him Little Nigger and he called my Dad "Big Nigger."

Kilgore went crazy, slamming his gavel and shouting, "You're in contempt! Court will be in recess."

John Thurman and I followed the court into his chambers, but I was wondering what the court was doing. I was not, and could not be, in contempt when I was simply reciting exactly what had been said. I wanted the court to know the relationship that existed between Ham and Wayne Harris. And I argued with the court that there was no contempt.

"Well," he said, "I wish you had told me you were going to say that." And the trial was resumed.

By the time Everett had finished his testimony, it was almost lunch time, and we recessed for lunch.

* * *

From the beginning Mr. Harris had tried to buy his partner's interest in the mini-storage. He was extremely bitter, alleging that Ham did nothing, and from my experience with Ham, I didn't doubt it! But the proof was that Ham owned a one-half interest in the property and the business. John Thurman had told us from the beginning that Harris wanted to purchase the interest that Ham and his children had, and he offered a $100,000.

"Is that a buy or sell offer?" I asked.

"Oh, no," Harris replied, which made me think the property was worth more.

I had tried to get Harris to have it appraised, or to join me in having it appraised, but his letter back left no doubt as to his position in the matter. In the May 2002 letter, he wrote, "I do not know the value of these properties, but I do know what they are worth to me. I do not want to spend any company or my personal money to determine what they are worth to the Hams." So I had it appraised by Tom Ferstil's company in March 2003 and nearly fainted when I read its value: $3 million. I guess Harris would pay $100,000! In a heartbeat!

I have been so thankful and relieved since I learned for sure what it is worth, because there will be money for Everett when I have gone to my reward.

* * *

But I digress. When we recessed for lunch, both accountants informed us that they wanted to talk to us, and the lawyers agreed. Both accountants told us if we continued with the lawsuit and the property was sold, which is what Harris wanted, nobody would make anything except the federal government. The accountants explained that the land was practically worthless at the time the Mini Storage business was begun, and that it is very valuable now, and capital gains would eat up everything. Nobody wanted that result.

The court gave us time to try to work it out when all sides indicated that they needed to rethink the matter. First of all, I was demanding that Harris pay back what he had illegally taken, because he had given Ham $1,000 a month—and nothing more—for years! He was not willing to pay what he really owed.

He admitted that he had managed the business as a sole practitioner, and he added that Ham had done nothing to deserve anything. We accepted a small amount, relatively speaking, but I was determined that Harris pay back some of the money he had stolen. In fact, we were elated at the settlement because we had never wanted the property sold. We wanted the business to thrive and the heirs of the man who owned half of it to get their half of the income! And that is substantially what happened.

The settlement agreement provides that the accountants of the respective parties are to be provided copies of the monthly financial statement and a detailed general ledger for each entity. After the tax returns are prepared, each party and their accountants receive copies of them. The days of Wayne Harris being the only person with any knowledge of what is going on at the American Mini Storage and Retail Sites are over!

Occasionally, Harris still tries to buy the children's interest in the business, but Gretel, whose husband could outbid Harris, and would, stops any further discussion.

Everett has told us that Mary Ballard Ham, to whom he was married at the time of our lawsuit, was ecstatic about the settlement and wanted to quit her job and live off the money Everett was receiving, particularly when Harris was repaying the money he had taken illegally. I did not know that was going on and never discussed anything about the settlement with Mary, but Everett was smart enough to inform her that the money he was receiving was money his father had acquired for him and his sister, and he did not mix any of it with his and Mary's money. I guess that listening to his mother try lawsuits for 50 years rubbed off, and he knew just how to handle it.

The surprising thing that has transpired is that Wayne Harris and Everett have a good relationship, with Harris making regular payments to Everett, which he shares with Gretel. Occasionally, Wayne even takes Everett to lunch, and they talk about their bad backs, Wayne having suffered from back pain, although not as severe as Everett. The business has suffered some difficulties, too—their main source of income having taken bankruptcy—but the mortgage is almost paid off, and Harris never misses paying the monthly amount due.

It has been a godsend.

Epilogue

So there you have it. As a girl born in Booneville, Arkansas, by all rights I should have maybe finished high school, married some local boy with a pickup truck, and had a bunch of babies. But through hard work and with damn little luck, I went on to become a college English teacher, a Phi Beta Kappa law school graduate, and both a prosecutor and defense attorney—and I still managed to marry and have two wonderful children.

Through attitude, determination, and perhaps some help from above, I was able to realize most of my wildest dreams, including many I never could have dreamt as a young woman in rural Arkansas. I have spent nearly 60 years as a practicing attorney, traveled every continent, and seen many things change for the better for women over the last seven decades—and my journey continues. While I no longer practice law, I am a great-grandmother with a wonderful family, which is the only thing I truly ever wanted.

I am still Virginia Estella Harkey Keeney Ham Atkinson. Many have said I was a pioneer. Others said, "She'll give up and stay home," but one man inspired me by saying, "We do not have room in our practice for a woman. Perhaps you should go home and be a good wife. Regardless, I hope you *find your niche.*"

I'm proud to say I did just that—and a lot more.